Latin America and Contemporary Modernity

Routledge Advances in Sociology

1. Virtual Globalization
Virtual Spaces / Tourist Spaces
Edited by David Holmes

2. The Criminal Spectre in Law, Literature and Aesthetics
Peter Hutchings

3. Immigrants and National Identity in Europe
Anna Triandafyllidou

4. Constructing Risk and Safety in Technological Practice
Edited by Jane Summerton and Boel Berner

5. Europeanisation, National Identities and Migration
Changes in Boundary Constructions Between Western and Eastern Europe
Willfried Spohn and Anna Triandafyllidou

6. Language, Identity and Conflict
A Comparative Study of Language in Ethnic Conflict in Europe and Eurasia
Diarmait Mac Giolla Chríost

7. Immigrant Life in the U.S.
Multi-disciplinary Perspectives
Edited by Donna R. Gabaccia and Colin Wayne Leach

8. Rave Culture and Religion
Edited by Graham St. John

9. Creation and Returns of Social Capital
A New Research Program
Edited by Henk Flap and Beate Völker

10. Self-Care
Embodiment, Personal Autonomy and the Shaping of Health Consciousness
Christopher Ziguras

11. Mechanisms of Cooperation
Werner Raub and Jeroen Weesie

12. After the Bell
Educational Success, Public Policy and Family Background
Edited by Dalton Conley and Karen Albright

13. Youth Crime and Youth Culture in the Inner City
Bill Sanders

14. Emotions and Social Movements
Edited by Helena Flam and Debra King

15. Globalization, Uncertainty and Youth in Society
Edited by Hans-Peter Blossfeld, Erik Klijzing, Melinda Mills and Karin Kurz

16. Love, Heterosexuality and Society
Paul Johnson

17. Agricultural Governance
Globalization and the New Politics of Regulation
Edited by Vaughan Higgins and Geoffrey Lawrence

18. Challenging Hegemonic Masculinity
Richard Howson

19. Social Isolation in Modern Society
Roelof Hortulanus, Anja Machielse and Ludwien Meeuwesen

20. Weber and the Persistence of Religion
Social Theory, Capitalism and the Sublime
Joseph W. H. Lough

21. Globalization, Uncertainty and Late Careers in Society
Edited by Hans-Peter Blossfeld, Sandra Buchholz and Dirk Hofäcker

22. Bourdieu's Politics
Problems and Possibilities
Jeremy F. Lane

23. Media Bias in Reporting Social Research?
The Case of Reviewing Ethnic Inequalities in Education
Martyn Hammersley

24. A General Theory of Emotions and Social Life
Warren D. TenHouten

25. Sociology, Religion and Grace
Arpad Szakolczai

26. Youth Cultures
Scenes, Subcultures and Tribes
Edited by Paul Hodkinson and Wolfgang Deicke

27. The Obituary as Collective Memory
Bridget Fowler

28. Tocqueville's Virus
Utopia and Dystopia in Western Social and Political Thought
Mark Featherstone

29. Jewish Eating and Identity Through the Ages
David Kraemer

30. The Institutionalization of Social Welfare
A Study of Medicalizing Management
Mikael Holmqvist

31. The Role of Religion in Modern Societies
Edited by Detlef Pollack and Daniel V. A. Olson

32. Sex Research and Sex Therapy
A Sociology Analysis of Masters and Johnson
Ross Morrow

33. A Crisis of Waste?
Understanding the Rubbish Society
Martin O'Brien

34. Globalization and Transformations of Local Socioeconomic Practices
Edited by Ulrike Schuerkens

35. The Culture of Welfare Markets
The International Recasting of Pension and Care Systems
Ingo Bode

36. Cohabitation, Family and Society
Tiziana Nazio

37. Latin America and Contemporary Modernity
A Sociological Interpretation
José Maurício Domingues

Latin America and Contemporary Modernity

A Sociological Interpretation

José Maurício Domingues

First published 2008
by Routledge
270 Madison Ave, New York, NY 10016

Simultaneously published in the UK
by Routledge
2 Park Square, Milton Park, Abingdon, Oxon OX14 4RN

Routledge is an imprint of the Taylor & Francis Group, an informa business

© 2008 Taylor and Francis Group

Typeset in Sabon by IBT Global

All rights reserved. No part of this book may be reprinted or reproduced or utilised
in any form or by any electronic, mechanical, or other means, now known or hereaf-
ter invented, including photocopying and recording, or in any information storage or
retrieval system, without permission in writing from the publishers.

Trademark Notice: Product or corporate names may be trademarks or registered trademarks, and are used only for identification and explanation without intent to infringe.

Library of Congress Cataloging-in-Publication Data
Domingues, José Maurício.
Latin America and contemporary modernity : a sociological interpretation / José Maurí-
cio Domingues.
p. cm.— (Routledge advances in sociology)
Includes bibliographical references (p.) and index.
ISBN 978-0-415-96467-8 (hardback : alk. paper)
1. Latin America—Social conditions—1982- 2. Latin America—Politics and govern-
ment—1980- 3. Latin America—Economic conditions—1982- 4. Civil rights—Latin
America. 5. Globalization—Economic aspects—Latin America I. Title.

HN110.5.A8D66 2008
303.48'280182109045—dc22   2007027485

ISBN10: 0-415-96467-9 (hbk)
ISBN10: 0–203–93239–0 (ebk)

ISBN13: 978-0-415-96467-8 (hbk)
ISBN13: 978–0–203–93239–1(ebk)

Contents

Introduction		*ix*
	Latin America and Modernity	ix
	Multidimensionality and Agency, Imaginary and Institutions	xiii
	The Structure of the Book	xvii
	Acknowledgments	xix
1	**Law, Rights, and Justice**	**1**
	Introduction	1
	The Pulse of Freedom	3
	Intermediate Reflections—Real Abstractions, Disembeddings, and Re-embeddings	11
	The New Faces of Rights, Law, and Justice	13
	Partial Conclusions: Real Abstractions, Social Coordination, and the (Renewed) Relations between Concreteness and Universality	33
2	**Development, Globalization, and the Search for Alternatives**	**39**
	Introduction	39
	Capitalism and the Modern Project, Markets and the State	40
	Intermediate Reflections—Accumulation, Regulation, and Development	47
	New Regulations, Economic Restructuring, and the Patterns of Capital Accumulation	51
	Partial Conclusions: A New Mode of Regulation Indeed, but a New Regime of Accumulation?	71

viii   Contents

3   Identities and Domination, Solidarity and Projects   76

Introduction   76

The Build-Up of a Region   77

Intermediate Reflections—Collective Subjectivities and Sites of Solidarity   84

Collective Subjectivities and Modernizing Moves Today   92

Partial Conclusions: Modernizing Moves, Transformism, and Molecular Change   119

Conclusion   123

A Recapitulation of Basic Issues   123

Modernization, Civilization, and Development   125

Shortcomings of the Present, Possibilities of the Future   130

Notes   133
Bibliography   165
Index   181

Introduction

LATIN AMERICA AND MODERNITY

This is a book about a particular phase of modernity in a particular region of the world. What is today called "Latin" America, an obvious misnomer, came into being with the very first expansion of the modern world in its making, through the mercantile and colonizing ventures of the Iberian monarchies. It has been part and parcel of the developments of modernity, albeit always at its periphery or semiperiphery, that is, as integral to it but without being able to pull the main strings of the process. This peculiar position has given occasion to a particularly deep-seated feature of this subcontinent when looking at itself, especially from the standpoint of its intellectuals, as either an incomplete or a degraded form of modernity. To approach it as a mere selection of traits of the modern civilization has been another manner of putting the issue that also misses its particular, rather than incomplete, features. It mistakenly assumes that modernity in its concrete settings reproduces an a priori design, providing in fact a metaphysical perspective on the subject, as though modernity was somewhere waiting in the clouds to be brought down to earth.

I take therefore the contours of modernity in Latin America, in the past and at present, as the outcome of specific, "path dependent" social processes. One aspect of these is that the dynamic of the center of modernity—still very much within the confines of Europe and the United States, though now including Japan—has had a disproportionate weight in that region, something that does not work the other way round. The point is not to say that modernity has not developed its own dynamic in Latin America, but rather that imbalances of power shaped, and carry on doing so, the outlook of social life in the subcontinent. Neither Brazil nor Mexico, Bolivia or Argentina have had the same possibility of defining the evolution of Britain, France, the United States, or Germany to an extent comparable to the impact on Latin America that these Western countries have had, in an intended or unintended manner.

Somewhat at variance with some of the analyses of the contemporary world, I will therefore hold to the old notion of a division between the center and the periphery that in particular Raúl Prebisch introduced in Latin

x Introduction

American thinking and made fortune thereafter across the world, with the idea of a semiperiphery being introduced later on.[1] I shall not, however, reduce it to the economic dimension, or even the political one, since this basic feature tends to structure the whole range of social systems and interactions across the planet. That is not to say, of course, that the internal dynamics of such countries is secondary. On the contrary, it is the peculiar combination of inner drives and impulses coming from the outside that defines the peculiar paths each of them has taken, with that particular element of power differentials having to be taken into account—which does not mean it necessarily yields negative outcomes. At both the imaginary and the institutional levels, Latin America has embraced modernity and its continuous developments, for bad or good, filtering them through the particular interests and identities that emerge therein (and the coalitions they are able to build), but also providing innovations of its own in the course especially of the last two centuries, that is, since the nineteenth-century independences. Of course, while their effects spill over social life as a whole, it is at the economic and the geopolitical levels that those imbalances of power are felt with special intensity.

A particular way of looking at the impact of the "West" on Latin America vis-à-vis modernity was modernization theory. According to it, these were merely backward, tradition-laden societies that had to catch up with the more advanced countries of the modern civilization. It had a very strong evolutionist basis. A special topic of modernization theory, or one that was argued in parallel to it, often reproducing some of its basic tenets—hence its mistakes—is found in the idea that these would be "dual" societies, split between modernity and tradition or something similar (formal versus informal, for instance). Dependency theory was a means to put the issue another way and showed that power relations at the global level in fact mattered a lot; its most clever versions were also aware of the importance of inner dynamics and modernizing coalitions, nonetheless stopping there.[2] My approach here is to basically try to understand how such processes operate at the internal level. I will thus concentrate on Latin America as my *unit of analysis*—without searching for the analysis at each country in a systematic way; but I shall frame those processes within the more general unfolding of contemporary modernity, which includes at several points the general trends and issues of power at the global level. My goal is to grasp how what I have called the "third phase of modernity"—in terms of general sociological theory the core of this book—has developed in Latin America since the mid-1980s, in its contradictory and multifaceted dynamics.[3] I eschew of course the highly Occidentocentric tenets of modernization theory in the following pages. Evolution as such should not be totally discarded from social theory, but this is true only insofar as contingency and history are and should be at the core of reconstructive approaches to its understanding. The *modernizing moves* carried out by all sorts of collectivities during the last centuries are, on the other hand, studied here as a central feature of moder-

Introduction xi

nity and decisive for its character today, whether they are more centered or more decentered. In the first case, such modernizing moves imply at times quite clear-cut collective projects—modernizing "offensives" we may say, in this connection; in the second, they happen without such a teleological perspective of social change, taking place hence in a looser and more or less unintended way from the collective point of view, with individuals and more restricted collectivities contributing to them as they further their desires and interests, being conscious or not, sympathetic or not if they are conscious, of the consequences of their acts and movements. A continuum must be projected, stretching from modernizing "offensives" (relatively highly centered) to extremely decentered moves. Ruling, intermediate, and subordinated collectivities appear in this connection as crucial for Latin America modernity, as they do for modernity in general. In addition, specific heritages and traditions—including some very modern ones, notwithstanding their difference vis-à-vis Northern Europe and the United States—are combined and changed, modernized, in the course of the unfolding of modernity in Latin America, in fact a phenomenon to be found elsewhere with greater or lesser intensity. All such moves are contingent, that is, "episodic," though path-dependent, as I shall show throughout the book, and will elaborate in the Conclusion.

One general contention of the book is that modernization has assumed distinct features in the areas where processes are more strongly driven by local dynamics and those sites whose dynamic forces reside to a large extent outside Latin America. This does not mean that some important changes and adaptations have not occurred, or that one can be sharply distinguished from the other. Regulatory processes linked to the neoliberal offensive and economic changes as well as identities and sites of solidarity were very much influenced by "exogenous" processes. Some of the collectivities and practices attached to them have modernized fast and deeply, something that often happens in a rather passive way with respect to those former elements. Meanwhile the state, in great measure based on an internal balance of forces, to which the external sway of sheer power as well as of "epistemic communities" must be added, has not moved, beyond its neoliberal reformulation, very far in its modernization, especially as a site of national and subcontinental mobilization and solidarity construction. In turn, the processes of modernization that are internally driven are especially important in what concerns the law, rights, and justice. Their momentum has been great since the 1980s. Such distinct directions of modernization entail, as we shall see, a tense dialectical development, with no unequivocal end point.

No doubts must remain here about what I understand as modernity or modernization—the former a global, multifaceted and varied civilization, the latter pointing to concrete and specific processes, without any metaphysical or a priori teleology, except that sustained by the collectivities that carry them out, in a more or less intended manner, in terms of what they pose to themselves as the horizon for social development. To

xii *Introduction*

be sure exogenous and endogenous are relative categories and often escape the control of the state, which has been especially important for the conformation of modern "societies." Nonetheless, inasmuch as the nation-state remains a crucial power container in the modern world (with the predominance of the "core" states plus the existence of one exclusive hegemon) and the "dialectic of control" between it and its citizenry is paramount in terms of possible national developments, these categories do have a role to play, which must not be overlooked.[4] This is by no means detrimental to the fact that "societies" thus composed are cut across by trends coming from many distinct sources. What is the meaning then of globalization in this book? I take it as a long-term process that has involved the whole world from the sixteenth century onward and has speeded up in the last decades. To a large extent an unintended consequence of social processes, more recently it has been actively pursed by a number of powerful collectivities and by others not so powerful, which, when trying to tackle its negative effects, push it forward in distinct directions. Integration of markets, production links crossing countries, political and cultural trends with great impact on identity building are the most salient features of such a process, as much as cross-border movements and networks. The nation state has indeed lost some of its power, or at least has changed in some measure its role in the global arena and with reference to how it regulates its internal territory, but by no means has it become a weak player. Capitalism, as a key institution within modern civilization and one that has a tremendous expansive drive, is of course a powerful force behind globalizing processes. It is in no way its exclusive mover. If the national dimension cannot be forgotten, we must not be oblivious to local conditions either, which vary today much more within countries than by and large it had done in the former stages of modernity. The neologism "glocalization" seems to be useful to frame this situation.[5]

An issue of periodization must be mentioned here, preparing the terrain so that we venture into an analysis of the three phases of modernity that will historically frame the analytical arguments to be developed in each chapter. Some would argue that modernity would have started in the sixteenth century—or, emblematically, in 1492.[6] It is true that a world market emerged and that some themes, in either Northern, Italian, or Iberian—and by derivation American—Renaissances were already played out, which outline the further paths taken by modernity later on. But such imaginary elements would be further developed and decanted in the following centuries, especially in the Atlantic Northwestern area. Besides, and more important than that, modern "societies" from an institutional standpoint, including capitalism as a "mode of production" and really modern states, with "rational-legal" features, can be recognized, even if in a very restricted way, from only the nineteenth century onward. Before that a conundrum of social forms sprung up in European soil and in the Americas, without minimally configuring what we can discern as modern social formations.

Introduction xiii

Finally, it is necessary to note that there is today much talk about modernity and globalization, but at least in what concerns Latin America the powerful sociological tradition represented by authors such a Gino Germani and Florestan Fernandes has not as yet found replication, especially in terms of a general synthesis of the situation and as to placing it within that more general framework. I hope I have advanced in this direction.

MULTIDIMENSIONALITY AND AGENCY, IMAGINARY AND INSTITUTIONS

The views developed in this book assume, without a sustained argument—since I think that by now it should not be necessary—that social life is a multidimensional phenomenon, whose concrete entanglements and dialectic must be analyzed according to each concrete process, even if we take a large space-time view (which includes the long historical *durée* and a wide geographical reach, as is the case here). More important than that is to point to the way agency is dealt with in this book and how I understand the imaginary and institutions, especially with respect to modernity.[7]

I reject both an individualistic and what might be called a "collectivist" standpoint (a perspective whose definition in such terms is besides not very accurate) in what concerns the "action-structure" debate. I have elsewhere argued at length about the role of *collective subjectivities* in social life; this is what actually authorizes at a more general theoretical level my dwelling on modernizing moves by all sorts of, more or less (de)centered, collectivities. States, classes, genders, "races" and ethnic collectivities, social movements, small groups, firms, international agencies, and many other collectivities, with variable levels of centering (identity and organization) weave social life. They do so within limits posed by their relationships—based on interests and power differentials—as well as by sedimented patterns of social interaction. Usually people speak about "elite" behavior, firms' strategy, and social movements. While, to be sure, many people who use it do not share an "elitist" view, the former is a problematic term—and it is embedded in fact in a Moscan-Paretian or Weberian-Schumpeterian conception, implying serious differences of rationality—and will be substituted for here by the notions such as ruling groups; the two other surely have their place guaranteed in this book. But other, less centered and varied collectivities, as well as the notion of unintended consequences of action, are supposed throughout, as a key mechanism of a social life whose contingency emerges to a great extent from the intertwined and unexpected manner desires, projects, and movements impact on the short and the long duration of daily life and history. Power and privileged access to information, facilities, and time to craft strategies are surely unevenly distributed in unequal societies, but I suppose that all individuals belonging to the human species, in this subcontinent and anywhere in the world, possess fundamentally the same reflexive powers.

xiv *Introduction*

There is no reason to think that they do not usually activate them, in politics as in any other field in which they are immersed.

Social life is thus seen here as a continuous process of movement and change. Its relative stability does not detract from that: In fact, it is through those aforementioned relations and patterns that collectivities reproduce social life and we can explain why it may be seen as static (or at least as captured by "stasis") at many points in history. Transformation is, however, omnipresent, regardless of its slow rhythm and the strong resilience of a great many key social arrangements. *Social creativity* (which includes and does not do without individual creativity) is always at work and to avoid its effects the dominant collectivities have to work very hard, sometimes adapting themselves or else accepting changes that they cannot eventually control, unless they cling to hopeless traditions. Creativity does not operate in a vacuum, though: It is always closely knit with individual and social *memories*, which are more or less recurrently reproduced traits of social life, assuming a whole range of expressions.

The most (relatively) stable, sedimented arrangements of social life must be seen as *institutions;* that is, they appear as the most permanent and structuring features of social relations, irrespective of how they come into and remain in being. Institutions that develop slowly may generate effects in the hermeneutical universe of social life, influencing cognition, values and norms, and aesthetic patterns. Marx stressed of course this point when he spoke of "social being" as conditioning consciousness. In many instances he was surely right. But often it is the other way round that things occur. Ideas appear, may consolidate an *imaginary* (implying memories, specific or "magmatic," justifications of the present and expectations for the future), and then strongly influence social praxis, being at once stable and shifting, depending also on how interests and power influence its evolution. Usually, it may be suggested, it is a dialectical interplay between institutions and the imaginary that actually obtains, including individuals as well as collective subjectivities in its making.

It is worth noting that this book draws upon Marxist authors, as well as upon Weberian, and functionalists. It should be clear, nonetheless, that it is a peculiar standpoint that I have tried to present in it. Surely it is not a Marxist perspective that underlies my arguments and positions. I have tried to incorporate many of Marx's insights into the theory of collective subjectivity, at the most general theoretical level and in its more specific expressions, while transforming his views usually in a rather radical direction. Even his economic theory appears here as mediated by the French regulation school. More concrete analyses in this book often owe a lot to Marxist authors, when they are interesting and sound. But neither Marx's view of the relation between economic infrastructure and the superstructures nor his view of social classes (especially their Cartesian-Hobbesian underpinnings in his writings), neither his almost deterministic hopes for socialism and communism nor, even less so, his political strategy in this regard, are

Introduction xv

supposed here (or elsewhere in my work indeed). Democracy, at best a moot point and often a real difficulty for Marxism (despite rhetorical proclamations and recent ad hoc solutions), enjoys, in contradistinction, center stage in my analytical efforts and in the normative perspective that accompanies them. The theory of dependence is, in addition, present in my arguments in a rather revised way. This relates to the issues just mentioned as well as to the economic one-sidedness of the several versions of such an approach. Similar questions must be raised vis-à-vis modernization theory. The idea of tradition and modernity taken as opposites is refused here as much as the role "elites" as such play in their writings. The simple-minded unilinearity of their evolutionary standpoint is deemed inappropriate and their view of integration as the normal state of society dismissed. Modernity and modernization are key issues, of course, but they must not be reified. The concept of modernizing moves, which can assume the aspect of (centered) modernizing offensives, is thus introduced from the very start so as to avoid such a reifying perspective.

I have elaborated my theoretical views at the most general level in former books and will not expand on them here. The more particular and empirically oriented discussions enacted in the following pages will at many points work out the implications of such arguments at more empirically oriented levels. When necessary those general theoretical elements will be brought to the fore. I have also filtered, often without pointing that out, the debates within the varied specific fields of theorizing that I bring together here through the lenses that theoretical perspective has suggested to me. At a few junctures, I would have liked to dive deep into such debates; I refrained from doing so especially because that would lead me far into complex subjects and overburden and imbalance the exposition of the main issues that after all furnish the line of argument of the book—the general characteristics of contemporary modernity in Latin America.

The modern imaginary has had freedom, equality, solidarity, and responsibility at its core (contrary notions pointing to domination and inequality, fragmentation and irresponsibility are as always present, remaining less often or less clearly formulated). The domination of nature has been central therein as well. The main institutions of modernity, which have of course a historical developmental dynamic, remain citizenship, the legal-rational state, nationhood, capitalism, racism, patriarchy, although mostly weakened and changed, as well as the more specific ways in which they are regulated today. If they include the concretization of the key elements of that imaginary, they very often provide for domination too. As a sociologist, I see no reason whatsoever for a definition of postmodernity, not even with respect to a supposed closure of the social imaginary in relation to the future—something that seemed plausible perhaps during the years characterized by the most recent general crisis of modernity (especially the 1980s). If anything, we will have to come to grips with the looser sense in which the institutionalization and the identities that weave social life are looked at now, which in some

xvi *Introduction*

degree forego the homogenizing thrust modernity had hitherto evinced, now rather changed.

Modernization theory was not capable in particular of understanding the historicity as well as the close link with the West that the modern civilization has always evinced in Latin America. Modernity was not simply there and was then transplanted to the subcontinent. Instead it has developed simultaneously in the West and in Latin America. Trends and periods are often similar—the West is also unavoidably linked to Latin America—and at times it may seem that modernizing moves merely try to reproduce in Latin American countries what has become the norm in Europe and the United States. To be sure, some projects are understood by their agents as exactly that; more loosely, the mirror of the West has always accompanied the unfolding of the modern imaginary in Latin America. This is not the same as to say that a reproduction of that imaginary and the mere effort of replicating it here is what has happened. To a large extent we must say that the modern imaginary is as much Latin American and peripheral as it is Western and rooted in the center: Modernity has been at the horizon of the subcontinent more or less from the same period as it was posed in Europe and the United States. Again, specificities and particular dynamics must not be overlooked.

The same is true of course with respect to institutions. This is one element that clearly defines modernity too. In connection with Western developments, the Latin American region, since colonial times, has had its institutions influenced by modernity, especially at the state level and in terms of its contribution to capital's "primitive accumulation." With the independences, the very moment the modern imaginary became paramount, modern institutions emerged in Latin America and matured in the twentieth century. Once again they did so with peculiar characteristics and through specific paths. If dependency theory was perceptive when it introduced the path dependent processes that led Latin America to its dependent and underdeveloped position, and the power relations that accounted for that in a large measure, its focus was too narrow and it often evinced problematic, catastrophic economic overtones.

It is important also to note that during colonial times the enunciations were controlled directly via the circuits of power that the Portuguese and Spanish colonial empires maintained. Things changed after the end of colonialism. Surely a relation of subordination and the power to enunciate were kept to a great extent, however now via indirect circuits of power in variable measure. These may include, in order to be really effective, relatively independent internal ruling collectivities that cannot see themselves detached from the hegemonic view of global ruling classes, as well as intellectuals who, due to their place in the division of labor (generating a sort of metaphysics in which the West becomes the measure of reality) and/or their connections with ruling collectivities, internal or external, espouse an "Occidentalist" view. Aspects external as well as internal to the new

Introduction xvii

nation-states have therefore to be taken into account. Is it useful to call this the "coloniality of power," as though there was an unbroken continuity in the process? The issues that Quijano points out are real enough, indeed crucial.[8] But center-periphery relations of distinct sorts—within the uneven and combined development of modernity—have to be dealt with, rather than assumed away or treated in what seems to me an excessively flat framework, which tends furthermore to date modernity too early and overlook the utopian, emancipatory horizon of modernity, concentrating only on the elements of domination it embodies. Thereby also the emergence of worldviews, sociopolitical movements, and social practices could be better situated, since in this regard a break with peripheral conditions may be achieved, as is the case in some part today. I hope to show this at least partly in the course of the book.

Finally, it must be said that Western social theory—including evidently the theorization of modernity—is present here throughout. This is so because its contributions are very important and because the connection between Latin America, the West, and modernity is inescapable. This does not mean, nevertheless, that I try to frame Latin America's processes as a reproduction of or as deviant cases vis-à-vis the West. The opposite is actually true: My aim is to construct a theoretical interpretation that, positing Latin American in a general way within modern civilization, grasps its specific and often pathdependent processes of modernization. Thereby we can perhaps achieve a more encompassing view of modernity.

THE STRUCTURE OF THE BOOK

This book intends to develop an at once empirically oriented and theoretically sustained argument about contemporary modernity in Latin America. Indeed, it is based on a massive amount of secondhand material collected between 2003 and 2007, which is visible along the text, although transmuted into a conceptual structure. Since contemporary modernity is a moving object, very much in its making, which has happened at a fast pace, a certain amount of anxiety to finish and publish the book has accompanied me in the latter part of this period. To some extent it is as if social life has already changed a lot between the times of writing and of publication. In any case, things have not changed that much and the main theses presented here seem to me valid overall, to my best knowledge. Moreover, I have covered a vast amount of middle-range theories and empirical data in this book. This is in principle a risky enterprise, for which in any case there are a few very good and respectable examples in the last decades. I have surely missed some material; maybe I have misunderstood a few others. I hope and trust this has been reduced to a minimum. That said, I think the general result in terms of a theoretical contribution outweighs the possible shortcomings and drawbacks of the project. At least we can see the contours of the forest, with

xviii *Introduction*

many of the largest trees standing out there too. These last observations lead me to a general theoretical or methodological question.

I of course accept many of the arguments of the discursive turn in the social sciences, but remain attached to a quite straightforward view of the relation between the reality of social life and statements about it. We cannot by any means hold to any simple correspondence theory, such as thoroughly and correctly criticized by Wittgenstein. Yet, general as well as partial theories build an interlinked set of statements that are more or less, *qua* a conceptual construction (whether their authors are aware of that or not), *adequate* to social life (and to nature). To be sure, nobody now—or just the philosophically naïve—believe in anything resembling a "social physics," as Parsons could still do in the late 1930s. Those conceptual constructions are certainly not exclusive or absolute; nor do they exhaust reality.[9] That said, I hope I have managed to advance an understanding of Latin America at present that would be capable of a theoretical grasp of its social reality. I expect I have provided a general conceptual framework, within the range of my knowledge and abilities, which therefore adequately corresponds as well as possible to Latin America's social life in the third phase of global modernity. In this regard, I agree with the idea that postcolonial thinking reproduces much of what had already been said by older Latin American philosophies in the 1960s and 1970s, although more open to the pluralism of social life than they were.[10] Besides, something that is in fact more problematic, its view of modernity and globalization is sociologically rather poor and one-sided, regardless of general interesting insights they may provide.[11] In contradistinction, I am after indeed a theoretical construction that combines concepts and empirical information, in a critical perspective; their undertaking goes by and large in a distinct direction. I hope to tackle their specific contribution in the near future. The good combination of general (and critical) theory and empirical investigation plus the outcomes it may yield is what should serve as the yardstick to judge the adequacy of any body of work. In the Conclusion to the book, the specific outcomes of the research will be framed by a critical discussion of modernity as a civilization, whereby this term as such and the universalizing effects of its global expansion will be systematically tackled, as will the renitent particularities (or multiplicity if one wishes) be systematically analyzed (and in the Conclusion I shall deal with Eisenstadt's and Arnason's approaches). Surely, one always speaks from somewhere. I myself speak from Latin America, Brazil, and find it fitting to advance an approach to this subcontinent from my (semi)peripheral—but not colonized—point of view. In addition, at this point it might be useful to state clearly that this is not a book by a Latin Americanist, but rather a work on the sociological theory of modernity with special reference to Latin America. That is, it does not actually fit traditional area studies.

In order to articulate and buttress my exposition, some clusters of concepts are introduced in each chapter, especially in the "intermediate reflections"

Introduction xix

they contain. "Real abstractions" plus the "instituting" and "instituted" aspects of social life in relation to citizenship stand out in Chapter 1; the revision of contemporary political economy, especially the French theory of regulation, combined with traditional Latin American approaches (especially so-called "historical-structuralism"), features prominently in Chapter 2; the concept of collective subjectivity—in its concrete expressions in families and generations, social classes, genders, races and ethnicities, the state, parties, and social movements—organizes much of the discussion of Chapter 3. More generally, an analytical distinction presented in some of my other publications plays an important role in the book. I distinguish between markets, coordinated through voluntary exchange; hierarchies, which have command performing coordination; and networks, which count on voluntary collaboration in order to achieve coordination.[12] All social formations and all dimensions of social process have these mechanisms of coordination, usually in some sort of mix, as the means whereby social life moves on. I will make recourse to these general ideas so as to understand modernity and in particular modernity at the turn of the Latin American twenty-first century. I explicitly include myself therefore into an ecumenically grasped branch of critical theory, with its traditional ambivalent embattlement with modernity.

I have in this Introduction taken some space to briefly define some basic concepts and offer thereby a chart to the reader, since not all of them appear explicitly at every stage of my exposition. The substance of the argument must be kept to the recesses of each of its chapters. I see no reason to abridge them here. I think it is better that the reader accesses them step by step; the Conclusion, indeed, will provide a more general and problematized view of the whole subject, but only after we traverse the empirical material that furnishes substance to the argument.

Whether I have been successful thereby in presenting an integrated, general, and plausible view of the contemporary subcontinent is for the reader to judge. All key issues pertaining to the theme have in any case been dealt with in the pages that follow, encompassed by the definition of a third phase of modernity as developing in this specific global space-time.

ACKNOWLEDGMENTS

Before concluding I must express my debts in relation to the making of this book. They are first and foremost to my research assistants at the Rio de Janeiro University Research Institute (IUPERJ), where I have carried out the bulk of the work. Nobody has helped as much as María Maneiro, Fabrício Pereira da Silva, and Thamy Pogrebinschi. I thank them very much for their collaboration, in the literal sense of the term. Alice Guimarães has been also important in what regards the Bolivian situation. To be sure, many people, students and colleagues, have at different stages helped me

xx *Introduction*

with the confusions and mistakes I kept incurring all along the way. Short stays in Argentina, where I taught at the University of Buenos Aires and at the University of San Martín, as well as a brief period at El Colégio de México, in Mexico City, were also extremely relevant for my research. I thank these Latin American travel mates, were they aware of their role in my endeavor or not, as much as I thank my Brazilian colleagues and students. I would especially like to thank Cesar Guimarães for regular discussions on the recent political evolution of Latin America as well as Frederic Vandenberghe, Manuela Boatca, and Wolfgang Knöbl for their careful reading of former versions of the text. Without the support of the Brazilian Scientific Research Council (CNPq) and the Funding for Research and Projects (FINEP), both belonging to the Brazilian Ministry for Science and Technology (MCT), it would be much less likely that this book would be completed. In too many ways, intellectually as well as emotionally, this book is connected to Andrea Pontual.

1 Law, Rights, and Justice

INTRODUCTION

One of the core elements of modern civilization, at the *imaginary* level as well as *institutionally*, is the system of rights that it has established with reference mainly to individuals (collectivities featuring almost residually in this regard). Law embodies such rights and, to sustain it practically, another institutional element was created—the judicial system. It was part and parcel of modernity at its inception and has, on the other hand, undergone change throughout its evolution. A bureaucratic body to deal especially with social rights complemented it. Of course the political system relates to a crucial aspect of the system of rights. To a large extent it is on the functioning of these elements that justice in modernity rests. As an aspiration and as a reality, *citizenship* has been the utmost expression of this imaginary and institutional core of this civilization. This set of imaginary and institutional elements, in its intertwinement with practices, offers the concrete articulation of democracy. Latin America shares in this sort of development. The understanding of this particular sort of issue, which is on the other hand general enough, allows for a good entrance into the development of modern civilization in Latin America and is crucial to understanding some of its pivotal contemporary features.

Can we accept Hartlyn's claim that the history of Latin America in the last two centuries has been a relentless, albeit at times interrupted, effort toward the realization of sovereignty, democracy, citizenship, pluralism, the rule of law, and accountability—which he summed up as the "quest" for "liberal ideals"?[1] Not exactly. But there is more than a grain of truth in his suggestion, let alone the fact that he perceives that this has happened more or less the same way on "both sides of the Atlantic." The fact is that the core values of modernity (which is surely broader than liberalism) have oriented, in a specific manner, the imaginary and practical deeds of social agents south of the Rio Grande. The system of rights in particular has been at the center of such a dispute. But so are conceptions of justice and the forms and contents of law in some measure. There are, practically, at times contradictions between the main elements of this imaginary—freedom, equality, solidarity—particularly when institutionalization is at stake. By and large they

2 Latin America and Contemporary Modernity

tend, however, especially in the long run, to reinforce each other, although freedom may eschew to some extent deeper equality and above all solidarity. Moreover, there is also an underside, more camouflaged ideologically but just too visible in real life, which expresses what then may be called a relentless effort at maintaining domination, inequality, and privilege—the other side of modernity, less obvious and outspoken in terms of the imaginary, more explicit as to institutions. These will be more at the center of the other parts of this book. Especially important here is the idea that *equal freedom,* that is, a unitary concept that eschews domination, inequality, and privilege in the relations between individuals, has been, despite entrenched difficulties, contradictions, and fluctuations of meaning, the main innovation modernity has introduced in the history of humanity as something to be achieved in this world. History, as a teleological process, has unfolded in the last centuries, especially in the West and Latin America, albeit encompassing somehow all areas connected to modernity, and can be understood as in part the pursuit and efforts by individuals and varied sorts of collectivities to make such paramount value come true.[2]

A central question to be answered throughout this chapter relates to the very idea of democracy. One of the tenets of modernization theory was that democracy was intrinsic to modernity, and exactly in the form and with the content it had acquired in the West, still more specifically, as it was supposedly in being in the United States. It would moreover emerge in the course of the evolutionary passage from traditional to modern society. Rational and universalistic norms, a consensus on political values and expectations, with strong, independent elites and a participant citizenry, it was held, would be the expression of that.[3] Parsons' view of democracy as a "universal evolutionary" is, at a high theoretical level, one of the main elaborations of this kind of belief.[4] Which is present also in authors such as Habermas, at least insofar as the full accomplishment of modernity in evolutionary terms, through the flourishing and political translation of its rationalized "life-world," is at stake.[5] This is not the view to be taken here. Instead, while recognizing that certain social developments, to be explored below, are conditions of possibility for democracy, I take its emergence and consolidation as a contingent event. To be sure, in a general way the imaginary of modernity, cutting across "societies" and continents, furnishes parameters and motivational elements for the search for democracy—law, rights, and justice. How this imaginary develops in each social formation is, nevertheless, contingent. The same happens in what regards its institutionalization. Both are closely connected to *specific* modernizing moves, which in some instances may assume the countenance of modernizing offensives when they imply clear political projects and a reasonably high level of centering of the collectivities that pursue them. The aspirations and struggle for equal freedom will stand out in these moves, which are relentlessly counteracted by attempts to curtail their more or less clearly defined goals. Other modern forces, connected to systems of domination

Law, Rights, and Justice   3

and inequality, are at the basis of such antidemocratic—or democratically limited—modernizing moves.

THE PULSE OF FREEDOM

To start our analysis we need to return to the division of modernity by and large and in particular in Latin America initially into two phases–the restricted liberal and the state-organized phases. The third, contemporary phase will concentrate our efforts in the remainder of the chapter. They all go hand in hand with similar developments in Europe and the United States, which in fact were the centers from which impulse to move in such directions came, with surely local re-elaborations of the principles on which each of them was based and inventions of its own making. Each of those two phases was followed by a crisis. Here I draw upon Wagner's view of those two phases—adding the third one myself. For him, liberty—associated with the contingency of the workings of the market—and the state—which imposes discipline—stand out in those two phases. I alter his view in the sense that freedom and contingency are seen as resting not essentially within the market, a principle of organization too, but also through the intervention of the state—based overall on hierarchies as a principle of organization, which can increase freedom and contingency for some collectivities and individuals—by giving them some basic security in areas essential for their survival. To be sure reducing contingency was partly an aim of the organization of modernity by the state; but raising general standards of welfare, thus of conditions for the exercise of freedom, hence of contingency by individual and collective agents until then unable to enjoy such promises of modernity, was also crucial for the emergence and expansion of social policies beyond philanthropy. In any case, all social formations are somehow organized, even though it is not necessarily the state that carries this out (markets and networks operate in this direction too).[6]

Within this general framework we have to bear in mind that restricted liberal modernity was even more restricted in Latin America, since the liberal state and the market only in a very approximate way were dominant in the subcontinent, while state-organized modernity assumed basically the form of the developmental state. In fact, in spite of the lack of a more general vision of the process in Spanish America (notwithstanding good historical information being of course available), we can take Fernandes' view of nineteenth-century Brazil as to a great extent applicable to its Spanish-speaking neighbors. He spoke of a "veiled revolution" during the process of independence in which the utopia of liberalism was imperfectly realized, remaining as the unswerving horizon of social development, though, and precisely because of that.[7] As he synthetically put it:

> The independence was thus undermined as a revolutionary process, thanks to the predominance of social-historical influences that confined

4   *Latin America and Contemporary Modernity*

the depth of the rupture with the past . . . However, the revolutionary element was the truly dynamic and propelling component. Because of that, albeit either dulled or deformed, it became the "'historical ferment'" of intelligent social behavior. In the short run it fed and oriented the options that delimitated, on the ideological and utopian planes, the ideals of organization of the national state. In the long run, in whichever level or sphere national integration occurred structurally, it produced effects that went beyond the mere alleviation of the heteronomical features of the old social order, leading indeed to its desegregation and to the concomitant intensification of the formation of autonomous features typical of a national society. This implied the constant re-elaboration of that revolutionary element, which surfaced again and again, within more or less favorable socio-dynamic conditions for its acting as a constructive social-historical factor.[8]

Rights remained themselves therefore the imaginary telos of social development, with movements from time to time struggling to make them come true. More conservative liberals, who used liberalism in an ideological way to justify an agrarian society that included slavery and other forms of personal domination, held sway over society and politics during the mid-period of the century—basically from the 1830s to the 1880s. Slavery was progressively abolished; land became a property to be bought and sold, the same happening with capital. And by the 1870s the liberal movement, in a Republican and in a radical antislavery guise, was reborn, its influence lasting until the consolidation of the "Old Republic," the liberal conservative regime that, dominated by big landowners, lasted for the first thirty years of the Brazilian twentieth century. Modernity and liberalism entered a deep crisis in the 1920s, in parallel with other national developments elsewhere, from which they emerged only with a renewed political and ideological outlook.

I shall not follow the development of each country in Latin America, but a periodization would not be, in this broad sketch, very distinct from Brazil, notwithstanding the obvious difference between the latter monarchical regime until 1890 and the other countries' republican regimes.[9] Independences—powerful modernizing offensives—occurred in the beginning of the eighteenth century, and a more open and radical stance was assumed by many of their promoters. From the 1830s to the 1870s, however, more conservative republics (with caudillos or not) had been established. By then liberalism resumed its utopian force to some extent; the beginning of the twentieth century witnessed a continuous upsurge of movements aimed at expanding the horizon of modernity and the incorporation of more collectivities into the rather restricted mould allowed for by oligarchic domination. Modernizing offensives as well as more decentered modernizing moves were staged, abandoned, and resumed throughout the period. The Mexican Revolution and Yrigoyen's Radical Civic Union (UCR) in Argentina expressed initially this push perhaps better than any other developments in the region. The "rights discourse," to use Strydom's phrase,[10] was then, if not dominant, rather important, along with, in the later period, the "justice discourse," mirroring developments in Europe since the 1848 *social* revolutions. In fact, there is some strong overlapping of course between rights and—social—justice in this period, as there is throughout modernity, since the latter finds expression in this civilization in the system of rights erected and expanded since the eighteenth century. While formerly freedom guaranteed justice, which was based on individual achievements and the ever greater domination and exploitation of nature it allowed for, later on the role of state and society in assuring that people would get what they should increased in a variable degree. In any case, although freedom, in civil terms, that is, as the absence of personal domination and constraints, was limited in the subcontinent, from the 1920s onward Latin America as a whole experienced the crisis of the restricted model of modernity it had built in the previous period.

As argued above, equal freedom has been at the core of modern values, notwithstanding the difficulty modern societies have had in transforming such value in institutional designs, since systems of *domination* and social *inequality* necessarily frustrate its coming true. It is worth stressing that while in Europe and the United States this drawback was constituted by systems of domination and inequality that had already to a great extent found in capitalism its main expression, in Latin America until at least the first decades of the twentieth century it was still the big agrarian property with personal relations of domination and very often forced labor that embodied domination and inequality. It was this form of private property that the system of rights—and the right to property in particular—supported. To be sure, adaptations had to be made, especially when it came to personal subordination and above all slavery. At the same time, it preserved a utopian horizon for liberalism, which could be exhausted only when it was further implemented or when its principles sounded incapable of delivering the equal freedom modernity had initially promised. In Latin America, it was a combination of both that came about, to some extent under the influence of external processes. Modernizing—and conservative at once—moves and offensives were carried out geared to maintain and adapt such institutional elements.

The system of rights expresses to a great extent what a society believes to be fair for its members—in universal or more particularistic terms—but the specific character and extension of such rights depends on how collectively, in a conflict-laden manner, we define justice in distinct countries and in different periods. In other words, it hinges on the concrete ethic of a given society, which is in modernity a mix of the rights-justice discourse with specific notions and practices, institutions and imaginary constructions. In Latin America, justice found its narrow confines in the limitations imposed by the heritage of slavery and other forms of personal domination, entwined with

6   Latin America and Contemporary Modernity

the lack of a contractual tradition (differently from the feudal West[11]), the tough hierarchical character it entailed for social relations, and the highly exploitative character of the colonization of the subcontinent, let alone the in many cases thorny problem of harsh oppression of ethnic minorities or even majorities (indians, blacks, the poor in general). This is a problem, as we shall see, that lingers on today and besets the achievements of present-day democracies.

A complexification of society, which had to a great extent the sway of capitalist development (but also of immigration, the emancipation of women, the reduction of personal forms of domination, albeit still limited in many places), came about from the turn of the century onward. And, as elsewhere, liberalism proved too narrow a doctrine to accommodate the emergence of these new collectivities and the demands for inclusion and rights they then raised. Social rights but also the respect for political rights, falsified by fraud and oligarchic mechanisms everywhere in the subcontinent, became key issues in stark political disputes. A democratizing modernization was sought for. These battles were fought in general by the new professional middle classes, the new working classes, peasants and women, as well as, more timidly, non-white people in several of these countries. In the case of the latter, rights was not usually the issue at stake: Inclusion without discrimination was the main point on the agenda. Mexico pioneered the changes with its 1910 revolution, the first of the new century. Otherwise, by the 1930s and the 1940s the subcontinent had become a convulsed area. Only new solutions, such as Brazil's protracted process of change, initiated with the 1930 Revolution, the mass mobilization that found in Peronism in Argentina and the 1952 National Revolution in Bolivia their outlet, as the most prominent examples of change, were really able to accommodate those clashes. Conversely, countries such as Colombia and Venezuela lagged behind under a tighter, though apparently more benign, form of oligarchic domination. Curiously enough liberal party systems have made them what was usually thought of as consolidated democracies, in which in fact widespread violence and clienteles dominated for a long time—counting on oil money in the case of the latter, and a murderous behavior by ruling groups in the former (the period became known simply as "La Violencia").[12] Once again, modernizing moves of distinct sorts are to be found here, some searching for the realization of aspects of the modern emancipatory imaginary linked to equal freedom, others trying to defend and adapt the systems of domination and inequality that prevailed at the time.

In the process of change, a new form of social solidarity—namely, inclusion and recognition, featuring the attribution of rights and prerogatives— had to be weaved. Liberalism initially projected this in terms of the basic system of civil and political rights established by the social pact between individuals that founded the state. Full inclusion and recognition in social life at this stage, throughout the world as well as in Latin America, required more than that: Social rights, as a means of leveling out at a modicum the

Law, Rights, and Justice 7

inequalities typical of modern social formations—which run counter to equal freedom—were introduced, in a very uneven, fragmented, and piecemeal way. This was often accompanied by a reduction of political freedom and rights and in particular the crafting of a specific pattern of incorporation of the working classes in the region: Corporatism. Whereas in economic terms the developmental state was the Latin American counterpoint to Keynesianism in Europe and the United States, as we shall see in Chapter 2, corporatism or later and diluted variants of that original model did the same vis-à-vis what in Europe came to be known as neocorporatism.[13] Corporatism had as its main feature not only the public and legal definition by the state of collective bodies; it also implied a specific, rather authoritarian relation between the state and such bodies, especially in the case of the working classes and their unions. It encompassed also, to a great extent, the middle classes and their union or professional associations as well as the upper classes, which, remaining however much less under the tutelage of the state, entertained also many informal links with politicians and public officials. The state helped establish or transformed the organization of collectivities, became responsive to their demands, and to a variable extent brought their leadership into the decision making-processes relative to specific areas (economic development for the bourgeois classes, social insurance and retirement pension funds for workers). Corporatism was seen as a mechanism of mediation. A basic idea was that society would be represented in the state through formal channels, alongside or not (depending on the more or less authoritarian doctrine being implemented) individual voting and parties. Those formal collectivities would also operate in relation to society partly as an instrument of state.[14]

On the other hand, what might be seen as a rephrasing of the neo-Thomist tradition that stemmed from the colonial period implied an "architectonic" conception of society according to which individual rights were subordinated to the inclusive collectivity, an imaginary pillar that may have facilitated the broadening of the state presence in social life, as well as to some extent the view of rights as an emanation of the political body rather than something pertaining in an immediate way to individuals *qua* individuals.[15] That does not mean that individualism has not enjoyed a paramount position, practically and ideologically. But the state has appeared, in turn, as the agency responsible for assigning to each individual and collectivity its proper and fair place in social life. By and large a new dialectic, or rather a new form of expressing such a dialectic, between *freedom* and *equality* unfolded during a large part of the Latin American twentieth century. *Solidarity* and *responsibility* now pass to some extent from the individual to the state, which assumes more clearly the burden of creating social cohesion. This happens without detriment to the fact that individuals remain the matrix of social life and are also seen as responsible for their lives and destiny to a large extent. At rock bottom, we do not by any means leave the world of liberalism, actual shifts in the phrasing of those issues notwithstanding.[16]

8 *Latin America and Contemporary Modernity*

In any case, step by step, starting with public officials and then embracing workers from key export sectors and financial services, to reach large industrial companies, social security spread to the waged proletariat of Latin American countries. And, as a means of incorporating the mass—or at least a great amount—of people in that piecemeal way, granting differentiated social rights and symbolic recognition, corporatism was a powerful tool in the creation of new forms of solidarity in Latin America, though some countries remained bound to oligarchy while others developed more peculiar mechanisms to build allegiances and identities (for instance Chile, through political parties, and Colombia, combining this with strong and pervasive clienteles) and corporatism as such has rarely achieved complete institutionalization in Latin America. But if neocorporatism was based on liberal democracy and social democracy, Latin American corporatist-like arrangements were modernizing moves based much more on a pattern of "cooptation-repression" that implied fewer rights and more political control on the part of the state over workers organizations and movements. In Mexico this went very far (including participation of unions leadership in parliaments and state bureaucracy), while Argentina had a much more mobilized mass movement and in Brazil it was perhaps, above all, a legislated model of labor relations that prevailed, meaning in fact juridification but little participation of the working class in decision-making processes at the state level.[17] This was the main face of the Latin American second, state-organized phase of modernity—which some, such as Germani originally and Touraine afterwards, have called the "national-popular" movement and state, a problematic definition that in any case captures the theme of solidarity and popular inclusion that was typical of this period of Latin American national developments.[18] Let me add that justice and welfare were during this period expressed to a large extent, whether in corporatist regimes or not, through labor legislation enacted by the state granting rights, protection, and benefits, in a variable degree, to those who were in the formal labor market.[19]

Contrary to conventional wisdom, in Latin America the state is not as strong as it is in Europe. It has not enjoyed the same "infrastructural power" to rule through society. Paradoxically, it has often had capacities that other social agents have lacked or had enjoyed in a lesser degree, as well as being capable of exerting "despotic power" with fewer constraints—a point to be elaborated later on.[20] Within this framework, army-based and variably violent regimes took power almost everywhere in Latin America between the 1960s and the 1970s—with almost genocidal features in Chile, Argentina, and Uruguay. In fact, they themselves expressed the impossibility of maintaining social exclusion (or reversing to it) after years of modernization, complexification, and social and political mobilization in Latin America. But they carried further the path of state-organized modernity, in a very authoritarian way and with lots of variation among them (often as "authoritarian corporative" regimes). A few wanted to move forward

Law, Rights, and Justice   9

toward industrialization, in Brazil especially, or pretended to be socially progressive, in the case of Peru, with its leftist "revolutionary" outlook, while others fancied a reversal of history in order to destroy the power of the popular classes, above all in Chile and Argentina. [21]

From the late 1960s onward, economically, socially, and politically state-organized modernity underwent a deep crisis (during which, by the way, the idea of "postmodernity" came to the fore—more as a symptom, I think, than as a diagnosis, in any case with much less impact in Latin America than in the West). The welfare state in Europe, Keynesianism, Fordist-like arrangements, and the developmental state: They all proved out of step or even out of date with deep social change across the world, as we will see in the following chapter. The crisis of state-organized modernity hit therefore not only the state but also and especially the organized working class, whose strong status as a publicly recognized agent (especially in Europe) was diminished, in particular due to underlying powerful socioeconomic change and the crisis of neocorporatism.[22] At the same time, the transition to democracy in Latin America in the 1980s brought up new demands, politically and socially, for full incorporation of unions and popular movements in the political order as well as for social rights. They were therefore to be answered in a moment of major transformations in the modern, and ever more global, social formation.

It is important to stress that the transition and consolidation of democratic regimes, with eventually the establishment of full political rights, and even new constitutions, was based on a combination of factors: the exhaustion of economic models (already in the 1970s or later on, as we shall see in Chapter 2), a new understanding by the main political collectivities that a new deal was required (even in the case of the military, who were everywhere defeated and ousted one way or another), the introduction of new institutions, and a change of so-called "political culture." Ruling groups had to grapple with freer subjects and social movements, hence their moves aimed at adjusting to change, developing a liberal-democratic view of politics, and creating some new institutions. While they might prefer a quieter "demos," what came about was not simply the assumption of power by new competitive "elites," as those following in the footsteps of Mosca and Pareto or Weber and Schumpeter might argue. If new political ruling groups did take over power, this occurred alongside with not only the rise of so-called "poliarchic" institutions (which established rules of competition and freedom of opinion), but also of mass participation and a change in the hermeneutic fabric of social life. The latter in particular brought forward a different way of looking at participation and rights, conflict and consensus, developing during the twentieth century and especially in the struggle against the dictatorial regimes. As an outcome of such modernizing moves, as Avritzer stressed, " . . . a central development . . . was a renewal in the constitution of the public sphere." The democratizing wave that swept the subcontinent and the world as a whole since the 1980s—what some have

10 Latin America and Contemporary Modernity

called the third global "wave" of democratization—was pretty strong and did not leave any country of Latin America untouched. Problems remain for the full consolidation of democracy in a number of them, which have also been beset by poor economic performance and perennial inequality. A new international political environment, with the end of the Cold War, was at least positive for democratization insofar as the United States withdrew support for military coups (with the recent exception of an anti–Hugo Chávez putsch in Venezuela).[23]

With the defeat of the military in the 1980s, by the beginning of the 1990s citizenship, now with a clear political aspect, was established in basically all the countries of the subcontinent. In some of them, such as Chile, there were severe formal restrictions to the exercise of political rights, recently lifted, while civil rights remained a problem in many parts of the subcontinent. Social rights were limited and unevenly distributed between distinct classes, professions, and regions. At the same time that the state has chronically evinced problems to develop its "infrastructural power," the incorporation of the population to citizenship stopped short of being complete, remaining formal in many cases and selectively implemented, which means also state weakness, since it cannot penetrate deeply into society and count on its institutions to implement its own policies. Moreover, the homogenizing trust of Western states was not taken to its conclusion in many instances, although certainly in several of them it was pursued at least at the ideological level. It has had thus to work on its own from the top and with of course less legitimacy.[24]

We may say that the *instituting* aspect of citizenship was especially interesting in this period of democratic renewal, so that a democratic system of rights, the *instituted* aspect of citizenship,[25] notwithstanding its limitations, was established by the end of the twentieth century. The instituting aspect of citizenship corresponds to powerful modernizing moves, which at times produced rather centered collective subjectivities that converged to yield a democratizing push. In former periods this was true too, although at times it might seem that the state was merely handing down rights. In fact, during the whole process of expansion of rights and the development of law and justice in the region, the instituting aspect of citizenship played a decisive role, at times being answered by the state in terms of democratizing processes, sometimes in a pre-emptive manner and often through authoritarianism. But eventually the emergence of a citizenry that could no longer and by no means just be suppressed affirmed itself through political mobilization and, as a consequence, this imperfect and limited system of rights gained space in the imaginary and made some concrete and important advances in terms of institutionalization.[26] Even the left, which in the previous period was prone to reject the framework of rights (or at least treated it in an instrumental way), privileging the socialist revolution and the proletariat (or the peasantry depending on the country and the political force at stake), embraced the rights-justice discourse and citizens in general as agents of change in an incisive manner. It bet on the instituting character of citizenship, whether as party discourses or as social movement contentions. It is true, however, that at times, for reasons I want to develop below, these demands for rights have tended to be more fragmented and/or plural.[27]

Just one more issue must be dealt with here before we move further. As is well known, the Latin American tradition stems from the so-called Western "civil law," in contradistinction to the "common law" tradition of the United States.[28] State centrism, codification in constitutions and other subordinated juridical systems, formalism, and the rejection of judge-made law are some key aspects of such a tradition. Since independence this has been the dominant pattern of the judicial system in Latin America, which is not the same as to say that juridification and the legal state actually have been operative in such nations, since political power has been intrusive and used to manipulate law and courts.[29] The democratic transition has indeed changed this in large measure. This is a process that has however not carried on unaccompanied. Along with features of the development of law, justice, and rights, this is one of the issues we will tackle after the following, intermediate section.

INTERMEDIATE REFLECTIONS—REAL ABSTRACTIONS, DISEMBEDDINGS, AND RE-EMBEDDINGS

The concept of "real abstraction" has a long history within the field of critical theory, from Marx through Lukács and Adorno and Horkheimer to Habermas. It was used of course in different ways, but only Marx, in a youthful text, employed it to speak about citizenship. In *The Jewish Question,* he stressed the abstract (and deceitful) character of the *citoyen* as against the concrete individual, who belonged to a specific class and supported specific interests.[30] The critical theory of the Frankfurt School was an important moment for the reproduction of this perspective, culminating in Habermas' work which, in my view, wrongly linked real abstractions to supposedly self-regulating systems in his *Theory of Communicative Action,* just to leave the issue on his way to a more liberal-democratic (though based on intersubjectivity) view of law and the state. Moreover, unfortunately at no point does he perceive the links of real abstractions to citizenship.[31] I shall not carry out here a reconstruction of the issue in that tradition, which I have put forward in detail elsewhere.[32] Let me in what follows propose some theses in relation to citizenship as a real abstraction and then frame the problem in Latin America with reference to this conceptual construction. As a background, a more agency-oriented approach (which however does not deny the role, not necessarily simply reifying, of institutions) will be operative, pointing also to the role of collective subjectivities in all social processes.

Before doing so, it is worth introducing Marshall's classical definition of citizenship. He saw it as introducing a *universal egalitarian status versus the*

12   *Latin America and Contemporary Modernity*

class structures of capitalist systems. Universalist social policies were thus at the core of citizenship; means-tested schemes were also accepted by him only in some cases, as well as some prioritization of those very poor (for instance in issues such as housing) or the handout of services (*viz.* university education) in terms of merit alone when what might be seen as rights became too expensive.[33] But we must stress too that universalism has distinct meanings in what regards, on the one hand, civil and political citizenship, and social citizenship, on the other. This is a rather subtle point. Those are at the basis of the legal or constitutional state, while the latter is, at least in its concrete workings, produced by the bureaucratic apparatus of welfare systems. It is, despite its universality, less systematic and homogeneous, since many distinct situations and discretion in the dispensation of benefits often have to be tackled.[34]

Modernity has developed through powerful processes of "disembedding," which reorganized identities and the space-time coordinates in which people lived, individualizing them, making their lives more contingent, and throwing them onto the national plane. People have been regularly "lifted out" of previous social relationships, which in the past tended to evince, in their fundamental elements, greater stability—that is, they changed in the long duration of history rather than on the short run, something that has become more common in modernity, since "all that is solid melts in the air."[35] The first, fundamental (individual and collective) re-embedding of modernity, through which people build novel identities and new social relationships, is offered by citizenship. Thereby people are taken as equally free, regardless of any specific traits, which they maintain, of course, as members of classes, genders, ethnic groups, and so on. To be workable, we must add, this sort of identity must be abstract but also real, in the sense that the world around the individual is structured according to such principles. These have at their core the system of rights, civil, political, and eventually social, and the abolition of personal forms of domination. Therefore, through "real abstractions" key imaginary and institutional aspects of modernity come together. Identity based on citizenship is in any case excessively thin, although most of modern institutions—including capitalism, through property rights—rest upon it. Other identities are therefore necessary to make life meaningful and society does not restrict itself to citizenship as a principle of organization. Especially those other relationships and identities linked to systems of domination—based on class, gender, race, and other collective subjectivities—are especially important, though other, more neutral (such as religious, cultural, sportive) individual and collective types of identity are operative in social life and provide for several other forms of re-embedding (which I shall discuss in Chapter 3). Citizenship, with its abstract character, has partaken in that decisive ("logocentric") aspect of modernity that derives from its *homogenizing utopia* and evinces a sharp tendency to reject particularities. Adorno was particularly aware of that when he spoke of the need to deflect reasoning from "the abstract equality of human beings," a "bad equality," toward the particularities (*das Besondere*) and the concreteness of social existence, lest we buy into that homogenizing project due to a misperception and lack of attention to this crucial problem.[36] This is an issue we must retain, despite the philosophy of history upon which his theory rests, and irrespective of contemporary modernity having forced some changes on this homogenizing thrust of citizenship.

As an encompassing collective subjectivity, the nation also often related to citizenship, whereby the latter receives a positive configuration beyond the "rights of man." It has been particularly relevant in this regard and central for the universalizing and homogenizing utopia of modernity, although it already lent it a particularized expression (which of course has implied always some sort of tension). The restless development of modernity, increasingly leading to pluralism, produces ever more numerous types of identity. While social rights themselves evince problems in terms of their universalization—thus of abstractness, especially though not only in welfare states based on corporatist systems—such identities tend to create a potentially fragmented social life, in which solidarity becomes much more difficult to ensure, a problem that is very much related to the crisis of the welfare state in Europe. That notwithstanding, citizenship remains the basic element in the imaginary and institutional articulation of modernity. To be sure, the generalization of a discourse that emphasizes plurality and the adaptation of institutions to such a reality further reinforce the very pluralization that lies at the basis of such developments in the first instance. A new relation between abstractness and concreteness seemingly starts to unfold.

A last issue must be stressed, connecting real abstractions and instituted citizenship. Appearing to their producers as given and external products, real abstractions, as Lukács pointed out, turn individuals and collectivities into passive, contemplative beings, bereft of initiative.[37] This comes up in the instituted character of citizenship since citizens enjoy rights that, once turned into law, must be secured or sponsored by the state, those agents henceforth deprived of activity. On the other hand, the instituting aspect of citizenship has been particularly important in the subcontinent in the last two centuries (a point that Lukács probably would have trouble considering). Thereby real abstractions dialectically expanded their role in the course of this larger social process. This carries on, despite the effort of neoliberalism to block developments beyond civil and political rights. The third phase of modernity has brought about changes in this regard too.

THE NEW FACES OF RIGHTS, LAW, AND JUSTICE

I have thus far constructed my argument by means of a historical-developmental approach to law, rights, and justice in the subcontinent. This served my purposes as for the two first phases of modernity. I want now to change my tack and carry out a more analytical discussion of the main trends and

14 *Latin America and Contemporary Modernity*

the modernizing moves vis-à-vis those issues at present. Before doing so, it is instructive to resume briefly the elements proposed in the first sections of this chapter bearing in mind the issues related to the conceptualization of real abstractions just introduced. What to say of Latin America and its development in the nineteenth and twentieth centuries in this regard? If the restrictive character of modernity during its first phase in the West meant that citizenship did not wholly embrace the population of those countries, the even more limited character of modernity in Latin America implied an even weaker power for citizenship, in the imaginary and the institutional domains. Personal relations of domination continued to be extremely important; rights were only imperfectly and incompletely respected in practice, whence social relations and identities had citizenship as, if not a minor, a less weighty element in daily life. Nevertheless, not only did the utopian element of history remain tied in with citizenship and the possibility of the expansion of the reach of the system of rights, as private property was based on the individual *right* to property, with the state formally built in a way such that courts, elections, and so forth found their articulation through the notion of the citizen. Therefore, while real abstractions played a less relevant role, they played it all the same. Moreover, not only did citizenship remain at the forefront of social development: It was piecemeal, in an uneven and combined manner, expanded up to the 1960s at least, going on further in some countries, to find an utterly renewed place and role in the process of democratic struggle against the military dictatorships and authoritarianism in general (cf. the Mexican regime) in the subcontinent. Besides, social citizenship, with its own contradictions, as seen in the previous section, performed an important part, as a horizon but also practically, to some extent, in the conformation of solidarity in the subcontinent.

We will see now how such issues have appeared during the third phase of modernity in Latin America. A negative backdrop must be pointed out before we tackle these issues. The conception of freedom has to a great extent suffered the impact of neoliberalism, in particular with respect to its link with equality and citizenship. More room for the exercise of choice in some domains, due to the decline of personal forms of domination and less state intervention, has arisen but has been strongly counteracted by the stark grip of the market and the increasing inequalities economic and social policies produced in the last decades. Neoliberal reforms in the economy and their accompanying attempt to limit the political space have entailed the material impoverishment of the population and the emptying out of political life, insofar as alternatives were from the very start utterly ruled out. The emphasis neoliberalism has placed on individual freedom in the market as the freedom to be cherished (as against equality) has not led to the expansion of rights: Much to the contrary, it has meant a battle to reduce rights or their efficacy, politically and socially, for most citizens of Latin America, substituted by compensatory policies aimed at the "losers" created by those very reforms. The subcontinent still has to grapple with the hegemony of

Law, Rights, and Justice   15

neoliberalism and the effects of that process, which has spanned especially the 1990s, but has not been actually reversed. Solidarity tends to shrink or apply to more limited domains while responsibility either resumes pristine liberal forms or begins to find new articulations.[38]

This does not mean that changes, and in a positive direction, have not occurred in relation to justice, rights, and law, notwithstanding a in a large measure hostile environment. In order to tackle that, we must make a first foray into the main forms of articulation between state and society in contemporary Latin America (a topic that will take on centrality in Chapter 3). Then I will try to extract a conception of justice from these forms. The role of rights and citizenship will be the focus of the discussion. Next the transformations of the judiciary will be accounted for. A further section will dwell upon a number of countries that will furnish more concrete elements for the discussion. Concluding reflections will follow, resuming a more general view of the third phase of modernity. The importance of "real abstractions" will be reaffirmed, but an orientation to the concrete, that is, to definitions that take into account more directly specific individuals and collectivities, will come to the fore. The decline of the working class as a more or less unified and homogeneous collectivity underlies much of these developments, implying the end or the reshaping—in the amazing Mexican case—of corporatism. The rise of pluralism, in the tracks of the increased complexity of social life, to which the deepening of globalization also contributes, is the other face of such developments. In one way or another, through difficulties and contradictory tendencies, the struggle for freedom and equality, in other words, equal freedom, in different languages and stances, stands out in the study of the third phase of modernity in this region.

Yet, distinct modernizing moves vie for direction of the definition of freedom and, more generally, the horizons of development of social life in Latin American societies at present. A progressive "project" may be spotted; in fact we had better speak of the outcome of a more decentered set of modernizing moves, in which some modernizing offensives can be discerned. A neoliberal or even liberal view is concerned with basic rights and philanthropy, with participation and social rights receiving as little heed as possible. An authoritarian perspective, which lurks almost silent today, would opt for domination alone. For now, it has no room to thrive.[39] We will have now the opportunity to analyze their distinct aspects in the following pages.

Disembeddings and Freedom

A first, important element to stress at this point relates to formidable changes that occurred in the Latin American rural world in the last three decades. As noted above, personal domination, especially in the countryside, was a dominant feature of the reality of the subcontinent. The development of agrarian capitalism has entirely transformed this situation, in an unprecedented way. This has entailed overwhelming processes of "disembedding,"

16 *Latin America and Contemporary Modernity*

as I have called them above, hence far-reaching modernization. Most peasants are no longer peasants—and yet there are still many of them! They share in widespread poverty; at this stage most of them have become free, wage workers, who have to deal with the contingency of social life and even subsistence almost on a daily basis. Others have become small proprietors who lack resources for land cultivation and decent survival. Either the failure of the agrarian reform or the straightforward development of agribusiness, including the end of protection of communal, *ejido* land in Mexico, has propelled a more typically modern subjectivity—at the individual and the collective levels.[40] To be sure, lack of resources and information, as well as the continued failure of the state to enforce basic civil rights—against the operations of its own repressive police forces or private militias or else outbursts of violence—limits the reach of this newly established freedom (not to speak of social rights, the possible antidote to the insecurity of the labor market).

But the fact is that both individually and collectively the new rural-urban poor are free to choose their ways of life and circulate around the national territory—looking for work and new re-embeddings—pursuing new modernizing moves and at times political offensives. Later on we shall see how this impacts on ethnic identities. If small proprietors surely exist, scattered across Latin America, and some sort of neopeasant identity lingers on—as in the case of the Brazilian Landless Workers' Movement (MST), the only one in the subcontinent that really raises this sort of issue today—once again we can see that they frame their demands for land and against the big rural property in the language of rights.[41] Civil freedom and rights demands clearly point to the further development of citizenship on a very concrete basis. Moreover, the enforcement of liberal democracies in the aftermath of the defeat of dictatorships, or authoritarian regimes as in the Mexican case, has led to more deeply rooted political rights throughout Latin America. Many consequences arise from that, as we shall see.

In the cities, which concentrate at present most of the Latin American population, this issue assumes a more problematic countenance, often directly connected to urban poverty and deprivation, but also to widespread violence and common crime. Historically violent societies, such as Brazil, and rampant and increasing inequalities, forced upon formally free peoples, have had the effect of promoting a situation of social strife and discontent that not always finds expression in social movements, but instead in crime, drug–dealing, and gratuitous violence. A few decades ago, even in the cities, personal domination and clienteles worked well—and the police was overall capable of keeping a small population, the "dangerous classes," under control. The "despotic power" of the state was enough at this stage; or else corporatism—of a more inclusive kind, such as in Argentina, or more restrictive, as in Brazil—was effective in controlling the better established working classes, in this case through a more subtle form of infrastructural power based on unions and professional associations. But now that personal forms of domination are almost totally gone, that corporatism has either disappeared or faces problems, and that the state would need a more inclusive form of citizenship in order to be capable of increasing its "infrastructural power," such a combination is not enough. The concrete limitations of citizenship have proved fatal in the last decades (with freedom crippled and deep inequalities as a constant as well as in terms of offering a stronger exercise of solidarity and providing for social integration).[42] If we add to that the especially important role and segmentation of markets (see Chapter 2) as well as the feeling of exclusion that arises from being at the losers' end of such a stratification system, it is not difficult to understand why these societies have faced such high levels of insecurity.

Finally, it is important to note a widespread lack of responsibility and the impossibility of solidarity beyond armed bands,[43] which can be witnessed above all with respect to the abandoned and poor young populations of such countries. It has often been coupled with the hierarchical, carcerary option that has taken over the United States and serves as an example for Latin America.[44]

The Persistence of Clientelism

This relates directly to the decay or demise of corporatism, the main form of articulation of the working classes to the state during the state organized phase of modernity, implying control and authoritarianism, a modern form of state-bureaucratic domination, which was completed by clientelism, another well-known form of relation between the population, on the one hand, and politicians and the state, on the other, across Latin America for a long time. Let me stress also that Mexico is in this regard an exception, since corporatism and the control of the unions' bureaucracy (linked to state and party—the Revolutionary Institutional Party, PRI) remains relatively strong. This shows that, even if the state is rolled back and underlying social changes continue, the political and institutional responses to this are neither automatic nor univocal. But in most countries where corporatism was somehow or another important—in Argentina and Brazil as to the urban working class, with more mobilization in the case of the former, in Bolivia as to the peasantry—it has starkly declined. Many developments may derive from this. By and large this connects not only to neoliberal reforms of the state and of legislation, but also to social changes that have led to a decrease in numbers and to the fragmentation of the working classes. Pluralism, in terms both of social situations and of responses to the new availability of the masses, has been the norm, including, as we can clearly see in the case of the *piqueteros* in Argentina, the organization of jobless "workers."[45] Freedom from corporatism has come about at the same time that savage markets and loss of jobs as well as worsening working and general social conditions have hit the popular classes.

18   *Latin America and Contemporary Modernity*

One response to this, harking back to former practices spread throughout Latin America, is clientelism, which provides for some sort of integration and a sort of solidarity, which is however skewed, insofar as equal freedom is of course absent from this arrangement. The reinforcement of this type of practice has expressed a mildly authoritarian modernizing move; or, put another way, the conservative counterpoint to neoliberal state reforms. A renewed link is established between the state and poor social strata, whereby greater control of society by the state may be established and the increase of infrastructural power by the latter may come about. Is clientelism a "traditional" practice, as many are prone to believe? I do not think so. In the absence of other mechanisms of representation and channeling of demands especially of the more deprived populations, there opens room for the activity of political entrepreneurs who either establish or bank on clienteles to give them leverage within poor "communities" (which somehow then have their demands heard and attended to) and force as for the political system.[46] But especially with the dominant forms of clientelism today, there is little of "traditional" in this relationship, especially when we speak of "thin" and "bureaucratic," in contradistinction to "denser" forms of clientelism (that is, more personal and implying a more direct exchange of benefits for votes). There seems to be no doubt that particularistic forms of political relationship—which would be typical of what O'Donnell has called "delegative democracy"—are then in place.[47] But there has been nothing really traditional in this. Instead we witness a very modern way of the unfolding of some of the possibilities of modern systems of representation, whose workings are by no means univocal—indeed it is in this space that clientelism has appeared and thrived. This does not mean that we should like it, or that we should not oppose other normative standards to it. I will come back to that. Meanwhile let me further explore clientelism.

The transformation of Argentinean Peronism has opened the opportunity for a reconsideration of the issue in a Latin American country in which—being present there—it had not played such an outstanding part. As unions declined, the working class pulverized, and Peronism had to shift its bases of support, clientelism assumed a much more prominent role in the Justicialista Party (PJ) than before, being also resumed by the UCR in a more bureaucratic, less personalist form. Therefore, regardless of the fact that this happened in the midst of a deep and dramatic crisis, the social sciences had to confront the rise of clientelism in a political system that was modernizing fast. It was not a lingering phenomenon, a witness of the past; rather, it expressed the emergence of a new, more liberal and democratic political system, which sprang from the floundering of the brutal military dictatorship that took over power in the 1970s. In Mexico, clientelism has been also an important topic of debate ever since, but more recently especially (though not only) with reference to the National Solidarity Program (PRONASOL), with compensatory policies that should operate as a buffer

Law, Rights, and Justice   19

in the face of the neoliberal reforms implemented in the 1990s, buttressing also the (eventually frustrated) permanence of the PRI in power. Some even speak of a "semi-clientelist" model, which combines targeted benefits with control of social organizations created to deliver and oversee them plus the electoral exploitation of the outcomes of the program, or of an uneasy compromise, which the World Bank, short of any other solution, has accepted, between general, quasi universalistic programs and targeted social policy. In any case, targeted policies remained at the core of Mexican social policy henceforth—such as expressed originally in Progressa and later on in Oportunities (Oportunidades) programs—in levels of reach and expenditure in fact lower than the Chilean ones, both showing clearly the centrality of neoliberal perspectives (aiding the very poor without "distorting" market allocation mechanisms).[48]

In Brazil, clientelism was an important issue in the social sciences literature,[49] but disappeared more recently. More "traditional" forms remain, in any case, and a new form of clientelism, exactly what I would like to call *bureaucratic clientelism*, has emerged more recently. It represents a cunning modernization of old formulas, while at the same time it may embody promises of citizenship further development. Empirically it is not so dependent on single politicians, nor does a socially organized network of agents, which are of course very often dependent on the access to state resources, basically articulate it. Conceptually it is distinct in that it is counts on a large-scale bureaucratic apparatus, in the case of Brazil centrally based, having at its center the Ministry of Social Development and Hunger Combat (MDS). This is not inimical to a more direct political clientelistic use at the end of the system of social assistance oriented to focalization and a specific, supposedly up-to-date and technically sharp sort of social policy. These programs do not differ much from compensatory policies (more on that below), although supposedly having as a target the definite removal of these people from present conditions, enabling them to carry on with their lives autonomously in the future.

The corollary is that these people can be selected more or less at will, especially in the Family Grant (Bolsa Família) program, whose participants receive a small amount of money from the federal government to escape hunger, since they are below a very low income threshold (as part, the only one in fact thus far implemented, of the Zero Hunger Program). This is especially true since technical indications have to be politically mediated— by municipal governments—in order to be implemented, *pace* local committees (with a majority of members stemming from "civil society") being in principle neutral as to who is selected. These must be the poorest among the poor. A strategy of political benefiting from this may be put in place by the opening of municipal directories by the party (or parties) in office and the formation of leadership in connection with the program where it is implemented, regardless of whether it is the municipality and its bureaucracy or local, civil society based, committees who control the

20   Latin America and Contemporary Modernity

distribution of benefits. Rationalization and bureaucratization may go hand in hand with the instrumentalization of social programs, vis-à-vis populations with very few social and political resources, which are more easily coopted by ruling political forces and may become their electoral bases in forthcoming disputes. In practice, there is often a mix between older and these more recent forms of clientelism, regardless of the impact such programs do have in the reduction of extreme poverty. In a more critical vein, it can also be argued that rather than eliminating poverty such programs aim at overseeing, secluding, and containing it as a means of social and political control of a threatening population as well as answering to a problematic issue posed on the public agenda.[50] There is apparently a great distance between this bureaucratic distribution of benefits and the personalized clientelist strategies. Can we not, however, make out the link between the manipulation of poverty and destitution, on the one hand, and electoral and political gains, on the other? The issue becomes more complicated once truly popular governments resort to this sort of poverty alleviation scheme, for instance Bolivia's "Bono Juancito Pinto."

The problem there is of course that clientelism eschews a relationship based on rights, even in cases in which it seems to be bureaucratically implemented. Instead of rights, we are still close to "favor"; it is still to a great extent a dispensation from above to the poorest—even if in a more impersonal manner and with some vague reference to the idea of rights—that has the upper hand. Experiences such as the Participatory Budget developed by the Workers' Party (PT), in several Brazilian cities, or the decentralization and public discussion of priorities put forward by the Broad Front (FA) in Montevideo, Uruguay's capital, aimed at breaking away from this. The concrete record of such innovations seems to be more mixed than the celebratory assessment of their virtues, by far exaggerated.[51] Insofar as citizenship is based on universalizing rights and clientelism is, at least in its older forms, steered by particularism and personal relations, real abstractions do not play a decisive role in such arrangements. They appear as real alternatives and attempts at more deeply though limitedly democratizing politics. This changes, however, to some extent with bureaucratic clientelism, since its more impersonal and rationalized form has similarities with the rights enjoyed by citizens, although this is not actually the case, since poverty and not a universal and common status and condition (that is, equal freedom) is aimed at by targeted social policies. In any case, it must be said that clientelism is as modern as citizenship. In Latin America, they often make up a *hybrid* that has nothing to do with the combination of "modern" and "traditional" links between people and the state.[52] It is a normative struggle *within* modernity that is therefore at stake when we opt for one or the other. We cannot investigate this here, but there are surely other situations in modern civilization—including in this central, original countries—that reproduce, with distinct traits, exactly this sort of hybridization and struggle.

Citizenship and Rights

We have seen above that the idea of social rights as introducing a counterpoint to inequality and establishing a universal status was at the bottom of social security systems in Europe. We have previously examined how this idea of social citizenship had influenced, within much less generous limits, Latin American experiences. Today, in contradistinction, it is extreme poverty (of the so-called "excluded") that has become the mainstay of social policy. Initially as a consequence of compensatory programs related to neoliberal "adjustment" schemes, targeted, focused social policies were staged throughout Latin America. They have become, however, the standard pattern of social policy, under the allegation of shortage of resources or provisory schemes until people emerge out of poverty, as against citizenship-based, universalistic social policies. This, as seen above, may connect to old and new forms of clientelism. An especially important point in this regard, too, is of course the trend toward the "flexibilization" of labor legislation, making workers more vulnerable, taxes less weighty, and capital more comfortable. This implies that justice and welfare are handed to the market, according to neoliberalism supposedly the best means to distribute rewards to individuals, entailing immediate freedom as against citizenship rights, which in fact create, especially through social rights, conditions that free workers from the immediate pressure of capitalist markets and the risk of poverty, increasing also general solidarity. Responsibility, at a certain point to a great extent directed toward the state, is returned to the individual alone, who has now to care for employability and destiny in life. At the same it was often under neoliberal regimes, or governments whose policy was at least very close to such a model, that social expenditure once again increased in Latin America, during the 1990s, after having fallen sharply during the 1980s. Thus, from 1990 to 1999, in the countries (Mexico, Colombia, and Venezuela) with middle levels of expenditure, this increased from US$ 251 to 365, while those with higher expenditure (Argentina, Brazil, Costa Rica, Chile, Panamá, and Uruguay) the increase was from US$ 796 to 1,055; in those with very low levels (Bolivia, El Salvador, Guatemala, Honduras, Nicaragua, Paraguay, Peru, and the Dominican Republic) the amounts were, respectively, US$ 58 and 113. This happened, however, within a general framework in which social assistance and focalization rather than security and rights became the core of social policy (with exceptions). Simply more money, which was not enough in any case, has had limited effect against poverty.[53]

This is all reasonably well known. Less clear are two aspects of these contemporary attempts at modernization—which have indeed modernizing offensives coordinated by international organizations now at their core.[54] First we must be wary of how they break with the modern project, reshaped during the second phase of modernity via social rights, of at least approximate equality of conditions working as the presupposition for the freedom of all. That is to say, it entails a break with equal freedom. Moreover, little

22 Latin America and Contemporary Modernity

attention has been paid to the tutelage aspects of such programs, which fit well together with bureaucratic clientelism. Thereby the state decides who the deserving poor are, that is, those who follow the rules related to work and the care of their children, besides being very poor, hence becoming entitled to such benefits, taken not as a citizenship right but rather as a benevolent and targeted handout from the state. And above all, instead of equality it is "equity" that becomes the centerpiece of the credo of contemporary social policy. Instead of universal services serving equal freedom, whatever the limits of citizenship and real abstractions, it is rather the selective targeting of groups according to the logic of giving a bit more to those who have much less. This not only divides the poor from the very poor—even though separating them and establishing the "deserving" ones sounds quite bizarre in a continent plagued by widespread and deep poverty—but also produces a fuzzy mix of targeting with general assistance, depoliticizes the social question, tends to freeze the issue of progressive equality, and discards both the universal status of citizenship and its tension with class stratification.[55]

We may confront this, and the functioning of most social services in Latin America (despite at times constitutional provisions that establish universal health care and educational rights), with Esping-Andersen's welfare states' classification.[56] We clearly see that Latin America has been moving from a variably effective corporatist welfarism toward a feeble liberal, residual welfare state (mainly in basic education and health care, while the pension system has been capitalized or even privatized).[57] To be sure, developments in a distinct direction are, due mostly to the left and frequently rhetorically, at times on the agenda. Hope may be derived from the fact that, according to historical reconstructions, a universalistic welfare state was not by any means a straightforward project in Europe. It was rather the outcome of disparate and sometimes contradictory effects of state and private social policies geared toward alleviating the suffering of the poor and the intentional search for solidary inclusion. But at least we have to be clear on the problems and the shortcomings contained in this sort of social policy, which is at the center of Luis Inácio Lula da Silva's government in Brazil from 2002 onward and was perhaps the main popular catch for his re-election in 2006.[58]

Can we just criticize the enormous effort programs such as the aforementioned Family Grant imply? That would be too short-sighted. Nevertheless, the program—the most comprehensive of its sort in Latin America today, though Brazil itself has other cash transfer programs—is very close to the neoliberal focused programs and one should not forget how distant it remains from actually developing a citizenship-oriented strategy, let alone the problems of deeper redistribution that remain untouched and the welfare dependency mechanism that may creep in thereby. The state assumes responsibility and solidarity is increased, but hitherto these programs remain basically at the level of social assistance and poverty alleviation.

In any case, the language of rights has become widespread in Latin America. Here the idea of a powerful, yet decentered, modernizing *qua* democratizing move takes on a stronger significance. A problem has been its indiscriminate use, referring to anything, hence losing its edge.[59] More positively it may be said that, however the shortcomings of such a loose usage, the issue has been placed at the center of the national imaginary and as a horizon of development throughout the subcontinent. This is how the last century ended up; this is how the new one has begun. Individual rights in the civil, political, and social dimensions have had evolutions that are not convergent, with the second faring better than the other two, a new dimension has been added to the debate, especially in countries with large "pre-Columbian" populations (Ecuador, Bolivia, Mexico, but also Chile, Colombia, Venezuela, and even Brazil, Argentina). Collective rights of indigenous peoples have come to the forefront of the debate, in cultural terms, in the legal dimension (see below) as well as in what concerns territorial claims. As elsewhere, a departure from the basically individualistic character of modern citizenship rights has happened in Latin America.[60] Yet, there may be more continuity in this regard than it might seem. Take the case of Zapatism, for some a radical departure from citizenship and an antistate movement. A very plausible reading of their documents and action is that the Zapatistas basically and originally demanded citizenship for the indian as indian, beyond the ideology of *mestizaje;* that is where the Mexican government broke off negotiations, not at the demand for autonomy, which it has granted to other regions of indigenous people (i.e., Oaxaca). If theirs is not an individualist, by no means is it merely a collectivist antimodern and anticitizenship view what they have supported either.[61]

Citizenship and Participation

During most of the twentieth century, unionism has been by far the major social movement in Latin America, the same as in other parts of the world. In Argentina, Uruguay, Brazil, Chile, and Mexico, the urban working classes performed a decisive role, while in others peasant unionism was as important as the mobilization the former achieved, as was the case in Bolivia. Even the transitions to democracy in the late 1970s and the early 1980s witnessed strong union movements at the forefront of social struggles—the Brazilian PT was itself partly a result of a renewal of the working classes and of unionism. This has dramatically changed more recently. If the countryside was swept by a capitalist tide and the (in both, Marxian senses) free rural-urban poor increased dramatically, in the urban areas change was also widespread. Industrial restructuration (implying permanent unemployment for many), the tertiarization of the economy (as in Lima, Peru's capital city), the segmentation of the labor markets, and economic recession have had, all taken together, devastating effects over unionism. That is not to say that it does not have any importance today, which would be patently a mistake. But it implies indeed that other social movements, within or without the working classes, or entertaining a more

24   *Latin America and Contemporary Modernity*

perpendicular relation with them, have increased their importance and that modernizing moves stem also to a great extent from them. That is what social movement analysts have consistently stressed in the last decade; this is also what has marked the left across the subcontinent.[62] We will be back to them in Chapter 3.

On the other hand, due to this more heterogeneous social tissue, but also due to the pressures toward pluralization, the national state has been shown less capable of imposing a homogenous national identity, which, for at least a while and in some countries, had to do with the homogeneity of the working class. Neither can this furnish such bases any longer, nor can the state block off the alternative identities that the deepening of globalization has been offering to all the collectivities that comprise the Latin American nations (providing some more freedom as to state power). This favors also the rise of social pluralism in what regards citizenship demands, since it is not only one issue or a tightly woven bunch of issues the population as a whole is prone to present to the state. Pluralism entails also plurality of demands and the relative weakening of the state contributes decisively in this direction.[63] A shift in modernization is thus under way.

Either mobilizing specific sectors of the population (women, indigenous people, blacks, the jobless, territorially based communities, etc.) or organizing specific sectors of the working class around specific demands (such as housing), social movements have therefore become much more plural and decentered than ever before. Within the left, this has also often entailed the need to build coalitions without any longer the possibility of standing alone at rock bottom as the only and true organization. Hierarchical relations between parties and movements, as well as within and between the latter, have therefore become more difficult to achieve, if anyone tries to stick to this former pattern. According to some, this has led to the development of networks—what I would like to define as collaborative endeavors—between movements and parties, especially, albeit not only, at the local level (with the proviso that we must be aware of the variable extent to which this diagnosis applies and without a direct derivation of organizational forms from levels of social pluralization):

> Against the backdrop of the left that preceded it—which, as we have seen, was adamant on theoretical unity and strategic centralization-, the new left distinguishes itself by a marked plurality. As to organizational strategies, instead of the unitary political subject of Leninism—the party vanguard or the state-party—the predominant forms are 'broad fronts' of parties and movements, the 'coordinators' of social movements or the 'meetings' of activist organizations. [. . . thus] coalitions or networks whose integrating organizations contribute to common political purposes—for instance, an election, a campaign or a protest cycle—without losing its organizational autonomy.[64]

Law, Rights, and Justice 25

Solidarity has therefore to find new paths and shapes, since neither the basic rights of pristine liberalism (not to speak of how neoliberalism poses the issue) nor the old all-embracing class or a state-based project can do the job any longer. This means also that a sort of shared, collective but not uniform responsibility has to be woven between the members of such coalitions and networks.

What some have internationally indicated as well is that a new sort of relationship between state and society has slowly been developing in the aftermath of the crisis of the second, state-organized phase of modernity. Now even European states must cope with pluralism rather than neocorporatism. Governance has become more complicated in a more complex, opaque, and uneven society.[65] New connections between state and society would be therefore necessary, in order to build bridges, channels of communication, coordination of programs, and so forth, as well as contributing to social integration. Little of that has thus far happened. A few openings are in process in Latin America, what can be seen in the relationships between the Lula government and the MST, in Brazil, or the Néstor Kirchner's government in Argentina and the social movement of the unemployed, the *piqueteros* (alongside his attempt to isolate the most radical, or divergent, currents within it). Networks of collaboration seem to be timidly developing. The problems that arise are pretty obvious: Does that mean actual networks or after all are we merely in presence of an attempt to return to clientelism or to the former highly hierarchical, cooptative-repressive model that was typical of corporatism, in a transformed situation? Be that as it may, the fact is that a coordination of this sort seems to be increasingly necessary if we do not want to leave social movements just cut off from the state and social solidarity to become a passive phenomenon rather than being built by active collective subjectivities in collaboration with the state, which can lend universal format to the demands of social movements. Cooptation is a problem that all social movements have to face when the state and/or parties are willing (truly or falsely, so as to subordinate them) to come to terms with social movements. We are in the midst of a changing situation, hence the problem comes back with different colors as well. The judiciary, especially in Brazil, also moves at times in the direction of weaving new links with social movements. We will look at that soon.

Another especially important development of this pluralization of social life has been the emergence of a multifarious public sphere, with "alternative publics" of various sorts, including alternative media, throughout the subcontinent, possible only insofar as political liberty exists. The importance of the main public sphere for the development of citizenship and rights is well established at least since Habermas studied it four decades ago. As a result of criticism, the *plurality of public spheres* and the existence of *alternative publics* have become issues widely shared in the recent bibliography, about Latin America as well as elsewhere.[66] Empirically this sort of question has popped up as a counterpoint to the study of social

26 *Latin America and Contemporary Modernity*

movements and has direct connection with the problem of citizenship as an instituting collective subjectivity—or, in other words, with so-called "active citizenship." Theoretically it has the advantage of being more precise than the generalized and loose use of the idea of "civil society." The latter has three sources: Either it derives from traditional Gramscian usage—and is therefore somewhat too narrow, although, correctly, it does not split state and society in a water-tight manner and stresses the class conflicts that structure it; or it stems from the Habermasian tripartite division between the economy, the political system, and civil society—being in fact too rigid and in my view patently inadequate; or else it is a poor and unnecessary substitute for the idea of society *tout court*.[67]

Modernity has become more complex (as partly seen here, a theme to be explored at greater length in Chapter 3); so has the public sphere. There came about the multiplication of (already plural) alternative publics, each with its own characteristics, its participants and audiences, plus proper issues. A molecular multiplication of modernizing moves is linked to this pluralization. Opinion and demands, as well as concrete orientations for action and movements, are forged there at the local, the national, and the globalized levels. Solidarity at different levels as well as partial forms of responsibility emerge in these plural alternative publics. Youth publics, ethnic publics, community radios, environmental concerns, these spheres multiply, fragment sometimes in their own directions and may converge, through more powerful and encompassing public spheres, such as those that have at their core mass media, or political processes. As any public sphere, alternative publics are articulated by a mix of hierarchical, mercantile, and networked principles and their accompanying mechanisms of organization.[68] They are usually based more on voluntary collaboration (networks) than on command (hierarchy) and voluntary exchange (market). It goes without saying that the two latter also play a role in their articulation.

The sense in which the notion of "civil society" can be accepted here stands as merely descriptive for what is a heterogeneous array of organizations that (though often linked to it) do not belong to the state. A Tocquevillian or pluralist view of society sits comfortably with such a perspective. The transition processes toward democracy in Latin America since the 1980s offered occasion for a proliferation of organizations expressing social movements and interest groups. Today, however, the massive emergence of nongovernmental organizations (NGOs), which has happened since the 1990s, has altered the landscape, forming what some would call a "third sector," an even looser and usually ideologically charged (antistate) notion than civil society, or one that is clearly connected to a neoliberal and de-politicized (and anticonflict) perspective of such a concept. Citizenship is certainly strengthened by the proliferation of associations expressing the population in a direct way and creating a new layer of more or less institutionalized organizations placed between society in general and the state. In what refers to NGOs the situation is, to say the least, less clear—to start with because such a term covers a wide range of entities. They may represent demands and shape agendas especially for the very poor and those who have trouble in organizing themselves, or in relation to questions that are diffuse and thus do not engage anyone in a very direct manner (cf. environmental problems); in addition, they may offer sources of independent criticism and programs. But they may also expropriate the opinion and the representation of people as well as establishing a new bureaucracy that is as self-oriented as that which belongs to the state, being even less accountable due to its nonrepublican character, therefore more freely operating according to its own interests and agendas or that of (especially international or state agencies) donors.[69] This is certainly not always the case, but in a rather critical vein it may be said that " . . . expectations regarding NGO potential for grassroots empowerment have been over-optimistic. NGOs have become harnessed by the state and been used to implement the neo-liberal model."[70] Moreover, the ambiguity and the not necessarily virtuous character of "civil society" is unmistakably expressed by the characteristics of some NGOs, meaning that they may be linked to modernizing moves and offensives of all sorts. This is not the only case in which "real civil societies" may evince antidemocratic and exclusionary views, let alone the class and conflictive character Gramsci attributed to it long ago, notwithstanding the fact that this has been more recently usually forgotten, especially in Habermasian approaches. The *heterogeneity* of civil societies, as well as their interpenetration with states—"political societies"—must be taken into account in this regard.[71]

In any case, a more positive view of the NGOs' role in the democratization in Latin America can be spotted in its participation in one of the main activities of what could be called a global, cosmopolitan civil society: the organization and global impact of the World Social Forum, which for many years met in Porto Alegre, Brazil, presenting what initially was thought of as a "counter-globalization movement," eventually being seen as a "counter-hegemonic" proposal for the new global society, in favor of democracy and as against the neoliberal model of globalization. While this is now a less important (or at least a less noisy) phenomenon and its organization and happening have spread across the world, it had a huge impact as one of the main fora where globalization such as it actually happens (that is, under, and at the height of, neoliberal hegemony) was contested, consisting largely in a Latin American invention.[72]

A Stronger and Plural Judiciary

The transformations of the judiciary are also an especially important area in which changes in citizenship have carried on in the last decade or so. As the keeper of rights, the judiciary is of course a key element in the articulation of citizenship, hence of social solidarity, through the distinct phases of modernity. As Pérez-Perdomo and Friedman observed in relation to the subcontinent,

28 *Latin America and Contemporary Modernity*

In all these countries, law has grown in importance—however we care to analyze or measure it. International investors pressure the system and create a climate in which lawyers and law become established; society as a whole also puts pressure on the system to produce results. Businesses employ thousands of lawyers; but ordinary people need the assistance of lawyers to buy houses, to get a divorce, and to do other mundane things. The growth of the middle class means more work for lawyers. Rights consciousness brings more claims against government and administrative agencies. There is a culture of claims developing.[73]

Among the changes that have affected the judiciary—modernizing it and lending it the potential to further carry out rather important modernizing moves—we can singularize three clusters: (1) the steady support for reform of judicial systems by the World Bank, other international as well as U.S.' agencies; (2) the tendency to widen the access of the population to justice; and (3) the rise (and fall) of pluralism.

1. While democratization is one chief aspect of the developments and moves mentioned above, the push of neoliberalism is the main feature of another far-reaching process of legal change and moves sweeping Latin America. Sponsored by the World Bank, reforms of the judiciary have been carried out in the subcontinent. The success of such reforms varies widely. For instance, in Peru they utterly failed, Brazil for a while lagged behind, whereas Argentina (which seems to have done well regarding cost and opportunities as well as process reform) and Ecuador had more positive outcomes to report. Central America and Colombia, where such reforms were enacted during a longer period and with more money, evince mixed results. According to a diagnosis that links this process negatively and critically to neoliberal economic globalization, the reform of judicial power in Latin America would be part of the agreement known as the "Washington Consensus," sold to and implemented in the Latin American countries in the 1990s by joint efforts of the World Bank and the International Monetary Fund (IMF). In fact, the broad reforms of law and judicial systems carried out by such countries aim at strengthening the rule of law, therefore facilitating the attraction of foreign investment. As usual, the World Bank has acted in this regard as both a think tank and a financial supporter of the reforms, which may be compared to the programs of "law and development" of the 1960s.[74]

The main suggestions and proposals contained in the World Bank documents, which in fact supported the effort toward what they themselves have called "second generation reforms" (see Chapter 2), can be summarized in four categories: (1) the assessment and reduction of costs and thus the increase of the economic benefits of the workings of the judicial power; (2) the unification of process law in a world scale; (3) the promotion of alternative forms of conflict resolution and access to justice; (4) the renewal of the selections and training of as well as incentives to judges, plus the reform of law teaching and the decentralization of justice administration. The rise of judges' wages, the increase in the number of courts, and the introduction of new technologies and computers, as well as even the creation of something such as a National Justice Council (to control the judiciary), are further issues on the World Bank's proposed agenda. More substantively, the reforms would aim at creating an adequate environment for the private sector, in particular for foreign investment, and the strengthening of liberal democracy, through a strong and autonomous judiciary. Secondarily, the opening of the access to justice for the population and the capacity of judges to investigate crimes would be also at stake.[75] There is little doubt that neoliberal reforms—and the neoliberal, business and market-based notion of freedom—lie at the bottom of such programs. But in touching the issue of access to justice, which they may mention merely to buttress their main aims, they point to the equal-freedom questions mentioned above. In addition, decentralization and access to justice bring us to a further problem in the process of legal and justice change in Latin America.

2. The worldwide movement to broaden the access to justice for the largest sectors of the population[76] has finally had its impact on Latin American countries. It could make sense only when these populations were actually freed at least from personal forms of domination. The end of the military dictatorships, as well as the transition to a more open political rule in Mexico, have given rise to this sort of move. Brazil is the outstanding example of this within the formal system of justice, especially through the creation of special courts to deal with the daily problems of the population. Therein what may be called the "judicialization" of social life and politics has been established—that is, the influence of the judiciary as a body drawing upon legislation that emanates from parliament, irrespective of how judges deal with it—in contrast to what has been called "juridification"—a typical formation of the welfare state, which implies the application by the bureaucracy of rules itself generates. In the case of countries with a "Latin" background, it is worth noting too that such developments are connected, or are at least parallel, to the attenuation of the distinction between civil and common law. This happens insofar as judge-made law becomes more important—in itself a modernizing move of deep significance, which has a professional corporation as its main carrier. Since the judiciary is called upon to intervene in many spheres and situations of social life, and here we find the other elements that trigger this specific process of modernization, it cannot rely on codes and the mere repetition and reposition of former situations. Instead, judges must be active and end up creating lively jurisprudence when intervening with a future-oriented attitude in addressing conflicts within social life.[77]

In Brazil, these new courts were combined with the emergence of a new generation of judges, who tend to mix in some measure the mere application of statutes with considerations of substantive issues related to justice, and with the Public Ministry—a specific state body that intends to represent the interests of society, created by the 1988 Constitution, with great autonomy

30   *Latin America and Contemporary Modernity*

from any state or society collectivities, although it often weaves alliances with many different sectors. Some even speak of a new form of "functional" representation within the judiciary, which would go further than that provided for by the parliament and representative democracy, in what consists in a polemical formulation. But it is quite arguable whether these reforms have actually facilitated the access to justice for most of the population, not to speak of the slow pace of the judicial system.[78] In Mexico, a similar process is under way, with more ambiguous results; likewise in Peru.[79] In Argentina too, one aspect of the reform of the judiciary was the expansion of services in order to open them up to the population. Some, nonetheless, sustain very pessimistic views regarding the possibilities of democratizing the system. It must be said, in addition, that some would speak in Argentina, especially as to social conflicts and "social protests," about "negative," that is, repressive "judicialization."[80] In Colombia, a clear politicization of the judiciary and the judicialization of conflicts have brought the judiciary to the center of the state, especially after the promulgation of the 1991 Constitution, with, on the other hand, neoliberalism standing out in terms of influence in the course of justice reforms. Besides, ordinary conflicts and penal issues that directly affect the population are not so well attended. Mention must be made to the figure of the ombudsman in a few countries of the subcontinent (such as Bolivia, Peru, Colombia, El Salvador, with several different names), who may be having increasing influence and gaining confidence from the population, regardless of difficulties for their work.[81]

In any case, it is clear that the importance of the judiciary is growing in Latin America, notwithstanding the real problems that beset the implementation of basic aspects of civil rights and the proviso introduced above about "negative judicialization" (certainly not exclusive to Argentina). The rule of law and the multiplication of issues that demand attention in legal regulations, implying both political stability and the pluralization of social life, are entwined in the present-day restructuring of the relation between state and society. Democratization, whatever the limits of such changes, is somehow strengthened by the virtues they usually evince. To some extent equal freedom, hence solidarity, is strengthened by such moves.

3. For many years, especially in some countries with either large indigenous populations (Bolivia and Ecuador, mainly) and/or a state that did not encompass its whole territory or had deep legitimacy (Colombia), strong modernizing offensives for alternative systems of rights, namely movements for "legal pluralism," were operative (the same happening in Mexico since the 1990s). Such movements mobilized relevant sectors of the population and many intellectuals, gathered in particular in the important journal *Otro derecho*, edited in Bogotá. In other countries, such as Brazil, mainly in the south, such a movement also thrived, alongside what some called "the law found in the garbage." It has inspired many activists and popular struggles against the authoritarian and/or exclusionary regimes that for a long time dominated these regions. For some, unfortunately, the movement was

expropriated by the reforms of the judiciary that were staged in the 1990s. In fact, the tendency toward decentralization they implied was similar to the points on the agenda of the World Bank for legal reform, as seen above, and was taken as part of the effort to provide access to justice to the poor and ethnically different.[82]

Pluralist movements in the terrain of law in Latin America, combining what was often named "alternative legal services" of various types, emerged in the context of the search for a reasoning and practice of the popular sectors and intellectuals who could challenge the hegemony of the powers to be in the region. They operated in a nongovernmental sphere. Often the support to the popular sectors was followed by professional practice and reflection, about the law and about broader social change. This is one of the elements that disappear from the practice and reflection oriented by the projects directed by the World Bank. Social movements have declined, leaving the realm of theory and normative thought for those who have frowned upon contemporary developments. At best there is networked collaboration between movements and the state, in an optimistic view, or cooptation of, in a pessimistic vein, of the former by the latter. What basically happens is the participation of those movements in the reform of justice and the development of alternative or extrajudicial spaces in the resolution of conflicts. This varies from country to country. Whereas in Mexico cooperation is rare, in Argentina and Brazil this happens more frequently. In any case, technicization and individualization are the outcome of such institutional changes.[83]

On the other hand, many of the innovations that are related to pluralism and the autonomous exercise of alternative legal systems have been implanted, especially in the context of constitutional reforms in countries such as Bolivia and Ecuador, as well as Colombia, enabling indigenous populations to exercise a transformed version of supposedly traditional legal practices. While this has strengthened freedom—democracy and autonomy—for these sectors, arbitrary procedures and decisions, as well as the reach of such alternative systems, have become a thorny problem to be solved in all these countries. Should the official, mainstream judiciary allow the burning of "witches" by people condemned by indigenous populations (as in Bolivia) or the expulsion and expropriation of minority Protestant groups in indigenous communities dominated by popular Catholicism and its "uses and mores" (as in Mexico)? If not, what is actually meant by legal pluralism in a constitutional state? Is there any actual possibility of the indigenous juridical rules being transplanted to the society at large, configuring what might be called a process of "interculturality" proper? This is a problematic issue for which there seem to be no ready-made answers at present. Responses have varied in terms of reach and consistency, short of the problems created by such hard cases.[84] While solidarity may thereby be increased at the local level, the overreach of the exercise of pluralism may threaten solidarity on a larger, national scale. A conflict of responsibilities, between local legal agents and national courts, becomes a delicate issue.

32 *Latin America and Contemporary Modernity*

Other manifestations of legal pluralism need to be mentioned as well. First of all, there is the spread of "arbitrage" by nonprofessional judges and away from the courts, speeding up and flexibilizing mainly the relationships between economic agents.[85] This is germane to the spread of a sort of legislation and legal procedures that unfold above the national state level, especially when large transnational corporations make business in Latin America as they do in other parts of the world (including the rules of global regulatory agencies—see Chapter 2). For some this would relate to the decline of the nation-state and the overcoming of "Fordism" (see Chapter 2), which demands greater flexibility in economic transactions and dispute resolution.[86] Neoliberal freedom and responsibility, even of a corporate sort, increases thereby, of course.[87]

Overall, however, it seems clear enough that social pluralism is eventually expressed especially in the institutionalization of legal pluralism in its distinct guises. But one may argue that it emerges in the access of the population to justice too. This happens not only because the scope and variety of issues becomes wider. Lay agents and their specific perspectives also gain space in an institutional terrain that has by and large been dominated exclusively by professionals and been largely formalistic and exclusionary.[88] What will become of it is still to be seen, to begin with because resistances are at work and problems abound. Popular participation is challenging and democratizing as well as often antiuniversalist, becoming dominated, as is the case everywhere the state withdraws from its role as a universalizing agent, by more powerful individuals or collectivities, whether within local and national conflicts or at the more global level.

A Tendency Toward Constitutionalization

A final issue that I want to tackle here refers to the heightened role of constitutions in the subcontinent. The end of military rule and of the PRI regime in Mexico brought about an importance to constitutional arrangements never before seen in Latin America. Either constitutional assemblies were elected or former, amended constitutions, resumed. Liberal democracy is of course at the center of such processes, although Chile, in particular until especially 2004–2005, still felt the weight of the power and the constitutional arrangements left over by the transition controlled by General Pinochet.[89] Overall, however, representative democracy, with varied degrees of attached participatory or directed democratic rules, is well in place.

Moreover, a development that has unfolded in most civil law countries seems to be operative in Latin America right now too. A move away from the predominance of specific codes (civil, penal, labor, among others) appears to be happening in favor of the constitution as a higher-level norm. More research into that would be necessary in order that a stronger and more substantiated argument could be done. But in two areas this seems to be clear. First, the role played by supreme courts and the constitution, in a way similar to what occurs in common law countries, has come about in the subcontinent, distortions and political manipulation notwithstanding (in which Mexico is a case with a terrible note of continuity between the previous PRI period and the present).[90] In a sense this contrasts with the flexibilization of law downwards; in another, it appears possibly as the other side of the same process. Instead of the rigidity of codes it is the compatibility of ordinary legislation with general and universal principles that is at stake. This happens regardless of problems that linger on as to implementation, especially of civil rights and often of state violence. Second, the new constitutions of Latin America, or reformed constitutional texts, have been framed by what may be called an "aspirational constitutionalism," which envisages social change rather than the preservation of order. This can and has been appropriated by social movements and judges to develop specific policies and projects. The problem here is that there is of course the risk of an accommodation based on rights already supposedly given (that is, what I have referred to above as the instituted aspect of citizenship in detriment of its instituting aspect).[91]

This is strong evidence. However, further social developments and deeper and more wide-ranging research has still to be carried out in Latin America in order to verify the correctness of this last hypothesis. Flexibilization of legal reasoning and new developments in law are mostly certainly in any case to occur due to the increasing complexity and demands upon the judicial system, in Latin America as elsewhere.

In what follows, I will frame more clearly the developments thus far analyzed within the previously introduced conception of the third phase of modernity.

PARTIAL CONCLUSIONS: REAL ABSTRACTIONS, SOCIAL COORDINATION, AND THE (RENEWED) RELATIONS BETWEEN CONCRETENESS AND UNIVERSALITY

As stated at the beginning of this chapter, law, rights, and justice have been shown to be pivotal elements whereby the general imaginary of modernity has been concretely expressed, in specific ways, in contemporary Latin America, linking up also with institutional forms. We have seen that much has changed and that citizenship has been at the center of the process of democratization, as a key form of re-embedding too. In this regard it has consisted in a form of construction of a more homogenous population, with some abstract elements in common, in each country. Other tendencies, however, press pluralism and a more heterogeneous view of rights to the forefront of the political agenda. There are limitations and restrictions to the expansion of rights, though. Civil rights have not been entirely guaranteed, especially for the poor, and a narrow, neoliberal conception of freedom, which is expressed in targeted social policies, has come up at the antipodes

34 *Latin America and Contemporary Modernity*

of the notion of equal freedom. Should that prevail in the long run, the third phase of modernity would move away from one of the paramount values of its imaginary. Thereby the richness of the pluralism that has been emerging would be crippled by an individualizing and shallow view of freedom that militates against its universalist and unitary character. If we add to this the widespread inequalities and capitalist as well bureaucratic forms of domination that pervade Latin America, it becomes clear that the institutionalization of modernity in the region might end up in a one-sided and antidemocratic mould.

The problematic character of parties today was only slightly mentioned, but a bottleneck for participation must be spotted there. The hierarchical character of much of the public sphere has to be emphasized too, since the commercial media (based on oligopolies) has enormous power. Both issues will be tackled in greater detail in Chapter 3. The end (or decay) of corporatism has proved difficult to overcome, especially with respect to alternative arrangements and beyond "poliarchical" electoral arrangements typical of liberal democracy. Overall, participation and representation (that is, the distinct and antagonistic logic of the "demos" and the "polis") are still to find a more advanced resolution, in Latin America as much as elsewhere.[92] Also negatively, clientelism, especially in its older forms, has additionally been a means whereby concrete demands of destitute populations are somehow attended by the state, combined or in parallel to the role played by real abstractions.

Yet, Latin America, despite the difficulties in finding its way into the third phase of modernity, has been capable of raising important issues vis-à-vis citizenship and of building coalitions and networks whereby plural demands and political voices can be articulated in this rather transformed situation. To this we must add the participation of the masses in electoral contests and debates, which has advanced enormously and become consolidated. Indeed, politics have been much more sensitive to mass participation than elsewhere (e.g., the United States and Europe). Therefore, in spite of the correctness of O'Donnell's criticism of "low intensity" democracies in Latin America, we must recognize, with Conighan, that the subcontinent is not stuck there. On the contrary, it has been often strongly on the move.[93] A renewed outlook for democracy has emerged from this; social movements and institutional alternatives have emerged and consolidated, in the midst of much suffering and fierce struggle. It is this dialectic between instituting and instituted citizenship that we see at work in Latin America today, meaning, on the other hand, that rights as "real abstractions" still hold pride of place in such countries. What may be seen as different here, at this very point in time, is that the expressions through which the language of rights remains powerful have assumed a much more plural and concrete countenance. Also, if we look at the functioning of the judiciary—an expanding force, propelled by popular demands and professional perspectives—we find that it tends to deal with plural demands and specific cases with a less abstract and a priori orientation than before. Once again, we spot a move away from abstractness to concrete social processes and situations, in a positive note. If the heterogeneity of social life has already appeared in this chapter, forcing itself against and penetrating even the structure of citizenship, in what lies in the pages ahead this feature shall be more salient. An encompassing modernizing move, including a myriad of more circumscribed ones as well as truly centered offensives, is responsible for this specific dynamic of the modern imaginary and institutions in Latin America today.

In terms of the dynamics and characteristics of social movements (whose precise contours will be dwelt on in Chapter 3), we begin to see new forms that have been slowly found to cope with changed social conditions such as described above when I characterized contemporary modernity in the subcontinent. Networks and alliances, more fleeting agreements and shared projects, sometimes of more limited reach and duration, have been attempted, especially at the local level. In what refers to the relation between state and society, however, there is a long way to go. Latin America has been beset by the problems generated by the passage to the third phase of modernity, but its development in this regard has been uneven and in many crucial areas it has been stuck with old solutions that are patently incapable of tackling these new problems. Representative democracy, the multiplication of public spheres, alternative forms of local government, the opening up of the judiciary—these are all developments that aim at organizing the population and channeling their "interests" and mobilization. New institutions emerge, old ones are refashioned, but serious problems linger on. Although networks—that is, voluntary collaboration between agents—can be in this respect spotted here and there, thus far only timid steps have been given in the direction of solving the problem, which is by no means merely a Latin American one.[94] Too often collaboration has been established between the state and NGOs, as though these represented society or were more accountable than the state. This is, however, something that only strong ideological presuppositions can take at face value.

So much for the time being for the mechanisms of articulation of social life, in other words, for those elements that organize the action of individuals and the movement of collectivities in practical terms.

In terms of principles, one further and probably very important element must be added to this discussion, which expresses as well, and in this case perhaps more auspiciously, the passage of Latin America into the third phase of modernity. The plurality of law and justice, as regards both institutions and conceptions, the greater orientation of the judiciary to concrete situations, emerging networks between state and social collectivities, as well as the build-up of rights coalitions are a set of developments that have a counterpoint in processes of universalization at the constitutional level. Could we say that value and norm generalization emerge in social consciousness and are expressed in constitutional arrangements that can therefore frame social pluralism and its consequences within a broader imaginary

36   *Latin America and Contemporary Modernity*

and institutional regime? I would think so. Constitutional principles are simultaneously universal and more flexible than the norms fixed by codes. A dialectical development would be at stake here: Some weakening of real abstractions (mainly on individuals rights) occurs inasmuch as individual cases receive consideration based on both real abstractions and the interpretation of the Constitution, implying a sort of judge-made law that is more sensitive to concrete, substantive issues. Juridical pragmatism may indeed gain ground in this process of universalization, flexibilization and (politically) judge-made law.[95]

These are ongoing developments in Latin America in which law and justice come to grips with the increasing complexity of social life. Real abstractions would thus be connected at rock bottom with concrete movements for rights and recognition.[96] But then, instead of a Kantian-Kelsian understanding of the process (notwithstanding for instance its renewed and more advanced intersubjective foundations, as delineated by Habermas[97]), it would be something closer to a Hegelian perspective that would underlie this normative sort of development. The "patriotism of the Constitution," to use Habermas' own phrase,[98] would result not from the desire of a general abstract framework that would be previous to concrete social life, but rather as an answer to the concrete dynamics of individual claims, social struggles, and general, augmented pluralization, which express themselves in other institutions in the state and society, as an answer of social agents (especially, though not only, judges and constitutionalists) to the problems entailed by those elements.

In this sense citizenship and rights, whatever their problems at all levels (civil, even political, social), remain as a mainstay of modernity and modernization. Nevertheless, in a subtle way, they appear, in their imaginary, institutional, and coordination aspects, in a different guise in contemporary Latin American societies, both expressing and contributing to the far-reaching changes that characterize the still developing global third phase of modernity in that region. We can relate and establish some process of diffusion and contagion linked to what was called the third "wave" of democratization, but then largely within Latin America itself; in some particular dimensions (such as law reform under the auspices of the World Bank), international agencies and powers do play at times a key role. Moreover the values of modernity have had a decisive and far-reaching impact on Latin American countries. But it must be said, with respect to these particular issues, that all these impulses have been filtered through the social conditions, relations, and struggles that since the nineteenth century and especially, in what concerns us here more directly, during the last decades and this bourgeoning third phase of modernity have characterized the subcontinent. To be sure, this happens in all dimensions of social life, but the cluster of law, justice, and citizenship has strongly displayed such a dynamic. This will be clearer when other dimensions come into the picture in the following chapters, by way of contrast and complement. All this depends on the

Law, Rights, and Justice 37

freer social conditions and the changing perspectives of Latin American populations, the forceful phrasing of their demands, and their more or less permanent, at times noisy, at times almost silent, mobilization in support of their values, interests, and goals.

In order to frame the discussion in an even broader conceptual field, we may say that this study shows clearly that modernity as a civilization is very much in a process of development. Within this global modern civilization, from a pattern that originally sprung up in the West, many variants have unfolded, combining also with other forms of interpreting that basic matrix. While in other parts of the world the mix of modernity with other civilizations, under the hegemony of the former, surely lent more room for the latter, in Latin America also particularities abound. I have not here referred to concrete re-embeddings in which this is even clearer—a task reserved for Chapter 3. But the original position and specific paths toward modernity, let alone legal pluralism, express this, all in all, in a straightforward way. In this case, however, we must note that this underlying heterogeneity of social life is somehow overcome formally either by the abstract universalism originally present in the concept of the citizen or, as more recently, by an architectonic solution that searches for a way to conciliate such abstract universalism and concrete heterogeneity, with problems and perhaps at times with failures. Also important for the sake of the argument I set forth here is the fact that today the third phase of modernity assumes distinct aspects according to regions and countries, changing, within a line of continuity, the original patterns, imaginary and institutional, of modernity, without breaking away from it (versus postmodernist or sheer "network" conceptions of contemporary societies, so common in the literature). It was a singular dimension of this process, in a specific region, that we have studied in this chapter.

In this regard the statement made at the very beginning of the chapter has been, I think, vindicated: Equal freedom has all the way stood at the center of the unfolding of history in the last two centuries of Latin American social life and popular struggles. Local ruling circles, bourgeois groups, democratic leaders have indeed played a role in the fight for liberty in the subcontinent, as they have done everywhere. In a more radical manner, since the 1920s at least, popular collectivities of different types have challenged the concentration of power—allocative in what regards nature, political in the general organization of society and state, symbolic-hermeneutic with respect to culture and identity—and the privileges that ruling collectivities enjoy. The realization of equal freedom as the main element in the emancipatory horizon of modernity and the deepening of democratic institutions and practices, along with renewed forms of solidarity, have become key issues in this connection, especially since socialism has showed itself a far more complicated project to be implemented (what implies, in contradistinction, the permanence of crucial forms of capitalist domination and limits for the realization of equal freedom within the bounds of modernity, in which capitalism consists in fact in a pivotal institutional cluster).[99] This

38 *Latin America and Contemporary Modernity*

renewal of equal freedom and democracy has been carried out in terms of the establishment of formal dispositions, in which "real abstractions" display centrality, in the civil, political, and social dimensions (at least as aspirations and goals, whatever limitations we actually find and the lurking tendency to twist the very meaning of freedom), but also in terms of an exploration of the potentialities of democratic practices and participation, that is, in what concerns the active aspect of citizenship, in many specific arenas and social practices.

Of the three views that fight for space in Latin American societies at the beginning of its third phase of modernity, it is the progressive "project"—or the outcome of its more decentered components—that would support more that instituting aspect. In contradistinction, the neoliberal or even a liberal view rests content with or would like to actively confine democracy to its institutionalized framework. Authoritarianism would totally reject or keep citizenship to a minimum even in its instituted moments (guaranteeing the rights necessary to capitalism, of course). Let us hope the democratic modernizing moves that thrive in the subcontinent come out of such contests as the bearers of the advancement of modern civilization through the activity of its emerging citizenry.

2 Development, Globalization, and the Search for Alternatives

INTRODUCTION

Latin America has not been very successful in remodeling its productive systems in order to reinsert itself in the new, globalized economy in a way such that it could take off in search of development in the turn of the century, at the economic as well as the social level. Once again it has become evident that there can be no simple reproduction of the stages central countries traversed. Economic, financial, and state reforms have been legion: No Latin American country, alas, including Cuba, has refrained from trying new economic paths. But the process of capital accumulation has not resumed with enough vigor and a clear direction, even after the overcoming of the dreadful financial crises that hit the subcontinent in 1990s. Nor have the Latin American countries been able really to take advantage of the positive, expansive condition of the global economy after the turn of the century. The prolonged crisis and finally death of "national developmentalism" has not meant that a successor with the same strength and legitimacy has thus far been found. The proposals of neoliberalism have by and large resulted in failure, harsh social conditions, relative stagnation, and backwardness.

Much of the general discussion about the Latin American predicament in the last decades has concentrated on so-called "macroeconomic" issues, mirroring, even if in a different and controversial manner, the concerns of neoliberals, who imagined (or at least publicly argued) that the mere opening of markets to foreign competition and the "rolling back" of the state would sort out the issue of growth and development. To be sure, other themes have also been discussed, such as labor markets, industrial restructuring, "reprimarization," and increasingly technology and innovation, as well as regulation and accumulation models, in a lesser scale but with a sharper conceptual edge. I will focus more on these last issues than on the 1990s reforms, although I shall also present them in their main elements. Special attention will be given to the possibilities of the (protracted) emergence of new modes of regulation and of new regimes of accumulation. Differences between Latin American countries will be surely pointed out. However, their common features and problems, needs and possibilities, as

40 *Latin America and Contemporary Modernity*

well as their peculiar inclusion in the global modern civilization, will often prove as strong as they did in the past. Capitalism is the "mode of production" that has organized economic life in the region especially during the twentieth century. Class domination will therefore come out clearly in this analysis, as will the mastery and domination of nature, although I shall tackle the former in greater detail only in Chapter 3.

Modernization theory—a liberal ideology indeed—had the market as a necessary feature of progressive evolution. Within it, "entrepreneurship" and the rationalization of economic practices should develop, against traditional ones (based on family, particularism, affectivity, nepotism, aversion to innovation and to risk taking). A lot of weight was usually placed on values and their transformation.[1] Once again it is worth pointing out that Parsons articulated this as a "universal evolutionary," stemming from social differentiation.[2] Habermas' evolutionism led him, in a strong criticism of Marx, to repeat Parsons' view and stress that markets were an evolutionary achievement, due to the complexity of modern societies and the need to unburden linguistically mediated communication (which, supposedly, markets exclude). In addition, Habermas saw markets in a very much neoclassical manner, as the stabilization of individual expectations entailing equilibrium, quite a flat description.[3] Markets are really a key institutional feature of modernity, but they are capitalist markets (class structured therefore, not markets *tout court,* in the abstract), on the one hand, while their specific imaginary and institutional constitution varies widely in space-time, to begin with due to the positioning of regions in distinct balances of global power. Finally, it must be said that capitalist economies include other elements that cannot, by any means, be reduced to the voluntary interchange between individuals and collectivities. Other mechanisms of coordination are present in modern economic systems, as we will see below. How such economic systems are shaped, at the local, regional, national, and global level, depends on modernizing moves by individuals and collectivities of distinct extraction and with varying goals. Concrete outcomes, rather than markets in the abstract, derive from economic, political, and cultural interactions, which have especially at present very powerful and well-organized players, often carrying out sharp modernizing offensives, as the elements that trigger social change.

CAPITALISM AND THE MODERN PROJECT, MARKETS AND THE STATE

The utopia of modernity—which stood at the kernel of many of its modernizing offensives—had, since its very beginning, a perspective of radical homogenization of the basic social conditions across national societies. Polanyi gave us a forceful, even if skewed, account of such a project, which, having taken over the state, created the conditions for what he called a

Development, Globalization, and the Search for Alternatives   41

"self-regulated" market (based thus on institutions). It should stretch across the social tissue, establishing the predominance of its mechanism of social coordination—*voluntary exchange*—over any other type of social relation. Freedom was basically freedom to sell and buy. A key element in our analysis in Chapter 1, the system of rights and especially the civil aspect of citizenship, was crucial for this, guaranteeing property rights as well as the right to sell one's labor force. Hierarchies certainly had a role to play in the relations between state and society, but the former would become a mere watchman, enforcing contracts and preventing that the freedom of one intruded on the freedom of another. Only in this limited sense (and in the penal procedures that were at the bitter end of such relations) did *command* have a part to perform. *Networks* in particular were eschewed in the full: Even unions were supposedly an infringement of the freedom of individual workers and of the freedom of contract in general. Hierarchies certainly had a further part to perform. This was true above all with respect to the factory and the family, through the labor and the marriage contracts. Thereby workers and women relinquished their sovereignty and thus became amenable to the exercise of command within these two settings. Even poverty would be totally overcome by this sort of revolutionary arrangement (which was taken, however, as the proper expression of the human species) and the homogenization of social conditions, except for those who did not assume responsibility for their individual destiny and chose to remain at the margins of society, needing therefore to be directed by those with superior enlightenment. In sum, the market—a capitalist one, which included hierarchical relations between social classes and genders—was at the core of the nineteenth-century first phase of modernity in the West, if not entirely in terms of its institutions (since many countries lagged behind in the transition from feudal to capitalist systems), at least in part in its imaginary, plus decisively as a socially hegemonic project.[4]

During this first phase of modernity, whose general outlook and specificities in what regards citizenship we have analyzed in Chapter 1, Latin America had the market also as its *telos* of development. Step by step, in a long, difficult, and protracted process, capitalist markets (and associated forms of private property) managed to deepen their roots in Latin America, pressed in by timid or bold modernizing moves, associated with modernizing offensives (usually carefully gauged) in terms of institutional arrangements. For this to come about, it was necessary that the manifold forms of personal domination and forced labor—slavery, peonage, and so on—that predominated in the subcontinent through the nineteenth century (living on during a large part of the following one) were eventually superseded, although the struggle for independence led to the freeing of slaves in many (though not all) places (being by and large disruptive of forced labor) while in mining in particular previous systems already incorporated basically waged laborers in that transition. It is curious to note that since its inception Latin America was connected to the global flows of primary commodities

42   *Latin America and Contemporary Modernity*

and precious metals (gold and silver), which were crucial for the process of capital accumulation, a feature that starkly marked such social formations and especially its ruling classes. Britain assumed a prominent position just after the independence of Latin American countries. But capitalist markets in a full sense had to wait for the aftermath of those wars in the nineteenth century to start to develop.[5]

Thus the liberation of labor was piecemeal, though widespread, as much as was that of land (belonging in archaic juridical arrangements to the Catholic Church and the indian communities) and capital (initially in great shortage, supplied now also via foreign investment).[6] Eventually, especially since the 1840s markets progressed, cities grew, a small internal market unfolded, and above all strong links with the global market either developed or were resumed by the middle of the century. In any case, Latin America remained the preserve of landlords—"latifundiários" and "hacendados"—whose wealth and power were guaranteed by the export of primary products to the central countries of the capitalist system, while in some cases (such as Argentina, Chile, or Mexico) the "modern" systems of production in mining or agriculture (especially in what regards basic processing and trade) were in the hands of foreign firms.[7] "Commodity of fetishism" in Marx's more traditional sense[8] (in this case only indirectly related to citizenship such as previously seen) held great sway in many areas and situations, since monetary-commodity links were pervasive especially in the cities and the "modern" systems of production. But the mentality associated with personal forms of domination—and their particular forms of hierarchies and command, in addition not based on contract, as pointed out in Chapter 1—was also pervasive. Therefore, homogenization could not come about in such a restricted form of liberal modernity, contrary to what market utopias proposed: The ideological side of the maintenance of private property and several forms of psychological and ideological rationalization of those forms of domination had the upper hand.

In any case—harking back now to some issues presented in Chapter 1—*responsibility* was thrusted upon the individual as the (free) agent solely responsible for his life, at least in what concerns the ideal to be followed in market economies as the organizing principle of social life, which would then result in growth and harmony. The "ferment" of the market utopia as well as the slow but steady change of social conditions by capitalist development eventually altered this situation. In fact, even a process of industrialization began to develop, especially in countries such as Argentina, wherein wealth was rapidly amassed and a free labor force emerged in a situation of empty space and scarce population, or even in situations where the mere development of more advanced products for the world market created a mass of waged laborers and a timid consumer market—such as was the case with the state of São Paulo, Brazil. A small working class emerged (often with a strong militant, anarchist, or socialist orientation), questioning modernity in its liberal guise, although for instance in Argentina it did not at

Development, Globalization, and the Search for Alternatives   43

first challenge the free-trade stance that the landed oligarchy and its foreign partners imposed to the country, in fact with very successful results.[9]

The crisis of liberal modernity was to a large extent a crisis of liberal capitalism. Economically it implied the shrinking of markets and devastating unemployment. Of course it was also a global crisis, hitting badly the periphery, Latin America in particular, since it was one of the main areas connected to the world market. State intervention in the economy mounted in this period in the subcontinent as it did elsewhere—initially to protect the prices of the primary goods exported by such countries, but later on also in order to lend impulse to industrialization. Keynesianism was of course the main outcome of this far-reaching change of mind away from liberal modernity in the economic terrain; other forms were however also being tried out (for instance in the Nazi project). Fordism in the United States on the other hand was an invention of the 1920s, but only with a general shift in regulation, the distribution of the fruits of increased productivity also through wages, and more generally the rise of the welfare state did it and similar forms of mass production in Western Europe take off as a steady solution for the rupture of the pattern of accumulation that came about between the 1890s and the 1920s. State-organized modernity (with its several specific forms of regulation according to each country) then saw the light of day in the economy, opening the way for the so-called "thirty glorious years," which stretched from the end of World War II to the 1970s. The second industrial revolution (providing for chemistry and steel), new technologies, advanced means of production, mass consumption, and durable goods were also key elements of the new equation.[10] Meanwhile, the First World War and restrictions to import due to the closure of Western markets to Latin American products allowed for an outburst of substitutive importation in some main cities of the subcontinent. Thus, as a composite outcome of modernizing moves and offensives, the second phase of modernity set in and spread across the world, articulated to the changes in the West and with specific characteristics and rhythms elsewhere.

Two new features were henceforth typical of western central countries. As a social form in which the generation of "aggregated demand" and "anti-cyclical" measures were a duty of the state, Keynesianism implied a new form of *responsibility* for development and growth, no longer merely individual and spontaneous; and Fordism, or whatever similar forms one may find in Europe, which depended on mass production and consumption. Homogenization remained, through the market but now counting strongly on state hierarchies and the verticalized and oligopoly firm, at the core of this renewed modern economic perspective. Not only was the diffusion of technologies in a more or less homogeneous manner throughout the productive tissue envisaged and mass production (via a few standardized products) generalized, but a homogenous working class should emerge, moreover organized in large and publicly regulated unions (on the other hand guaranteeing full employment). Neocorporatism was politically the

44   Latin America and Contemporary Modernity

main expression of economic life, in the agreements brokered by the state between workers and companies. The periphery had its own forms of state-organized modernity. Let me sketch the form it assumed in Latin America, wherein, as elsewhere, the "developmental state" appeared as its basic expression in the economic realm, leading the final and decisive phase of what became known as the "import substitution industrialization" and was successful to a variable extent.[11]

If the initial phase of industrialization arose from a process of accumulation and market expansion centered on the primary export sectors and the production of light consumer goods, the second phase had more to do with the limits Latin American countries faced to import. Department II—means of consumption for workers (especially textiles and food), since more sophisticated products were not internally produced—slowly developed; intermediate goods such as paper and rubber products also started to be produced. This remained basically within a liberal paradigm, although state intervention to support primary exports had been already under way. It was mainly in the 1940s that a new pattern emerged, which depended very much not only on protectionism, which indeed prevailed, but fundamentally on state action in order to create its "basic industry," thus part of Department I of the economy. Steel, mechanical industries, and chemicals, plus oil and electricity, all of them key industries of the second industrial revolution, were the main aspects of state intervention in economic life,[12] the core of its new modernizing offensive. In general terms, this was the further path taken by the import substitution process and the role of the state in generating aggregate demand was combined with its participation in the construction of the infrastructure for industrial development. In fact, the substitution of imports must be seen as a dynamic process, insofar as increased sophistication of internal production requires the importation of products of higher aggregated value, with, on the other hand, reduced endogenous innovation. In turn, this demands a permanent strength of the export sector of the economy, based either on primary goods, whose prices in the international market suffered a steady long-term decline in the world market, or increasingly on manufactured products.

By the end of the 1950s, the industrialization of Latin America slowed down. The disparity of income distribution and therefore the limits of the internal accumulation, problems of relative decline in exported value and of access to external credit, the low rate of internal capital formation, and the mounting costs demanded of the state to keep up with the needs of the construction of the Department I were stalemates difficult to overcome. Only Argentina had approached an "intensive" model of accumulation based on income distribution, which however went too far for the strength of the economy. Labor markets with low wages and that tended toward segmentation as well as large rural masses without monetary means to consume created problems for Department II. It was the establishment of transnational corporations in Latin America—for many an unexpected

Development, Globalization, and the Search for Alternatives   45

modernizing move—that gave further impulse to import substitution, in this case nevertheless with a more perverse edge. While durable goods were, at the center of the global system, available for the mass of waged workers, in the subcontinent they were directed to the middle classes and a smaller fraction of workers of those more advanced industries. The implantation of such a pattern, which was an extensive development in the periphery of the intensive mode of accumulation prevailing in the center, created further imbalances in the Latin American economies, since they required the expansion of Department II to an extent that generated severe tensions in those countries as well as stiffened the extremely unequal income distribution on which they were based. In the period of state-led import substitution, an alliance between state bureaucracies and rural oligarchic groups, on the one hand, and "national" bourgeoisies and the popular classes, on the other, tended to be woven (with corporatism, as already seen in Chapter 1, as a means of incorporating, regulating and controlling the working classes, being implanted and kept to a variable extent in the most advanced countries in the process of industrialization). The last phase of state-organized modernity was based on a new alliance between ruling collectivities with foreign capital and actually developed in two countries alone: Dictatorship, in Brazil, and a lasting authoritarian, postrevolutionary regime, in Mexico, answered for that politically.

Thus Brazil and Mexico managed to continue with industrialization. The oil boom in the latter provided for advancements especially in infrastructure, while the latter pushed forward with great voluntarism to complete what at the time were the fundamentals of its industry of "capital goods" (advanced chemicals) and its Department I, although it must be stressed that not even Brazil was successful in implanting an area of microelectronics, semiconductors, and informatics, notwithstanding some steady effort.[13] Argentina got caught in the relative decrease of agricultural productivity, due to the lack of investment in innovation, undergoing recurrent crises of the "stop-and-go" type since the 1960s and finally a politically oriented process of de-industrialization in 1970s. In any case, all three managed to control the technologies of the second industrial revolution. Chile tried without much success to move further in the construction of a Department I, Colombia and Uruguay advanced especially in terms of light industry, while Venezuela floated on top of its oil production, to be become a "rentier" society (pampering its upper and middle classes). Peru, Paraguay, Bolivia, Ecuador, and most countries of Central America did not overcome the narrow and tough combination of oligarchic domination and backward agriculture. In several countries, however, transnational corporations installed their plants and catered for the middle- and upper-classes market. To date, these developments mark strongly the character of these national economies.[14]

There is, finally, one more feature that deserves to be singularized here, since it clearly contradicts the homogenizing thrust of state-organized modernity in its attempt to replicate, with state help, that central element

46 *Latin America and Contemporary Modernity*

of the modern economic utopia. Labor markets tended to be segmented in formal and informal markets, with part of the a population occupied in "marginal" sectors, which could hardly be deemed an "industrial reserve army" in Marx's sense.[15] Moreover technologies were not evenly distributed across the productive tissue, especially since the large corporations not only did not transfer their technologies, but also prolonged their product and accumulation cycle by expanding them in Latin America. The same limitations were present to some degree in the workings of state-owned industries.[16] Latin America remained throughout (even in Mexico or Argentina, which approached more closely the status of homogeneous societies) highly *heterogeneous* in its economic and social fabric, indeed a problem for the ideologues of national development and nation building. In this case, however, it is worth stressing (an issue that will be of consequence later on in this chapter) that this form of social pluralism stemmed basically from difficulties of the modernization process rather than from its success.

This whole world came down, certainly not all of a sudden, but in any case in a definitive way in the early 1970s. There are several explanations for the crisis of Fordism (from the saturation of the norm of consumption, to the growth of the tertiary sector and unproductive labor, to productivity crises, through the disconnection between the national space and accumulation at a global level, plus the loss of hegemony of North American capitalism). But the fact is that a long and expansive cycle, based on the auto-industry oligopoly, the electro-electronic sector, and civil construction, came to an end. The renewal of technology was frozen (the sectors where it could occur were not capable of pulling the whole economy along) and too much fixed capital (basically equipment) had been recently immobilized. Rates of investment were also dropping. At the same time, international liquidity became suddenly short.[17] In the periphery and the semiperiphery, Latin America in particular, the crisis was superimposed upon severe difficulties, such as the former introduction of a new Department II in the economy that furnished products for the middle classes without a corresponding Department I. This was very hard for the state to build, due to the lack of ever increasing resources, whereas internal bourgeoisies had neither capital nor interest in providing such solutions. The vulnerability of Latin American economies worsened: Terms of interchange were falling, imports mounting (due also to the very success of import substitution, which raises the aggregated value of the necessary but not internally produced means of production) as well as debt and net export of capital increasing.[18] Whereas these "structural" blockages prevented a better relationship with an increasingly globalized market, the 1970s introduced the dramatic variable of global crisis, which continued in the 1980s (the "lost decade," during which the region saw its gross domestic product—GDP—per capita fall to levels of thirteen years before) with the debt crisis and the incapacity of the state to resume development in those former modes.[19]

INTERMEDIATE REFLECTIONS—ACCUMULATION, REGULATION, AND DEVELOPMENT

Political economy was a must for most of Latin American sociology in the 1960s and the 1970s—in connection with Marxism, deriving from the United Nations' Economic Commission for Latin America (ECLA, later ECLAC, since it now includes the Caribbean; or, in Portuguese and Spanish, "Cepal") or in connection with dependency theory. With the defeat of revolutionary and reformist efforts and the rise of dictatorships, as well as the so-called "crisis of Marxism" and the hegemonic position assumed by neoclassical economics, political economic approaches basically vanished from the subcontinental social sciences landscape.[20] Nevertheless, it seems to be slowly making a comeback. The French Theory of Regulation has been in the forefront of that. It is to such a development that this chapter is connected, although Marxism and Latin American "historical structuralism" (of an "Eclacian" or dependentist breed) are also theoretically (and politically) present in its making.

The regulationist approach appeared to great extent through Aglietta's study of the vicissitudes of the processes of capitalist accumulation in the United States and simultaneously as a critique of, and alternative to, the neoclassical theory of the general equilibrium. Although not exactly Marxist, his approach shared much with Marx and in particular stressed the role of *institutions* in the development and regulation of capitalism (although the Keynesian problematic is present as well).[21] Since then a very impressive body of work has developed. According to Boyer, the theory of regulation has a number of issues at its kernel: (1) Why is there a passage from growth to stagnation and instability? (2) Why do crises assume national forms? From these, the theory proceeds to work on a further number of "intermediate notions," the main of which is that of "regime of accumulation," implying an ensemble of regularities that assure a general and relatively coherent progression of the accumulation of capital, hence reabsorbing distortions and small imbalances. The third step in the construction of the theory leads to the definition of institutional forms in five aspects: (a) of the monetary constraint; (b) of the configurations of salary relationships; (c) of competition; (d) of the modalities of insertion in the international regime; (e) of the forms of the state. In turn, the "mode of regulation" refers to the whole of procedures and individual and collective behaviors that reproduce the fundamental social relations, sustain and "steer" the regime of accumulation, assuring the dynamic compatibility of a whole set of decentralized decisions. Together they characterize a "mode of development."[22] Moreover, crises have been from the beginning a key issue for regulationists—in fact their starting point vis-à-vis the critique of neoclassical economics. Among these Boyer singled out those that stem from (1) internal or external perturbations of a new type; (2) sociopolitical struggles—questioning the compromises that underlie institutional arrangements; (3) the deepening of the very logic

48 *Latin America and Contemporary Modernity*

of regulation. They may be focused crises, of adjustment, of the regime of development and, of course, of the "mode of production."[23]

Julliard elaborated on some of those general theses—stressing the importance of Marx for the theory—and noted that the regime of accumulation has at its core the relation between technical progress and wealth distribution, as well as growth per capita and the surge of new products. He notes too that accumulations can be intensive or extensive, the former dwelling on increased productivity of labor, hence the "stock of capital" by worker (which may be translated into a more orthodox Marxist language, but perhaps without the inevitability such approach entailed, as the growth of the "organic composition of capital"). This extensive form implied the colonization of new markets and the appearance of new products. Moreover, the balance—or imbalance—between Departments I and II (see Endnote 9) is crucial for the understanding of accumulation processes.[24] Thus, in Julliard's assessment technical change and progress is clearly present, as much as in Amable's claim that the theory is keen on the issue.[25] In Marxism or neo-Schumpeterian approaches, this theme has in any case featured with greater prominence. In sociology, specifically, certainly influenced by such currents, the greatest tour the force vis-à-vis contemporary developments of capitalism and technological change was offered by Castells' study of the "network society" and the informational revolution that, he claims, has ushered in a new era.[26] I want therefore to introduce more directly into the discussion of accumulation and regulation, as carried out in the next session, technical—or, as it is more appropriate today, scientific-technical—innovation and change at the core of the analyses. In any case, I do not pretend any economist's technical expertise. I shall rather aim at a general synthesis, specifically from a sociological perspective.

We must be careful not to take regulation as an institutional and institutionalized process that necessarily eschews heterogeneity and contingency. The market utopia of the nineteenth century and state-organized modernity of the twentieth bet on that in different ways, although the former professed faith in self-regulated (and perfect) markets. Regulation may occur in and through several dimensions (more at a state or more at a societary level) as well as allowing for great variation, flexibility, and complexity, which all imply a high level of contingency. And Keynesianism is certainly not the only model that gives people "conventions," anticipations about the future, and institutions, contrary to what an architectonic view of social life might suppose;[27] liberalism and the new "mode of development" we will analyze below have furnished both conventions and institutions. In fact the tendency of recent institutions, however badly suited yet for the creation and maintenance of social solidarity, has been to accept, deal with, and even further heterogeneity and contingency. That is the very meaning to some extent of what has been called "flexible accumulation," in which the division of labor, pluralism at large (in production and consumption), and shifting patterns of accumulation have developed at a very fast and uneven

Development, Globalization, and the Search for Alternatives   49

pace. Flexible accumulation would be defined by the end of mass production, segmentation of markets (plus "eclecticism" in labor practices), the curtailing of Taylorism, for which Toyotism (the work by teams and polyvalent workers, as against repetitive and unskilled tasks) substitutes, outsourcing, "just in time" (with commodity stocks reduced and tailored to customers' necessity at a high speed), while "lean production" (and hollowed-out firms) appeared at least at the historical onset of the restructuring of the corporate world. However, in the central countries or elsewhere, Fordism and similar systems do not necessarily disappear; in addition, "sweat shops" based on extensive use of cheap and overexploited labor have proliferated not only in the countries of the periphery but also within the internal peripheries of those central countries.[28]

Innovation became in the new regime of accumulation an even more important element in the competition between capitalist firms, either to guarantee particularly high profits or in order not to fall behind competitors,[29] especially in a situation of extremely fast change. But, as reflections coming from the neo-Schumpeterian bibliography warn us, due to the plural character and complexity of technological developments firms rarely innovate alone: They have become "more specialized, focusing their competencies." For complementary knowledge, they increasingly make recourse to interaction (through networks and common projects) with a variety of actors (other firms and universities, in particular).[30] It is true, nonetheless, that in central countries innovation has been much more spread across the economic social fabric. Informatics and microelectronics have pervaded the whole of the economy—something much more problematic in the Latin American subcontinent, as we shall see. Homogenization is thus at the service of complexity over there, while in that less favored situation heterogeneity stems in this particular aspect from the lack of dynamism of the regime of accumulation.

Here we must return to some issues introduced at the beginning of this chapter. While liberal modernity as well as state-organized modernity could imagine that the world could be coordinated basically through the market as well as state and verticalized firms' hierarchies, the present condition of economic life does not allow for that. Castells has stressed precisely the role of networks and their flexibility in this age of highly advanced scientific-technological development, although he did so one-sidedly and with an oscillating definition of network (at times meaning collaboration, at times implying merely a descriptive notion of nodes and connections). The same happens with Boltanski and Chiapello, whose work does not clearly define whether its depiction of the contemporary world is a direct description (and then it would be really exaggerated) or an analytical construction (in which case it would be closer to the truth). In fact I have criticized them all and pointed to both the particular importance of networks and voluntary collaboration (within common "projects," of a shorter or longer duration) in an age of increasing pluralism and complexity, and the continuing importance

50 *Latin America and Contemporary Modernity*

of markets and hierarchies.[31] Even though situations are obviously different, the peripheral or semiperipheral condition of Latin American countries does not detract from the importance of such distinctions or from the growing relevance of network arrangements.

This leads us at last to the question of how the theory of regulation relates to peripheral and semiperipheral economies. At least some of its versions tend to refuse the very division between center and periphery. Furthermore, some of those authors argue that while the theory of dependence (and the old ECLA) explained underdevelopment by external domination, regulationists stress the primacy of the "national" dimension or at least assert that the permanence of underdevelopment depends on internal forms of regulation (pointing out especially Korea's case).[32] Two main conceptual issues have been at stake in their discussion. First, the validity and distortions of the label "Fordism" when "de-localized" toward the periphery—"sub-Fordism" (in relation to import substitution) or "peripheral Fordism" (more generally applied, implying the lack of macroeconomic coherence)—have been main expressions of this problematic. Second, it has been observed that the inexistence or weakness of the Department I of the economy characterizes underdevelopment.[33] In my view, whatever the sensible reservations that can be drawn with regard to the transposition of concepts, the displacement and therefore torsion of Fordism are as much a conceptual necessity as an empirical reality of the extensive regime of accumulation developed in a global scale from the 1950s onward by transnational corporations all over the world. The same happens with the notion of "post-Fordism" and flexible accumulation: Latin America is placed within a much larger global economy, hence under the impact of the changes in technology and productive processes, although surely in an "uneven and combined way." It partakes of the new forms and regulations of capitalism in a global scale, which " . . . is becoming ever more tightly organized through dispersal, geographical mobility, and flexible responses in labor markets, labor processes and consumer markets, all accompanied by hefty doses of institutional, product, and technological innovation."[34] In any case, the imbalances between the Departments I and II seem to be a promising way of framing the issue of underdevelopment and the place of countries within the international division of labor and the center-periphery-semiperiphery relationships.

In the following assessment of the changes and new trends cutting across Latin American societies, I will try to cover precisely the issues and suggestions by regulationists, directly drawing upon their work at times and adding a perhaps stronger emphasis on innovation and technological change. I must say, however, also from the start, that this last point is taken not in the belief that it happens really often in the economies of the subcontinent, but as much as an issue to which attention has been more recently directed with great concern and in search for solutions. And I must say too that dependency and the place of Latin American countries in the periphery or

Development, Globalization, and the Search for Alternatives 51

the semiperiphery will remain, in accordance with Eclacian and dependentist views, either at the core or as the background of what will be discussed below.[35] Finally, in order to carry this out, I shall use a threefold analytical distinction when I refer to the new regulations (something implicit also in the foregoing discussion): the *collective agent (subjectivity)* of the regulation, the *institutions* that are brought about in the process (which includes interaction with that which is regulated), and the *mechanisms of coordination* that prevail in the process under consideration.

NEW REGULATIONS, ECONOMIC RESTRUCTURING, AND THE PATTERNS OF CAPITAL ACCUMULATION

The first, general thing to be taken into account when we assess the new, deeply changed conditions of Latin American economic life derives from the outcomes of the long crisis in which it was immersed, along with the whole world, from the mid-1980s to the early 1990s. The framework of state regulation greatly changed, following and giving impulse to the breathtaking transformation that was occurring at the societal level in that period, as an answer to the crisis. To start with, as already stated, Keynesianism no longer worked and was unable to pull national economies from the "stagflation" of those years. Besides, technological innovation on the scale it was taking demanded capital in brutal amounts (thus powerful financial markets) and worldwide markets in order to allow for profits compatible with those huge investments. Foreign direct investment (FDI) partly grew out of that. Radicalizing a strategy that emerged in the unfolding of the 1970s crisis, the U.S. government took the lead to "deregulate" markets and forced other countries, including those of Europe and of course the Latin American ones, to repeat its moves, due to its direct power or to the competition its companies put up in the global arena (and thereby even that government lost some of its power). This modernizing offensive meant a real break with former patterns and hammered in the beginnings of the new phase of modernity in the economy. Telecommunications were a prime, though not the only, example of such a decisive policy, with far-reaching implications, which included the privatizations of state-owned telecom companies all over the world, Latin America featuring also of course in this regard, with much ado.[36] High-tech and generally innovative and powerful firms, as well as financial markets, were the first and foremost to benefit from these changes, which led authority away from the state toward the market and networks—embodied henceforth in a plurality of agencies in an increasingly global landscape. Profits increased and there came about a recapitalization of firms and capitalism.[37]

In this new mode of global regulation, therefore, it is not only, and at times especially not, at the level of the national state that institutions and agents play their role. The International Monetary Fund (IMF), the Organization for Economic Development (OECD), the World Bank, the General

52 *Latin America and Contemporary Modernity*

Agreement on Trade and Tariffs (GATT), and the World Trade Organization (WTO) have become main regulating bodies. They had a strong position of authority in the past and still respond in large measure to the most powerful states, especially the United States. But their regulatory authority has greatly increased and the hierarchical power they enjoy is at present extremely large. Along with them, agencies of risk assessment and agreements between the gigantic transnationals that rule over the global economy offer other instances and institutions of regulation of the global economy. The former lay in fact at the core of finance capital coercive moves and blackmail: They command the flocking away of large masses of volatile money whenever conditions look bad from the point of view of the very high rates of profit they expect or whenever governments are perceived to be promoting policies detrimental to their interests. Latin America surely had been caught in this whirlpool, with the damaging distinguished feature that its states, including the strongest ones, are by no means as strong as those of the West and Japan. Contrary to the theoretical expectations of the theory of regulation, notwithstanding the fact that regulation remains partly national (and so does the regime of accumulation), it has moved to a great extent from that level onto the global one. All countries have to adapt to that.

That is what we see in Latin America, where for many years some held the dream of returning to what they saw as the golden era of national development(alism). The 1980s, the lost decade, saw spurts of growth in this direction. However, they were definitively left behind in the 1990s, in a more radical or in a more moderate manner. Without exception, although at different paces and times, all countries in the subcontinent changed their economic policies, privatized almost all of their state-owned companies (important exceptions were Brazil's Petrobras and Venezuela's PDVSA, their oil companies—as well as Paraguay overall, a bizarre case of quasi-confirmation of neoliberal rent-seeking theories[38]), "de-regulated" their markets, and opened up to international trade. To curb the crippling inflation and sometimes hyperinflation of the 1980s (in part a result of harsh distributive conflicts), tight monetary policies have been followed everywhere. Less spectacular, but equally decisive though not as encompassing and radical as they were carried out in the countries of the center, the features of firms and labor markets were drastically altered by processes of capitalist "restructuring." Networks advanced a bit, but not that much, in particular since the restructuring of productive processes and technological innovation have been the backward open secret, on the one hand, and the Achilles' heel, on the other, of the updating of Latin American national economies. In turn, labor markets have deepened some of their pristine characteristics in the subcontinent. An additional aspect of its development is what has been dismally called the "reprimarization" of the economic fabric. While state changes have been the result of an explicit and thought-out modernizing offensive, restructuration was mostly more decentered, configuring moves

Development, Globalization, and the Search for Alternatives   53

of variable intensity. In turn, unintended outcomes of such transformations pushed Latin America into what may be called a "back to the future" situation, with a sort of regressive specialization setting in.

Latin America arrives thus at the beginning of the new millennium with daunting challenges and a problematic economic and social situation.[39] By and large, these countries remain largely heterogeneous, of which Bolivia is a good albeit radical example, with its *abigarrada* (multicolored, fragmented) or *ch'enko* (a Quéchua word for confusion) economy, lacking an even basically integrated internal market. Some countries evince a great diversification of their economies, despite imbalances between productive sectors and often quite uneven processes of regional development. This is particularly the case of Brazil and Mexico, though the macrocephally and economic concentration of cities such as Lima and Buenos Aires, reproducing what happens especially with Mexico City and São Paulo, expresses this also in an exemplary fashion. Other countries moved backward, since the military dictatorships decided to de-industrialize them, betting on the new age of agricultural exportation; it was with this drawback that they faced the emergence of the new phase of modernity. Chile took this further than any other country, but Uruguay and Argentina went down the same road for a long time, although Chile was reasonably successful in finding a niche for itself in the world market with its primary products, while Argentina has undergone a steady decline, under also the brutal exploitation of finance capital, with the advantage of having kept a considerable industrial sector.[40]

Since the import substitution model was dead, a search for alternatives was in order but ended up captured by neoliberal tenets and offensives. A few industrial paths have been newly tried out or reinforced, with arguable results. In this latter case, the traditional and durable goods branches plus manufactured commodities keep the upper hand in Brazil—a traditional pattern, notwithstanding some niches of products of high technology being carved out even for exportation—while "maquiladoras" (or simply "maquilas") dominate the Mexican and Central American landscape. Other Latin American countries have remained largely agrarian, with industry having much less importance. This, of course, does not mean it does not exist: Traditional as well as durable goods industries are established in many of them, confirming variably sized Departments II of the economy. Everywhere—and especially in the most industrialized countries—the importation of capital goods for Department I of the economy puts pressure on their balance of payments. Some countries seem to reproduce their history of "magic wealth," Venezuela standing out in this regard with large reservoirs of petrol, while others try to follow in the same direction seeing in their oil and gas the salvation of their children, a to some extent correct but rather short-sighted view. Nevertheless, the traditional agrarian problem has been utterly transformed. Agribusiness emerged everywhere powerfully and new social relations as well as new products have spread across Latin America

54   Latin America and Contemporary Modernity

associated with the aforementioned process of "reprimarization." The analytical aspects dealt with below express this convergence and diversity of recent evolutions.

In the following sections, we will basically tackle two sorts of modernizing moves. The first, implying firms restructuring, takes place in a more or less decentered manner, since there has been no overall plan or even industrial police in this sense (although the sheer size of transnational corporations entails a high level of centering at least as for their own moves and the opening of national economies has forced such processes on many firms, sometimes in a desperate manner). The second, conforming an actual project in which international financial institutions and global capital are key players, has pitilessly advanced the third phase of modernity within the neoliberal framework. The remnants of national developmentalism have not for a long time been able to put a modernizing fight of their own against this offensive.

Economic Policies, Reforms, Privatizations

At what neoclassical economists call the "macroeconomic" level, we witness the first moves of Latin American countries toward a new phase. Mostly this happened against their will and, moreover, they really had no clue about where those moves would lead them. But if creditors were key players in this, they were not the only actors: This was also the case of the IMF, which was given a prominent role by the former as a political agent of debt renegotiations, and had already made up its mind, due to the new neoliberal outlook of the U.S. government and the already overwhelming influence of neoclassical economics. This meant a new agenda (which some countries such as Chile and Argentina had already taken, with very arguable outcomes), including basically the calling " . . . to reduce budget deficits and tighten monetary policy; to liberalize trade and exchange rate regimes; and most generally, to expand the role of market forces and the private sector" (including surely the privatization of state-owned enterprises, a sometimes very controversial, state-funded, and corrupted process).[41]

The "Washington consensus," defining what became later known as "first generation reforms," embodied the wisdom of that program, which became the hallmark of neoliberalism for Latin American countries. These reforms have considerably altered the situation of the Latin American economies. The state was "rolled back," there was a fiscal overhaul, and monetary policies were strict, with a new sort of contractive discipline, against expansionist Keynesian measures, counting on a direct anchorage on the dollar for sometime in some countries, with disastrous long-term effects for them, especially in the case of Argentina (and remains effective in the case of Ecuador, with problematic results in terms of trade deficit). The market took a larger share of economic life, denationalization of much of the economy ensued, import substitution policies found their ultimate death,

Development, Globalization, and the Search for Alternatives 55

and instead of an inner-oriented economy, it was outward-oriented strategies that began to develop, on the premise that foreign trade would do great good to modernize the subcontinent's economic infrastructure. Inflation was finally curbed, after the outburst of hyperinflation that plagued especially Brazil and Argentina, and foreign debt brought under control, though other prices were paid (such as the increase of internal public debt and, eventually, often a renewed foreign debt, plus widespread corruption and new private, badly regulated monopolies, in many cases of state-privatized companies). In fact, markets should be at the kernel of the whole of social life and should guarantee, once again freed from state controls and exploitation, including in particular the come and go across frontiers of finance capital and the development and well-being of the population.[42]

In any case, Latin America would never be the same. State and market would from now on entertain radically different relations. "Second generation reforms" were later on pushed forward, but their implementation has been much less thorough, even because they were more pulverized and often tackled contradictory goals. They implied basically further privatization, poverty combat, the strengthening of legal frameworks for investment, new forms of legislation, decentralization, and the reduction of corruption (as analyzed in Chapter 1). Flexibilization of labor legislation was also at their core, but the difficulty in implementing this stemmed from the variably vigorous resistance of organized labor; curtailing the power of workers' unions was thus decisive. Not only immediate conditions would be deeply altered thereby—and they were in a number of countries, such as Argentina, to a considerable extent.[43] We must remember (as seen also in Chapter 1) that perhaps the main characteristic of welfare measures in Latin America has been precisely proactive labor legislation and attached benefits.

Thus "deregulation" became a worldwide phenomenon, including Latin America. In fact, it was a new type of regulation—enforced by international organizations as agents, based on open markets as mechanisms of coordination, of course not "natural" at all, and new institutions as well as subsidiary-regulating agencies—that was enforced, by central countries themselves, especially the United States, and international organizations, such as the IMF, the World Bank, the OECD, the GATT, and others. The "conditionalities" underlying the loans of these agencies were closely related to those main objectives.[44] In this new situation, cash flows in and out of Latin America became much freer and mounted during the 1990s either as FDI (in large sums, in particular related to privatization processes, but concentrated on non-tradable and non-exportable products, namely, telecommunications, infrastructure, etc., but often consuming lots of imported capital goods) or as financial, speculative, and short-term capital, which benefited from the usually high rates of interest used to curb inflation (along with "stabilization plans") and the new liberal pro-market regulation. They meant of course denationalization too.

56 *Latin America and Contemporary Modernity*

Not even the major crisis of the 1990s in Mexico, Brazil, and Argentina provided for a change in the management of exchange and interest rates (though the exhaustion of privatization processes was one of the factors in the sharp reduction of FDI in the very turn of the century).[45] On the other hand, competition from abroad at least in the beginning represented an unbearable burden for national firms. Many died; others survived by adapting to the new conditions. Capitalist restructuring, carried out either by foreign firms or by national ones in their struggle to adjust and survive, thus came about, in the aftermath of those "macroeconomic" changes, contrary to what had happened in the center of the modern global economic system.

In relation to the large privatized state-owned enterprises, innovations, imported from the center too, were sometimes introduced: regulatory agencies, above all in telecommunications, as well as in basic services, oil production, and other areas, with relative autonomy and implying new rules as well for market functioning. Antitrust measures and a few social areas (for instance, health insurance and the environment) have been channeled through similar instruments. Such agencies clearly represent a new form of capitalist regulation.[46] They diffused across sectors and across countries, representing, at the institutional level and at least formally, one of the key modernizing offensives of the period. In 1979, 43 agencies existed (including central banks); 21 were formally autonomous. In 2002, there were already 119. Chile—without however granting them autonomy—established agencies in the 1970s–1980s and Argentina jumped in, creating many of them in the early 1990s. Brazil was a relative latecomer. The origin of such instruments of regulation lies in the United States during the nineteenth century and they were revised and strengthened by the Reagan government, expanding worldwide later on, including Latin America and especially Europe. They have been recommended by the World Bank as "best governance" practices, probably depend on communities of professionals (mainly economists trained in neoclassical departments in the United States, hired in the Latin American state sectors, private companies or international agencies), and work as a sign to investors about institutional stability. With reference to the latter region, it seems that the move away from the state has meant a number of compromises: between its executive branch (through the agencies) and business, plus between the executive and the agencies.

In the first case, this deal means that the autonomy of the agencies ensures non-state intervention, hence the protection of private inversions, and stability, also though not only at the legal level, hence guaranteeing in a particular way a form of rational-legal "authority" (definitely not "domination" in this case). In the second aspect, it is the degree of autonomy of the agency vis-à-vis the state that is at stake. Its bureaucracy must be in principle controlled by political authorities in a democratic order, but it is at the same time appointed for fixed periods and cannot be dismissed. In any case, all over the subcontinent this new form of business-friendly state

Development, Globalization, and the Search for Alternatives 57

regulation works as a sort of commitment of the state to defend society from abuses, while it remains to some extent absent from concrete decisions and is committed to economic freedom. Of course, the risk of capture of this bureaucracy by one or more corporations exists and can be indeed a thorny problem for other firms and the citizenry at large, whose participation is at best nonexistent. In any case, the power of the executive branch of the state appears as salient in relation to the agencies. But, even worse, as the example of the harshly privatized Mexican Telecom shows, new and very poorly regulated privatized monopolies often emerged from such processes.[47]

At last, a peculiar aspect of change in Latin America is the processes of integration carried out in the last decades, within what has been called the "second wave of regionalisms" (the first having taken place in the 1940s– 1950s). Contrary to most moves discussed above, they represented genuine internal modernizing offensives. The Common Market of the South (Mercosur), the Andean Community (CAN), and the South American Community of Nations are the main expressions of this process and have concentrated on opening markets through the establishment of common tariff regimes. Not much has been accomplished beyond that, although as such this may be seen as a great step, fraught with possible future consequences. The low level of state "infrastructural" capacity (see Chapter 1) is however reproduced in the case of the regional institutions, which penetrate superficially and do not strongly mobilize the societies of the countries they are supposed to bring closer. Once again, market integration, something especially visible in the case of Brazil and Argentina, has been a real achievement of the processes at stake. More arguable—in fact basically detrimental to the Mexican economy, as we will see below—was the establishment of the North American Free Trade Area (NAFTA), into which the northernmost Latin American country, along with smaller ones in Central America, was dragged.[48]

The Restructuring of Firms and Industrial Paths

One of the central aspects of capitalist development in last decades of the twentieth century has been the process of restructuring of firms, which has been known, as seen above, as "post-Fordism," encompassing a myriad of distinct situations. In the countries of the center of the global system, such modernizing moves have had far-reaching effects, with implications for patterns of accumulation, for forms of regulation, for labor markets, as well as for the insertion of those economies in the global market. Besides they were closely articulated with the technological revolution. Restructuring has been very important in Latin America too, in both industrial and service firms. But it has its own specificities. First, it happens with less general impact. In the subcontinent Fordism as such, or related forms of production (not the pattern of consumption, except in some degree in Argentina), was never by any means hegemonic—and some of its aspects are actually reinforced at present. Taylorism may have had greater impact, but previous forms of

58 *Latin America and Contemporary Modernity*

labor organization remain operative at large, as they were in the past, with great verticalization. Traditional industries, sometimes assuming the aspect of "sweatshops," have been pervasive. The thinking of ECLA, as mentioned above too, stressed the heterogeneity of technological absorption in Latin America and this had obvious and direct relation with firms' production processes. Now this often happens as well, albeit again via specific paths.[49] Garza Toledo has synthetically conceptualized the restructuring process as

> . . . the transformation of the sociotechnical basis of the productive processes, in its technological, organizational, of labor relations, of profile and labor culture. [. . .] the state, with its expenses, is no longer the leverage of aggregate demand, added to this the opening of internal markets to international competition. . . . Productive restructurings have been decided directly by firms in the face of new market conditions and the economic reorientation of the state; they have been related also to the specific change of industrial policy, of foment to industrialization, typical of the period of import substitution, to the new one, of less state intervention and the intent of conversion of the export sector into the dynamic sector of the economy.[50]

In some sectors, restructuring has included processes resembling Toyotism. That is, the development of workers' teams with greater autonomy, less segmentation of tasks (qualified and polyvalent workers thus becoming more usual), and much more collectively shared responsibility at the shop floor. However, this does not seen to be the most common situation: Restructuring has, since the 1980s, developed much more through "hard" than such "soft" forms. That is, the modernization of equipment, which often implies change of working conditions, appears as the strategy more utilized by firms, rather than flexibilized working processes, although in some countries of the region there are indeed organizational changes. These tendencies are true for both national and multinational companies. But even in this regard it has been largely confined to the biggest firms, it is concentrated in those linked to the world market, and usually does not imply last-generation changes. Not much microelectronics and computerized control are introduced (some more advances in this respect obtain in the service sector). Moreover, organizational changes often have entailed, paradoxically, even when "just in time" schemes come into being, a deepening of Taylorism, without much change of the working class as such (which remained in a considerable measure male, mature, and with a certain level of experience in mobilizations, although women and younger workers have been brought in and not seldom represent a less politically experienced labor force). By and large the flexibilization of legislation and the weakening of unions—commanded of course by the state—has been central for the process of change throughout the economy,[51] leading to workers' vulnerability, to greater exploitation of labor, to "extensive" accumulation (in the language of the

Development, Globalization, and the Search for Alternatives 59

theory of regulation), in relation to the spread of products designed for the world economy, and to the increase of what, in Marxist terminology, must be called "absolute surplus-value." A real modernizing counteroffensive was thus launched against labor, which had achieved progress in terms of legislation in the previous phase of modernity.

Another important aspect of industrial restructuring in particular has been an inclination toward vertical disintegration, though this is not, once again, an absolute tendency (and has happened alongside fusions and take-overs, with which it maintains no contradiction in principle). Oligopolies have resulted from or been strengthened by this, but a large sector of small and medium-size firms, often of family property, remain responsible for a large percentage of jobs, which are not however usually well-paid. Instead of trying to lower "transaction costs" through the "internalization" of external markets, typical of the second phase of modernity,[52] firms have been outsourcing tasks and building networks with suppliers and consumers. Market control is guaranteed to a great extent through the design, definition, and contracting of products rather than by sheer production. To be sure microelectronics was the main locus for such processes but it is now widespread in all industrial branches of the world economy. Textiles, for instance, a supposedly traditional branch, is especially pervaded by such practices in a local as well as in a global scale. This restructuring of production is often carried out through what has been called "global commodity chains." These chains may be "producer-driven" or "buyer-driven." A company may localize some parts of its own complex productive process in different countries—something that is by the way responsible for a large amount of the growth of global trade in the last decades: intracompany trade—or outsource to suppliers abroad. Both processes can be very volatile and imply quick changes in the localization of firms that, for varied reasons, may just move their plants from one country to the other.[53] Outsourcing for the internal market, as well as cutting across distinct countries, often implies the contracting of smaller firms with informally hired workers to do part of the production process for firms operating within the formal labor market.[54] Let us examine how the main industrial countries in the subcontinent have fared in this regard.

The Argentine situation expresses such mixed changes. The quasi-intensive model of accumulation adopted in the 1950s–1960s was already destroyed by a marked tendency toward de-industrialization carried out since the last military regimes. Restructuring was superimposed on such a process and did *not* revert it (an overvalued currency throughout the 1990s did not help either). Industry fell from 31 to 17 percent of GDP, with a deep disarticulation of the productive structure and the dissolution of production chains. Outsourcing has been a common strategy adopted by industrial firms, but there has not really come about what might be called "flexible specialization"; "deregulation" of labor markets and attempts at introducing "Japanese" forms of labor relations have been in place too. In

60 Latin America and Contemporary Modernity

the automobile industry, for instance, subcontracted firms are numerous and appear at varied levels of sophistication. The same happens in the privatized telecommunication industry, which on the other hand had more thoroughly modernized. A renewal of the labor force has come about in both branches. The use of more traditional knowledge and the introduction of more flexible working conditions have surprisingly taken place in the metal-mechanic and the steel industries.[55]

In Brazil, no de-industrializing process has ever come about. In fact the military changed the pattern of the Brazilian economy and pushed forward import substitution and the modernization of the country's economy, increasing the coefficient of industrial products in its exports and completing part of what was then the Department I of the national economy. In any case, trade liberalization and an overvalued currency in the beginning of the 1990s put local industry under heavy pressure. Many branches suffered badly, productive chains were broken, and the concentration on industrial commodities (such as steel) was reinforced, implying what might be called "regressive specialization." Heterogeneity has been kept as the norm of the economy. However, in the medium term this seems to have resulted in an increase of productivity in many firms, under strong external competition, though not for the capital goods industry: Especially those with higher levels of aggregate value, but surely not only them, increased their import coefficient—notwithstanding the fact that Brazil represents (along with India) the only developing country in the world that has a reasonable branch of "tool machines." The disproportional evolution of production vis-à-vis employment seems to indicate that labor-saving equipment and processes have been utilized in the course of industrial modernization, in fact the former being precisely the area in which modernization and innovation seem to be concentrated. Subcontracting expanded while fusions and denationalization came about. Authoritarianism, job insecurity, working-class fragmentation, and a sort of teamwork that make workers control each other (instead of instilling true, voluntary co-responsibility) are other outcomes of this process as well as geographical dispersion of industrial areas away from São Paulo's formerly militant working class.[56]

Yet, if Brazil seems to follow most Latin American countries in that restructuring has modernized its industry in authoritarian ways, some actual novelties here and there seem to have appeared. Agreements with workers mediated through the unions have happened in a few cases that are paradigmatic for Latin America in either the old automobile region of the ABC or elsewhere. This is particularly the case in a few, more advanced industries, for instance in the new automobile district of Rezende, where Volkswagen has installed an extremely modern plant, networked with suppliers and with the local administration, with new productive methods and new labor relations, counting on highly trained and skilled workers. The fact that the country has one of the largest economies in Latin America furnishes stimulus for it serving as the basis for companies drawing upon the global

Development, Globalization, and the Search for Alternatives 61

commodity scheme to explore also the other South Cone markets (including especially Argentina, although it exports to Brazil at this stage more or less the same amount of cars as the other way round).[57]

In Mexico, industry has been sharply transformed, first of all under the aegis of privatization, as well as under the impact of the new economic links with the United States. Along with the perverse effects of the commercial opening, with the rupture of many traditional industrial chains, change has been marked above all by the presence of "maquiladoras" or "maquilas," assemblage units, especially, though not exclusively, in its northern frontier with the United States. An institutional modernizing offensive opened room for a myriad of modernizing moves. In fact it has attracted a great many North American companies, as well as firms from other countries (European, Japanese, or Korean), which have used its much cheaper labor force to produce for the neighboring markets of the United States and Canada within the framework of the NAFTA. But the "maquiladoras" have not delivered what they promised: Although there has been indeed some upgrading, most plants are backward, merely assembling parts produced elsewhere, with very low wages, repression of labor organization (also from official unions backed by the state), and no technological innovation. In addition, they evince a particular and grave problem in comparison with other types of industry. Insofar as they depend on imported parts with high levels of aggregate value, they generate surplus incomes for the commercial balance but may be deleterious to it in that there is little value locally added in the exported production. Skewed regional development is another negative outcome of the "maquiladoras," which do not produce any so to speak "trickle down effects" upon the whole of the economy, although they provide for a certain amount of surplus in the commercial balance.[58]

Moreover, as part of "global commodity chains," Mexico's situation is highly volatile in terms of the mobility of firms and capital, since they can leave at any moment they decide that conditions are better elsewhere. This has happened indeed with at least part of the microelectronic industry, which has recently fled from the country. To be sure, some more stability has characterized many sectors and there are other types of "maquiladoras," of third and fourth "generation"—which perhaps should not be called "maquilas" at all. These have invested in technological innovation and hired highly qualified engineers in their headquarters in Mexico. This is especially the case, for instance, of the Technical Center of Delphi in Ciudad Juárez. However, such an example does not stand for the majority of the vast "maquiladora" industry.[59]

The Limits of Scientific and Technological Innovation

The development of capitalism in the last decades of the twentieth century and henceforth has been based, as seen above, in a number of crucial technological breakthroughs, especially in microelectronics and informatics.

62   *Latin America and Contemporary Modernity*

If we can speak of modernizing moves and offensives that will have a lasting effect in world economic history, it is perhaps in those areas that the most powerful of them may have happened, exactly the ones in which Latin America has done very badly. In fact, technology generation has been missing since the establishment of capitalism in the subcontinent. Levels of state and particularly private investment in science and technology (S&T) and research and development (R&D) have been consistently and by and large extremely low, in contrast to what happens in the United States above all, but also Europe and Japan, and even East Asia. On the other hand, if transnational firms may use advanced technologies in Latin America (though often they take there somewhat out-of-date plants and products, rarely investing locally in R&D) these technologies do not usually spill over the economy as a whole, contributing to a persistent heterogeneity of the social fabric in this regard. In fact, agribusiness is one of the few areas in which—though only in Brazil—there has been systematic local investment in R&D (but I will not dwell on it now, returning to this issue when analyzing agricultural modernization in the last section of this chapter). As a result of the 1990s reforms, low tariff protection was implemented, internal efforts in R&D in the privatized companies were reduced (they now import from their matrixes and global suppliers) or from locally based multinationals), informatics-related technologies of production spread in relation to the largely, usually transnational companies, the same not happening vis-à-vis small and medium-size firms. Local productive chains became less dense and there came about a privatization of universities and research institutes. Meanwhile intellectual property rights were strengthened.[60]

This type of shortcomings, though he does not discuss them directly from this angle, constitutes one of Castells' main concerns when analyzing contemporary Chilean society. While it is true that Chile has, according to him, fared well in its attempt at specialization in the world market and, within Latin America, sustains a reasonably well educated population with an above-average access to electronic means of communication and the Internet, it is far from having achieved a good situation in any of these aspects, keeping therefore low levels of productivity and lagging far behind developed societies.[61]

General data for the area, for which I especially draw upon the Interamerican Network for Science and Technology (RICYT), shows that most countries dedicate very little of their GDP to S&T and R&D. In the period between 1994 and 2003, global expending in R&D increased an amazing 82 percent, from $470 billion to $860 billion. Latin America slightly increased its expenses but decreased its share of the global rate from 1.6 to 1.3 percent, at current dollars; in terms of measurement according to buying power parity, the situation looks a bit better, but by no means satisfactory: From 3.1 it fell to 2.5 percent. While Brazil has managed to keep recently its expenses close to 1.0 percent of GDP, Mexico passed from 0.29 to 0.45 percent from 1994 to 2003. Argentina maintained its rate constant and low:

Development, Globalization, and the Search for Alternatives   63

0.44 percent of GDP. These three countries concentrate 90 percent of the regional investments in the area.[62] The private sector is very much absent from this picture. On the other hand, science—as a pure activity—has been the hallmark of Latin America, and this has led to a limitation concerning its entwinement with technology production, which is a salient characteristic of contemporary developments in the core countries of capitalism. In terms of organization, the subcontinent is conspicuous also for two features— whose most popular expression is to be found out in the North American Silicon Valley and the microelectronics and informatics industry, which was the main focus of Castells' "network society," discussed above. The first is the absence of "innovation clusters," which have been crucial for most of the forward leaps of the present—Brazil concentrates the few to be found; the second, as if that was not enough, is the "triple helix" scheme, bring- ing together firms, universities, and governmental funding or contracting agencies, which has made few inroads in the Latin American landscape.[63] In neither case do we find substantial modernizing moves. Let us examine that again at a more specific level—that is, the national innovation systems of its economically most developed countries.

Argentina has indeed a system of science, technology, and innovation. The first fact to come up in its analysis is that the private sector invests only a third of the in any event very low national average. Most activi- ties are concentrated in the capital Buenos Aires. Compared to Mexico and Brazil, which have 0.7 and 0.8 researchers for every 1,000 people, Argentina is in a better position—featuring 1.7 for every 1,000. But this is very low for international standards—for instance, the United States has 9.0 and France, 6.9, for every 1,000 people. Besides, Argentina's research- ers are rarely to be found in private firms, they do not perform very well, and few hold PhDs. Intellectual property rights are not established as they might be and venture capital is not available for scientific investigation. According to researches officially carried out, most Argentine firms do not innovate at all. As in other places—and counting with foreign firms— big companies are the most innovative ones. Unfortunately, there is very little networking between firms and universities—neither are universities adjusted to business, nor do firms possess adequate structure and interest in collaboration.[64]

We might expect that in Mexico things would look brighter but that is not the case. To start with, it seems clear that the "maquiladora" industry does not produce spill over effects in terms of technology for the economy as a whole, *pace* the few R&D centers established here and there by trans- national companies. And in terms of the national system of innovation, the picture is at best timid and similar to Argentina. There are no links between university and business, funding is low, credit for innovation is scarce and, even when new patents—which are few—have origin in the Mexican ter- ritory, they are bizarrely due more to foreigners than natives. But there is evidence, though studies are few, that firms that export innovate more—or

64 *Latin America and Contemporary Modernity*

vice versa—as well as that the number and the quality of the production of Mexican researchers has improved.[65]

For Brazil, data seem to be more precise; the situation, however, is similarly dismal. In the stronghold of Brazilian industry, metal-mechanic capital goods, innovation is slow compared to other breathtaking branches of the global economy—and we have seen above that Brazil does not fare well in the advanced sectors of such an industry. The microelectronics sector remains undeveloped.[66] Besides, detailed studies have shown that cooperation is rare, for several reasons. Lack of internal capacity and the small scale of companies, absence of interest, very few partnerships with universities and low governmental funding are among them. When there is cooperation, it is not for innovation, but for less noble tasks (such as joint training). Product innovation is not common and process innovation is not widespread. Public investment is at the core of S&T in Brazil, universities surely have expanded, and money for research has increased, but even in this regard there is a long way ahead if Brazil must persist in trying to at least to some extent catch up—or not fall even more behind—central countries in terms of S&T and R&D. In any case, as in Mexico—and better empirically established through research—there is a clear correlation between success in export activities and firms' investment in R&D.[67]

Cooperation between Latin American countries has been virtually nonexistent in this regard—and has only very recently been affected by regional integration processes, *viz.* the Mercosur, indeed between Brazil and Argentina. Until very recently biotechnology—concentrated in both countries on human health and agriculture—was one of their few areas of cooperation. There is not in fact much prospect of evolution in this regard since this theme is not really present in the public debate and few countries have developed capacities in S&T, which does not carry much weight in the processes of integration, though those two governments have been making some effort in this direction.[68] These poorly posed issues have as a consequence a very subordinate position of Latin American countries in the global division of labor, if not a desired outcome, an inevitable one all the same. These countries " . . . seem to specialize ever more in commodities of low aggregate value . . . ," with "'static' comparative advantages," rather than in "knowledge intensive" activities. This obviously implies fragilities in the long run.[69] If overall the situation does not look good, in what concerns labor and consumption things do not appear brighter.

The Evolution of Labor Markets and the Pattern of Consumption

Latin American societies have always had labor markets whose dynamism was not as intense as that of the central countries. They have never really enjoyed full employment in the Keynesian scheme. The theories of "marginality" that were quite common in the subcontinent reflected this sort of problem, but had as a drawback simply detaching a large part of the labor

Development, Globalization, and the Search for Alternatives   65

force from the actual process of the economy, claiming that a huge mass of people performed no role in the economic process. Moreover, this entailed a sharply dualistic view of labor markets and society, involving the function of informal labor markets. This is today a position almost consensually viewed as mistaken.[70] As we saw above, a Marxist standpoint was also present in the debate, stressing a phenomenon that stood beyond the "industrial reserve army," with arguable results. However, they touched on a real issue for Latin American societies: Insofar as a mass of people was only peripherally brought into the capitalist market, and had no actual means, in a traditional sense, of reproducing their labor force, it was questionable which role they played in the overall scheme of accumulation and development. To be sure, one could simply argue that they were integrated in the capitalist process of development by means of the "subsumption" of traditional forms of labor (either as small proprietors or via several forms of more personal domination), by lowering the price of labor force, producing means of consumption at very reduced prices, and by bringing the price of labor as such to lower levels. Patterns of consumption are closely associated to this.

Today, a complex debate has developed about the "end of work" in Western societies. Many of the positions are certainly far-fetched, but in any case they underscore a visible trend, that is, the development of labor-saving technologies and the role of concrete labor in capital accumulation, as well as the part performed by new identities, which do not have labor and class as their reference. "Structural unemployment" has been one of the main issues at stake, a consequence of modernizing moves aiming at labor-saving strategies.[71] I cannot deal with such a complex problem here. Suffice it to bring up the question and see how it has helped to give new life to standpoints long ago forgotten in the Latin America debate.

In particular Nun has drawn attention to this evolution of labor in Latin America, resuming his former contribution (which he deems now too "economicist") and arguing that the subcontinent, with its peculiar labor markets, was a pioneer in a sort of issue that today afflicts advanced capitalist societies. According to him, there is an unwarranted conflation between the notions of "industrial reserve army" and "relative surpluspopulation." The latter may produce in fact "dysfunctional" effects. For that he had introduced the notion of "marginal mass." This was related to the passage from the competitive to the monopolist phase of capital, its internationalization, and deep changes in the occupational structure, all leading to a segmentation of the labor market. Now he clearly stresses that the end of stable wage labor is not at all an issue, but his former basic theses are revised and understood as rather close to truth, against the functionalism of many Marxist authors at that time and today. He acknowledges too that a number of authors and the International Labor Organization (ILO) believe in the reversal of such trends. He also recognizes the role of strategies and regulatory institutions for capitalist accumulation—hence that there is no such direct relation between productivity gains and unemployment. But he

66 *Latin America and Contemporary Modernity*

is adamant that there is clearly at this point a relative surplus population and that it is not by chance that the debate about marginality started in Latin America. Nun does not talk of "exclusion"; instead, segmentation is pointed out as the central feature of especially, albeit not only, these labor markets. In addition, he appears to connect this phenomenon in a rather direct way with informality. However, he does not see all such developments as inevitable and that there is no alternative—in any case stark changes in regimes of accumulation and social alliances would be necessary to alter the situation.[72] It would be hard to make sense and thoroughly discuss Nun's thesis and their implications here. However, I think that, despite shortcomings, his arguments carry a lot of weight. The main problem for me, at least within the limits of this chapter, is that he himself conflates the "marginal mass" with informal labor markets.

It seems to be very clear that a large mass of people is of little importance for accumulation processes at this point—and many of them are found today in the swollen "service" sector of Latin American economies and in small firms, with loose capital labor relations, as well as in self-employment and underemployment. But many of the people in the informal sector are absolutely fundamental for the present regime of accumulation. Flexibilization of legislation and weakened unions allow for overexploitation of workers but the same is true as for the lack of enforcement of existing rules, which is so common in Latin America and is at the root of such huge informal labor markets, especially in the main metropolis of the subcontinent and in the service sector. Lima, Peru's capital, is only a particularly vivid example of this, giving room to a well-orchestrated and well-financed neoliberal campaign that uses informality as a banner for thorough "deregulation." Informality is also very important in industrial production, even by means of outsourcing of tasks—in the new global regime of accumulation, by internal networks or global commodity chains—needed by large firms that hire basically from the formal sector and subcontract firms that operate often with recourse to the informal labor market. Informal labor markets and informality in general undermine the power of labor (unions suffer badly) and de-collectivizes labor processes, especially by segmenting the labor force and the increasing heterogeneity of the work situation (whereby also class boundaries become more blurred). As for a definition, it is notorious that the informal economy is a vague term, hard to pin down. It includes both poorly and well-paid work, plus the behavior of even large firms in some aspects. We thus depart from notions of dualism and marginality. What is more interesting is the articulation of formal and informal activities, following the "requirements of profitability." Workers, even during the same working day, may shift from one sector to the other. And sweatshops are not only old, but new to capitalism. This is also true, of course, for Latin America, where informal labor remained almost at the same level despite growing industrialization between the 1950s and the 1980s. Now, almost everywhere, the informal economy—and this is the new trend to be stressed—has been growing at the

Development, Globalization, and the Search for Alternatives   67

expense of the formal one. Its persistence cannot be explained as a remaining feature of traditional relationships, such as for instance survival activities by the poor, but rather as new social relationships, which are always defined by their context.[73]

In terms of labor markets, therefore, the utopia of modernity no longer seems to hold—homogenization does not look as a possible goal. Beyond an industrial reserve army in Marx's sense we have to grapple with a population that does not play any significant part in capitalist accumulation. To be sure, the distinction proposed by Nun cannot be confused with that between formal and informal labor markets. And it has to be taken first of all as an analytical construction rather than as a concrete description of actual processes, although it does reflect developments in social life. People surely may be at some points of their life in a such a hopeless situation that they are part of the superfluous population that some deem "excluded" in contemporary societies—and so they main remain for the rest of their days. But this is not mandatory, since a few may be able to do the trick of passing to another situation, while others fall down into a less fortunate existence. In terms of the collectivities that make up the whole of a national and even international labor markets, this is of reduced importance and does not change the segmentation and heterogeneity that is a typical feature of contemporary societies, something that is particularly dramatized across the Latin American region.

In the context of such a discussion, it may be instructive to introduce the issue of the tertiarization of the economy. All over the world the service sector is growing at a faster pace than agriculture or industry. The same happens in Latin America. The first problem to be faced is that the service sector is highly heterogeneous and includes activities that cannot be easily lumped together: High-quality and very or extremely skilled jobs, requiring higher education, are very important in this regard (in medical, and educational services, financial companies and high-technology support, etc.); deriving often from outsourcing of new, specialized tasks, on one extreme, and very low-paid, unskilled, "survival" jobs, usually in trade as well as in informal schemes, and often on one's own, with very low "barriers of entry," since they demand very little capital, on the other extreme.

A further problem is that many have argued that, in contrast to developed countries, there has been a tendency toward a "spurious" tertiarization of Latin American economies, concentrated therefore in that degraded extreme. Latin America has had its share of advanced tertiarization—and in some periods it might be argued that productivity in the service sector was higher than in other areas of the economy. Moreover, economic restructuring and economic development have included in the last decades much of that positive tertiarization indeed. But much support, even for those with a mixed view, can be found for the much higher growth, especially in terms of employment, of that negative sort of tertiarization. This appears partly in connection with sluggish economic growth and, perhaps more important,

68   *Latin America and Contemporary Modernity*

lack of aggregate demand for labor (due to advances of productivity that dispense with labor-intensive activities), as well as with a huge amount of informal jobs and survival activities of people eking out in small trade "businesses" on their own (of which the neoliberal campaign mentioned above wants to make so much . . .). For instance, in Brazil and Mexico in the 1990s, a result that would be shared by most other countries in the region, around 15 percent of all jobs created corresponded to own-account (excluding professionals and technicians) or unpaid work in trade, restaurants, and hotels, the segment with the lowest educational level of all the tertiary sector.[74] Of course, this carries weight to Nun's approach, although it cannot of course validate it per se.

This structure of labor markets and the service sector, more indirectly and due to the more skewed character it evinces in Latin America, is of course associated with huge inequalities, of which these countries have sustained records year after year in the world. Large numbers of people go on with minimal consumption. The 1980s and the 1990s were overall very bad in this regard. Brazil excels in this but is not alone, having recently spread the use of "grants" in social policy (see Chapter 1) to alleviate the problem. Although these are data whose precision is very problematic, insofar as they do not actually reveal the class nature of society and how upper strata hold assets and property, nor are they disaggregate for the richest strata (the 0.5 percent richest, for instance), an approximation to the problem is given by data collected by the World Bank. In an assessment of the late 1990s and early 2000s, the richer one-tenth of the population kept 48 percent of the regions' total income and the poorest tenth, only 1.6 (while in "developed countries" that upper decile earned 29 percent and the lower one, 2.5—something that should not serve really as a consolation . . .). Gini coefficients averaged 0.52 percent in the 1990s in Latin America, while the same index was 0.34 for OECD countries (and, as is well known, the higher the figure, the worse the level of inequality).[75] Within this very unequal pattern of distribution, consumption is of course also starkly stratified.

The idea of reproducing the patterns of consumption of central countries is widespread in Latin America, albeit not only there, especially in the upper and upper middle classes. "Objects" are differentially distributed. The cheapest ones (beverages, food, clothes, and some electronic domestic appliances) reach even the popular classes (albeit sometimes at the very end and in very low quantities); consumption electronics and cars reach the middle classes, but, above that, sophisticated products, either internally produced or imported, are concentrated in the upper classes. Even the features of agriculture as well as the average intake of proteins in the distinct social classes are related to this, although this is certainly not an exclusivity of Latin America. Beyond many other situations, however, the lifestyle of reference in the subcontinent derives from countries—especially the United States—which are five, six times richer. This is an old problem, which reveals some aspects of a would-be "cultural dependency," since the patterns are mimicked rather

Development, Globalization, and the Search for Alternatives   69

than internally created, a cluster therefore of dependent modernizing moves by consumers. Latin American sociologists used to apply the term "demonstration effect" in order to characterize this dynamic.[76] With such a segmentation in acquisitive power and consumption markets (alongside now with some aspects of "post-Fordist" consumption markets, to be seen in Chapter 3), it seems pretty obvious that regimes of accumulation cannot be based on intensive accumulation and the generalization of the benefits of the rise in productivity. A rather uneven process of accumulation seems to develop from these premises: without sustainability vis-à-vis mass consumption, extensive in what regards the most profitable goods consumed by the classes posed on top of the consumer market. This is connected and allows for the repeated extension of product cycles and the continuity of accumulation at a global level, whereby the central markets are broadened with recourse to segments of Latin American peripheral markets.

The Role of Agribusiness and "Commodities"

The dreams of modernizing Latin America have been consistently built around the notion that industry should become the driving force of development. This was related to the diversification of social structure but also to the thesis that, in the long run, there was a tendency for the deterioration of terms of trade for primary products. Some might even argue that no such tendency exists, but the obvious fact is that central countries may have a strong agriculture—the United States' exports in this area have indeed battered the Mexican producers at home within the framework of NAFTA—which is, nevertheless, neither the driving force of their accumulation process nor the kernel of their foreign trade. Yet, Latin American economies have been to a great extent reprimarized in the last decades. This is especially true of their foreign trade, but stands more centrally for the accumulation process as a whole. Some countries, such as Chile, have decidedly de-industrialized and delved into primary production wholeheartedly, reversing the original import substitution industrialization, whereas others have never actually industrialized. Even in those countries where industry has developed, export of primary commodities has become highly important. All this hinges very much on the rise of agribusiness.[77]

This trend is, in the first place, associated with the transformation of the rural social structure in a radical manner. Latin America was until the 1970s and the 1980s, with a few national exceptions, a region of peasants. This is no longer the case. Wage labor has become even more widespread across the subcontinent. There are large sectors of peasants in a mosaic whose precise composition is marked by heterogeneity, but such small proprietors are not so numerous, which does not mean at all that rural poverty has been superseded. Overall, agribusiness, based on large productive properties and commodities such as soy and other grains, cellulose, but also meat, have

70 *Latin America and Contemporary Modernity*

made such powerful inroads in the economies and societies of the subcontinent that they have become a crucial component of their social life. Overall this implied a decrease or, alternatively, a change of form and substance of peasant movements fighting for land reform and distribution.[78]

In Argentina, after a long decline in a once powerful stock raising (which has not thus far recovered) and agriculture, due to the lack of technological innovation, crops have had their productivity increased. They have become crucial for the country's commercial balance. In Mexico, small producers were devastated by the NAFTA free-market and free-trade regulations as well as by the reforms that, aiming at the end of *ejido* land in peasant-indian communities, turned it into a sellable commodity. Also large farmers suffered. They have all become the victims of a debt system that enriched finance capital and has given origin to a powerful and mixed social movement—El Barzón. Only agribusiness for export has thrived in the new situation. Chile has indeed since 1970s found niches for exports especially to the United States, but, with low technologies and no innovation actually sustaining the agricultural and pisiculture systems, this makes its economy also vulnerable in the long run. Large foreign companies control now seeds and often commercialization, creating a new sort of dependency. While the twentieth century was the stage for the "green revolution," based on the use of heavy chemicals (defensive products and fertilizers), across the world and also in Latin America, the last developments are closely associated with the introduction of (especially for soy beans and corn) transgenic cultures. In this aspect, too, formerly and at present transnational companies have held the strings, controlling capital, patents, and products (above all seeds, although they refrained from introducing the "terminator" variety, which does not reproduce itself). Only in Brazil, through Embrapa and a myriad of state-owned and private research institutes, have endogenous technological investments actually developed in a significant scale (for soy, rice, beans, etc.).

In any case, the push to make the whole economy move seems to be more powerful in the agribusiness case than it is in the "maquiladora" industry, although commercialization is often carried out by foreign companies within the global commodity chains scheme.[79] If this much is true for legal cultures, it is as much for illegal ones, in which Latin America is particularly well-endowed in the area of coca and cocaine for export, supplying a large North American market for cocaine as such as well as for crack. Colombia is in the forefront of production. But in this case small producers, peasants looking for survival, especially at the Amazonian agrarian frontier, have been in the forefront of cultivation, even while they are integrated also within a global commodity chain, in which—as usual, as for other global commodities—profits remain concentrated in the countries where they are sold. In any case, strong technological advancements are constant in this sort of cultivation.[80] Meanwhile the main oil producing Latin American country, Venezuela, has lived, repeating what it did during the 1970s, in a

Development, Globalization, and the Search for Alternatives 71

state of "magic spelling" due to the easy wealth produced not so much by the exploitation of nature but rather the enjoyment of a trick afforded by its "black gold."[81] This may or may not last long, though it will inevitably become exhausted. Unfortunately, thus far no actual development scheme has been derived from such abundance.

PARTIAL CONCLUSIONS: A NEW MODE OF REGULATION INDEED, BUT A NEW REGIME OF ACCUMULATION?

Latin America has undergone a far-reaching transformation in the last two decades. The former regime of accumulation and the former mode of regulation—that is, its mode of development, to use the theory of regulation school's phrase—were deeply altered. But can we speak of a relaunching of accumulation and development, in the more general, traditional sense? Have those modernizing moves and offensives been successful in achieving this? Or have new modes of regulation been introduced that do not allow, in fact along with another series of factors, for a sustained process of economic growth? That is the question posed since the mid-1990s in a regulationist view, which points to weaknesses in terms of savings and accumulation, as well as to the lack of diversification of the productive structures, stressing that no Latin American economy could be by any means considered "advanced."[82] Economic growth has been sluggish compared to Asian countries, China and in India in particular; within the so-called "developing world" growth rates have been smaller in Latin America than elsewhere: Historical series for the last ten years or so tell a tale of stop and go, as well as of limited success in accumulation rates. Even if we compare it with the developed (OCDE) world, the region does not fare really well. There have been improvements in growth rates, internal debt, and external vulnerability since 2003—macroeconomic policies have taken advantage of the favorable global situation. But the general pull of the world economy and in particular the Asiatic demand have been fundamental for their performance, as well as the positive evolution of terms of interchange for commodities and the cash flow of resources provided by immigrants in Central America.[83] The sustainability of such a pattern in the long run is open to question, let alone its peculiar "style" of development.

If in this regard things do not look bright, even less is that the case in relation to transformations in the productive processes as such, as seen above, which have developed very unevenly and with technological changes lagging behind, let alone the absence of process changes that might be favorable to workers and the reiteration of exclusionary patterns of consumption. The predominance and sway of finance capital have been immense and the power of blackmail it can still exert was not actually curtailed across the subcontinent. It seems to be clear that neither is there a consistent pattern of accumulation, nor is finance capital leading a new "growth regime." It

72 *Latin America and Contemporary Modernity*

can, however, still exert enormous pressure over the economy and the polity, expressed in the strenuous efforts to keep "macroeconomic" stability, in which strong and largely independent central banks stand out. Moreover, the strong penetration of foreign banks in the region and the high concentration of bank markets (still the predominant form of financial institutions therein) have not shown positive effects in the conditions of credit.[84]

Elaborating the issue, we may summarize what has been analyzed in this chapter and, resuming with circumspection the conceptual scheme of the theory of regulation introduced above, suggest that the mode of development in Latin America seems to be by and large based at present on the following elements: (a) tight monetary discipline with a contractive basis and fluctuating exchange rates, with finance capital and central banks playing a crucial role (Argentina, Ecuador, but also Brazil to some extent for a shorter while, put the monetary parity with the dollar, a radical and unsustainable move, at the top of all institutional forms of regulation of the economy, which was at the core of the 2001 debacle of the former one)[85]; (b) a sharp division of labor markets into formal and informal, with an increasingly large superfluous population and an extensive regime of accumulation with a loose norm of consumption, implying very segmented markets for the working masses and the low middle classes, on the one hand, and the upper middle classes and the upper classes, on the other; (c) of oligopoly firms, derived from concentration and de-nationalization processes, with competition within a second lawyer of small and medium-size firms; (d) rather open economies and dependent insertion in the global economic system; (e) loose regulatory state, with not much capacity to implement its own laws and rules, as we shall see later on. To this we must add (generalizing Ferrer's conclusions about Argentina to the subcontinent as a whole, perhaps with less severity in some countries, although not even this proviso necessarily applies) that in " . . . no region . . . do we observe accumulation processes in a broad sense, that is, an overall development of the whole of society and the economic system."[86] Latin America seems to be stuck in its pattern of low consumption and low technological development, dependency on the power of and decisions by transnational firms, financial markets, and governments of central countries, without a clear future ahead. Much of the new regulations is clearly socially perverse and cannot be deemed conducive to success, regardless of the fact that they cannot be held alone responsible for all the shortcomings of the present, which must be distributed among other factors, external and internal alike.

It is interesting to note that although democracy and democratic waves had a kind of linkage with developments elsewhere, they largely stemmed from endogenous modernizing moves within Latin America, which eventually came to connect states and populations in a less despotic, more democratic manner (I will certainly return to that in the Conclusion). They are doing well too. If anything, so-called "diffusion" processes happened basically within the Latin American region and counted on the defeat of one

Development, Globalization, and the Search for Alternatives 73

dictatorship after another to undermine the solidarity the military could sustain across countries and rob those regimes of legitimacy. Shortly after economic reforms were enacted and, if they were implemented and seduced a great many of the ruling groups and upper classes of the subcontinent, such modernizing moves and offensives were in a good measure imposed by forces from outside Latin America. Since the 1960s and especially the 1970s, transnational corporations landed in the region; their presence was very much increased in the 1990s and they were at the forefront of firms' restructuring (and not always in the worse manner). Finance capital took over much of the wealth of the region in the course of its inward and outward flows during the 1990s. International agencies, the IMF, the WTO, the World Bank, the GATT, along with in particular, though not only, the U.S. government, imposed specific agendas, reforms of first, second, and never-ending "generations." Patterns of regulation were imported, through the diffusion of ideas and practices shared by professional communities, but also via the forceful creation of agencies such as demanded by those international organisms. Thus globalization is not just the outcome of the process; it is at its very root with deep intensity, crafting a new, the third, phase of modern civilization in Latin America in the economic dimension.

It is particularly sad to see that, in addition to the present inauspicious situation, there is no real alternative thinking in Latin America that could lead to a modernizing offensive capable of tackling the present unfolding of the third phase of modernity in the economic sphere in a more interesting way for the peoples of the region, certainly nothing that might resemble the old ECLA and its original blend of historical-structuralism at the analytical level and peculiar state interventionist instance at the programmatic one. Impasses abound; novel alleys are missing. It is not clear how the Latin American predicament will be sorted out.

In the 1970s, Cardoso and Falleto analytically differentiated between: (1) "development" and "underdevelopment," the latter referring to the degree of differentiation of the national economy, which is relative and can be seen only in comparison with other economies, and the subordinated position of the national economy within the international structure of production and distribution; (2) the situation of "dependency"—which took that latter aspect into account, but stressed the decision power those situations implied, hence summoning the political aspects of the issue; and (3) the center-periphery relation, for which the functions within the world market of the national economy was what mattered, without further consideration of the political aspects of dependency. Furthermore, they introduced an original point of view and argued that, within situations of dependency in Latin America, development was actually occurring in some countries, in a "dependent and associated" manner (Brazil, Argentina, Mexico).[87] Cardoso, later on, was rather circumspect about the reach of the "theory," which he proposed then to frame as a part of a theory of *imperialism,* in the sense Lenin defined it, irrespective of further changes in the global articulation of capital and

74   Latin America and Contemporary Modernity

the changing role of finance capital (once again transformed today, by the way).[88] If we take their assessment and concepts into account, the situation looks rather bleak now. Underdevelopment seems to be the norm, once we define development today in terms of the third technological revolution, which provides for the broader differentiation of productive systems and their leading role in the global process of accumulation. Latin American countries are, in addition, either in the periphery (Ecuador, Venezuela, Peru, Bolivia, Colombia, Uruguay, Chile, El Salvador, Guatemala, Nicaragua) or in the semiperiphery (Brazil, Mexico, Argentina) of the global civilization in economic terms, depending on their level of internal differentiation and industrialization. They all export basically commodities (often primary) or industrial goods, with a few exceptions, of internally low aggregated value (*pace* Brazil's appearance in a few areas of higher technologies—especially small aircraft). Petrol and gas have become recently dubious sources of wealth—as ethanol promises to be too, for ecological as well as economic reasons, reinforcing the reprimarization of the economy. As for dependency, it had been a long time since the political and economic systems of Latin American countries had been so openly subordinated to the dictates of external forces—finance capital and the international organizations mentioned above. And, in what regards imperialism, the power finance capital, transnational corporations, Western governments (especially the United States), and international organizations have acquired over Latin American economies, along with the continuing process of dependent underdevelopment, places the issue in a position similar to that which Cardoso stressed. We will come back to this in the following chapter and in the Conclusion. At any rate, it can be said that a long road was traveled and huge efforts made, but also that in a relative sense the subcontinent is back to where it started its efforts to alter underdevelopment and its position within global capitalism, regardless of absolute advancements during the twentieth century in some countries. And if imperialism is not exactly the same as in 1970s, it remains in place with a renewed role for finance capital and transnational corporations.

In addition to that, we must introduce an issue hitherto not mentioned in this chapter, that is, the tension between nature and development, environment and capitalism, which is a mark of the global debates today, and has a peculiar expression in Latin America. The critique of capitalism and the predatory style of development it implies was very strong in the sixties. Several answers were tried and Latin American social movements and NGOs played a very important role in the debate, as carriers of a true modernizing offensive that challenged one of the pillars of modernity. This culminated in a dismal resolution vis-à-vis world fora and the relations between "developed" and "developing" countries, with the former pulling out from any actual commitments to changes with respect to debt, lifestyle, and so on. The solution was a compromise category—that of *sustainable development*—according to which the two elements of the pair were compatible.

Development, Globalization, and the Search for Alternatives   75

No precise translation of such compatibility was proffered and since then emphasis has been put on one or the other element of the expression. Thus, while environmentalists have been putting weight on sustainability, governments, especially under pressure from the public and business to modernize their economies,that is, to grow, obviously stress development.[89] This, in a continent of large poverty and inequality, with a hunger for improvements in the lives of ordinary people, and where consumption patterns tend to mirror those of the center very strongly and business groups have a huge influence, could hardly be different.

The third of phase of modernity, in Latin America as elsewhere, cannot but keep a central feature of this civilization, that is, the *domination of nature,* at its core, implying intensive use of natural conditions and widespread destruction, and of course the multiplication of risks, of local, national, and global significance.[90] It is witness also to the consolidation, even within conditions of material deprivation of large sectors of its population, of commodity fetishism, which neoliberalism has taken as far as possible, by seeing societies basically as *markets* and by having consumption very much according to Western patterns as a goal for the rich and a sweet dream for most of the population, without much room for alternative values.[91] Capitalism is of course at the center of both these issues, as much as it is directly related to the existence and shifting identities of social classes, which we will examine in the next chapter. It is at present, as it has been from the very beginning, a crucial aspect of modern civilization, and its articulations have become ever more global. But now it is heterogeneity that appears to mark, beyond the generalization of market conditions, the establishment of capitalism in this third phase of modernity. This of course has important consequences for the modern imaginary and for the projects that may envisage development in a broad sense in the contemporary Latin American situation.

Yet, Latin America has not constantly grown, despite all reforms and promises neoliberalism, economic restructuring, and so forth, and the commitment to accumulation at a high social and environmental price. This is indeed a stark contrast with the flourishing, whatever its limitations, of democracy that we have examined in Chapter 1, and has indeed militated against it: The combination of at times relative, at times absolute stagnation, and some frightening disasters at the economic level, with electoral and sometimes participatory democracy, could not but harm the latter. This is especially true if we take into account that during the 1990s and to some extent into the 2000s, what some have even called "monolithic thought" consecrated the hegemony of neoliberalism and left no room for democratic debate. It seems to be high time to return to questions and dissent, in the search for real alternatives.

3 Identities and Domination, Solidarity and Projects

INTRODUCTION

The Iberian conquerors that arrived on the southern coasts of the New World were faced with an enormous quantity of populations of distinct ethnic origins distributed across the subcontinent. Languages and religions, mores and practices were legion. As if that were not enough, they brought to their new colonies millions of black slaves from Africa, also of different religious, linguistic, and ethnic origins. A highly heterogeneous social fabric resulted from this mix. Class, ethnic, and "racial" stratification converged.[1] Exploitation was tough. As a political body, the state of Iberian monarchies had a mission to fulfill, namely, civilize and integrate within a Christian political community the newfound peoples of the subcontinent; the church, as a mystical body, should carry out their evangelization. This perspective stemmed directly from the neo-Thomist view espoused by the main Iberian theologians at the time.[2] The final period of colonial life already witnessed changes, but it was with the independences that modernity set in. Continuities can, however, be discerned in the midst of ruptures.

This chapter will start with a consideration of social life at large in the nineteenth century and most of the twentieth. Which relations of domination and exploitation prevailed, which forms of solidarity were crafted, which identities did people recognize for themselves and in others? How did the state interact and mold these societies? How was the heterogeneity and pluralism of many of these countries dealt with by the homogenizing project of modernity? Which collectivities carried out modernizing moves? Initially, as in the former chapters, I will focus on the first and the second phases of modernity. I will then move on to tackle at greater length the traits of the third phase, which, as elsewhere, is marked by growing social heterogeneity, with peculiar characteristics in the region under study here. Throughout, neither "elites," the stuff of much of modernization theory (at least in its Latin American version), within its analysis of the passage of "traditional" to "modern" society, nor classes, "groups," and "elites," as in dependency theory,[3] will be taken as the only collective subjectivities that matter to modernization and modernizing moves. The theory of collective

Identities and Domination, Solidarity and Projects 77

subjectivity shall allow for a broader understanding of such processes and their increasingly plural character.

THE BUILD-UP OF A REGION

Due to the disembedding processes already conceptually defined in the intermediate reflections of Chapter 1, modernity presents individuals, *qua* subjectivities or citizens, with rather unspecific characteristics, as abstract beings. More consistent re-embeddings are thus necessary. A few sites of collective identity and solidarity have played a key role in this respect in Latin America.

The family has been crucial. Its heterogeneous character, a heritage of colonial times, was maintained. Sometimes a similar outlook enclosed different contents. By and large we can distinguish types of what has been called the "creole" family: white, nonwhite (indian and black), and mixed. In the aftermath of the independences, the Napoleonic French Civil Code—with its emphasis on male leadership, wifely duty and obedience, as well as civil incapacity—furnished the model for gender and marriage relations in Latin America. That said, informal unions, except for the ruling classes, were the norm rather than an exception. The colonial legacy of informality predominated. Ruling class families evinced a rigidification of "patriarchy" (i.e., the domination of women and the offspring by the male head of the family). Indian families often involved polygamy and were usually informal, based on "traditional" customs (rather changed, in fact, at this stage). In the Andean region, "tribal marriage" (*watanaki* or *servinakuy,* in Quéchua) developed from old customs—allowing for sexual experimentation, the possibility of dissolution, and a tendency to postpone formalization. While formerly black slaves were usually forbidden to marry (though not breed), freed blacks and "mestizos" now evinced the same informal pattern of marriage. Matrifocality and male absenteeism were common. The ruling classes, on the other hand, had a male ethos in which sexual predation of women of the subordinated popular classes was strong, especially, though not only, when they were slaves. According to Therborn, "[i]n the 1890s, Latin America and the Caribbean had the most complex and multifaceted socio-sexual order of the world."[4] Let us make no mistake, though: There was one paramount family pattern in these new countries. Based on the agrarian state, but with the city as its wider focus of action, the patriarch connected with extended kinship and forged alliances with other families, through personal domination plus ties of friendship, nepotism, paternalism, and authoritarianism.[5]

During the twentieth century the propensity to marry formally seemingly grew. By 1960, Brazil, Chile, and Uruguay had the strongest formal "marital order" in the region. In this the modern tendency towards homogenization, with greater control by state and church, can be discerned. Beginning in the

78 Latin America and Contemporary Modernity

1910s, the Mexican revolution gave the first important steps toward the emancipation of women and the weakening of patriarchy, a movement that traversed the twentieth century. While this tendency became stronger, the movement toward the formalization of unions was reversed in the 1970s. Since then, informality spread out as well as a sharp decline in fertility rates ensued (alongside birth control, by families or the state). Thus a profound change—what specialists call the "first demographic transition"—took place there, accompanying urbanization, the rise of the middle classes, and proletarianization, alongside the decrease in mortality and, somewhat later, fertility rates, similarly to what happened in the central countries of global modernity in a somewhat earlier stage. It took however a longer period of time to be fully accomplished, specific features are prominent, and it varied from country to country, being completed only in the 1970s. What some deem a new, the second, demographic transition started soon after—an issue we will discuss later on. The plurality of family life in the subcontinent, which has always included extended units and female leadership, in tandem with more traditional nuclear and male-dominated households (which are prevalent), has been maintained.[6]

These multiple features of the family had a direct relation with the plural social structuration of Latin America. In the new independent cities, a patrician "elite" ruled over poor white people, mixed people, indians, and blacks, which conformed a "baroque" social fabric, indeed a colonial heritage. These cities slowly massified and some embraced large waves of immigration mainly from southern European countries in the beginning of the twentieth century. The countryside was even more rebellious, mixed and often fragmented according to race, ethnicity, and social condition, although control over such rural masses was trusted to rural landlords and "caciques." The incorporation of such masses, their fusion or the attempt to make such countries whiter through European immigration, the contraposition between "civilization and barbarism," were long-lasting themes of Latin America's daily life, intellectual projects, and state policy.[7]

The nation, a crucial form of modern identity, beyond the level of abstractness and individual isolation, and beyond the family as a collective subjectivity as well, was also a means to overcome the blatant and problematic pluralism that characterized social life throughout the region. It emerged in the nineteenth century as a construct of vital importance. As elsewhere, it worked as a main focus of social solidarity, allowing for the imaginary, as well as, to some extent practically, overcoming of the entrenched divisions of society in terms of class, race, and ethnicity. It has consisted, alongside market and state as such, with which many would like to directly identify it, the collective subjectivity *par excellence* of modernity since its origins. Nationalism depends as much on the selections of traits capable of building that identity as on the forgetfulness of others, which might again and again rip apart the collectivity thus constituted. In the subcontinent, it featured prominently in the very beginning of the modern era and was one of the first

Identities and Domination, Solidarity and Projects   79

places where its potentialities were tested. In contrast to chauvinistic forms of nationalism, in the subcontinent, with the independences, its appeal was rather to emancipatory moves, against colonial domination.[8]

In Latin America, the state had a particularly strong role to play in the effort to craft new nations. This was so either in the amazingly large geographical area covered by the Brazilian Empire (whose central ruling groups had all been to the University of Coimbra, since there was none permitted in the colony, and shared a common view of the country) or in the mosaic of republics that emerged (in large measure thanks to the presence of local universities, hence local intellectual groups and leadership) across the subregions of the Spanish colonial empire. If in Europe and elsewhere a more homogenous fabric had already been prepared by many centuries of common life and shared social and material infrastructure, as well as by developing national markets and Absolutist states, in Latin America things were more complicated, since those elements were present with less intensity. The state then came in forcefully to bring people together, repress regional attempts at secession, and create a common culture and identity. Results varied widely. Differently from what happened in European countries, war was not especially important for Latin American nationalism—the wars of independence, crafting a defensive form of nationalism, were as far as that went, although in a few stances during the nineteenth and later on in the twentieth century such states battled with each other in territorial and geopolitical disputes. Reasons that contributed to the minor role of war for nationalism therein (but should we deem that always necessary?) were a small tax basis and weak bureaucracies, plus the incapacity of Latin American states to mobilize population and resources. An even more complicated problem was how to homogenize the populations under their rule. Education played now a role similar to evangelization during the colonial period. The mosaic of ethnicities and skin colors was an especially difficult issue, for which the colonial states did not really care, since theirs was not a view especially keen on homogeneity (in fact the segmentation of the social formations over which they ruled was taken for granted and assumed without further concern). But this was possible in the first place insofar as basic social control and domination were exercised through more personal ties and landlords had the necessary power and social conditions to guarantee order. With freer subjects and a more open identity, bringing people into a common frame, generating identity and solidarity within a common space, and offering a shared future were imperative if re-embeddings should occur that did not threaten the state and the position of the ruling collectivities that were favored by the independences, fulfilling also the task of assuring psychological well-being for those who thereby achieved a new place in the world. A national re-embedding and the homogenization of social identity were aimed at theoretically, but with limited reach in practice, since such a nation was to a great extent an abstraction.[9]

80 *Latin America and Contemporary Modernity*

With the piecemeal incorporation of the popular masses into the nation and the twentieth-century efforts to break free from economic dependency, a more mobilizing sort of nationalism tended to emerge in most Latin American countries. It substituted the milder, more liberal and cosmopolitan perspective that predominated during the nineteenth century and the first decades of the twentieth. It heralded the beginnings of the second phase of modernity ("state-organized" as previously defined in Chapters 1 and 2), in an internal expansionist move beyond its formerly highly restricted features, and resumed the emancipatory project of the independences. Education and cultural policies were prominent at this juncture, reinforcing the former project of nation building through state action, now vis-à-vis freer populations. This was often interwoven with projects to create or deepen what ideologies of miscegenation envisaged as a mixed, "cosmic" race or as "racial democracies," conforming new modern projects for re-embeddings, assimilationism, and the homogenization of society. If they might mean a *telos* of equality for the racial problematic, in practice such projects did not by any means do away with racism against blacks, indians, and all sorts of mixed people. In any case, in Brazil and Cuba black culture received pride of place in the imagining of the nation. Introducing a general revaluation, often praise, and an assimilationist view of indians, "indigenism" came about all over Latin America too. Nevertheless, especially in the Andean region, problems of communication, lack of state interest in the face of local schemes of personal domination, and the persistence of precolonial idioms were not conducive to the realization of nation building at all, something that Mexico overcame with its far-reaching revolution.[10]

Mexico, Cuba, Brazil, Argentina, Bolivia, and Chile, among others, saw national-popular movements grow in importance and strength, gathering urban workers and sometimes peasant masses: Economic development, social inclusion, and political independence (with a more complicated relation to democracy) were key issues from the 1930s to the 1980s. It came into being entwined, nevertheless, with attempts at controlling those same popular masses, which threatened sometimes to break loose from the limits imposed by still largely oligarchic societies and polis. Corporatism, which we have conceptually analyzed in Chapter 1, was the main instrument of such a regulated and authoritarian incorporation, which had nation and state building interwoven in its definition. As noted there, corporatism implied the incorporation of legally and formally defined organized collectivities within the framework of the state, representing society via channels other than the individual voting capacity and worked in society in part as an instrument of the state. It was probably the mechanism whereby the Latin American states ever achieved greater "infrastructural" power during their whole history (a topic to which I will return below). Thereby, also, all would find an—ideally domesticated—place in the frame of the nation and the state through a pattern of "cooptation-repression" of the working classes. Businesspeople were formally included in the corporatist regime,

Identities and Domination, Solidarity and Projects 81

mainly in the countries where the same obtained for the working classes. The system was usually looser and they tended to retain more independence, due of course to their greater social power in relation to the state, if compared to the working classes, furthermore differing a lot in terms of the variable capacity of such organizations to actually bring together and steer the bourgeois classes. That said, corporatism hardly achieved, with the exception of Mexico, a polished and complete institutionalization, for instance in Argentina and Brazil, while other countries, such as Chile, have never had a corporatist system, or had it belatedly and in a much weaker form, that is, Venezuela and Colombia.[11]

Parties grew either side by side with such corporatist arrangements, in Mexico, Brazil, and Argentina, or as alternative means to connect state and society, either as partisan organizations, especially in Chile, or as neo-oligarchic and clientelistic instruments, in Venezuela and Colombia. At times, as with Peronism or Chilean and Uruguayan left parties, they were capable of large mass mobilizations; in those neo-oligarchic regimes stability was, however, achieved against actual popular participation. Nevertheless, more generally they were not deeply rooted in social life and conformed rather unstable party systems, especially when mass mobilization entailed authoritarian solutions carried out by the military against actual processes of social change.[12] Bureaucratic-corporative and providing specific channels for different ruling classes in distinct countries (the industrial bourgeoisie in Brazil, mainly the reactionary landlords in Argentina, Uruguay, and Chile—and, as a passing exception, trying to reach out to the peasant masses in Peru), the military dictatorships did not change the main features of state power in Latin America (except for a few civil service reforms), accentuating its despotic character.[13]

The state in Latin America has been a crucial element in modernizing offensives, even in propelling politically capitalism and in the formation of capitalist classes. It did not, however, make a clear break with some of its pristine features. Patrimonialism or bureaucratic patrimonialism (with societary or state origins), as well as a "feudalized," or "prebendal," state of "assisted capitalism," have been widespread traits of Latin America. The bureaucratic but (neo)patrimonial features of such states—without detriment to their modernizing character, nor of the informal and illegal, corrupted practices such feature entails—have also been recognized by many authors, with distinct ideological and political persuasions. At the same time, bourgeois interests have found privileged channels through which they have had leverage over states' leadership and their main officials.[14] Nevertheless, contrary to conventional and recent ideological wisdom, these states were never actually strong—or at least were not as strong as their Western counterparts. They did have the means to integrate with the international market, to promote capitalism and support the powers and privileges of the upper classes. But they have always had trouble penetrating their "societies" and implementing policies and decisions through them, thus becoming more

82 *Latin America and Contemporary Modernity*

legitimate and establishing closer ties with their citizenry. "Despotic" rather than "infrastructural" power often characterized the actual constitution of such states, meaning that they did not have much power to shape their societies (whose precise traits only belatedly did they survey via statistics). Of course this did not prevent the military from taking this despotic character to its heights during especially in the 1960s–1970s. Since oligarchic domination prevailed in some important countries, such as Venezuela and Colombia, they did not need to resort to dictatorships.[15]

Even territorial control by the state in Latin America was fully achieved only in the second half of the twentieth century—an issue that has beset in particular Colombia. Besides, state machinery has been rather inefficient and for a long time they had trouble in taxing their societies. Colonial legacies live on to some extent also in this regard. Attempts at reforming the state have been numerous in Latin America, especially during the twentieth century: in the 1930s in Brazil, Colombia, and Argentina; in the 1940s in Paraguay and Panama; whereas in the 1960s the focus on economic development brought the topic once again into the limelight. Outcomes were only very partially successful—with military governments in the South Cone showing a more efficient record in this respect, as did the United States' occupation in some small Central American states. In any case, only with the second phase of modernity did the number of public officials and employees really go up, including those in state enterprises and in education and health care—a very uneven process according to different countries. On the other hand, if there were countries (Argentina, Chile, Uruguay) and regions within countries (especially vis-à-vis the urban working classes) wherein the disciplinarization of the population via political and bureaucratic means and clear patterns of what should be considered appropriate and civilized behavior were imposed by the state and other social agencies, by and large we cannot talk of a spread in "conventionalizations," at least with the same magnitude that was typical of the second phase of modernity in Europe and the United States. Lack of infrastructural power and even the continuous subordination of large parts of the population to forms of personal domination in the countryside prevented this sort of development. Direct violence was the main means of controlling most of the popular classes.[16]

Crucial actors in all such countries were also, though often grown under the protection of the state and even at times having it as their demiurges, the industrial (as well the commercial and financial) bourgeoisies, which were often enough allied, through politics and personal relationships, to the powerful landlords that emerged as the ruling classes in the aftermath of the independences and predominated until the middle of the twentieth century, whose influence, nonetheless, declined henceforth. Some in fact spoke of the most modernizing power blocs in the region at the outset of what I have defined as the second phase of modernity as crafting a compromise or alliances within the state between different—landlords, bourgeoisie, and middle class—collectivities, which set the limits for developmental policies

Identities and Domination, Solidarity and Projects 83

in the region: The more oligarchic elements predominated, the less likely was industrialization.[17] These links and the restricted space such bourgeoisies have found, due to the pressure imperialism and the subordinated position of these countries in the global system, have lent them very defensive features. They have refused "plebeization" and the democratizing outcomes brought about by the development of a "competitive order," supporting thus a strong differentiation of status within these societies and against the popular sectors. They have looked for allies abroad as well, instead of internally. Fernandes spoke in fact of a "plutocracy" as for the second half of the twentieth century in order to characterize the Latin American ruling classes: Oligarchies, internal bourgeoisies, and foreign partners (as well as the highest levels of the middle classes) were fused in a collectivity marked by the "overpriviledge" of class and rooted " . . . in power founded on wealth, in the availability of property and in the capacity to speculate with money." They evinced a very authoritarian and exclusivist character. Since the 1960s, an association with foreign firms and international capital had guaranteed the continuous economic development of a few countries, especially Mexico and Brazil, in the subcontinent, accounting for the shift in the import substitution process and a dependent development pattern in a few countries, as analyzed in the foregoing chapter. Overall, however, the Latin American bourgeoisies seemed to evince a rather adaptive attitude—instead of the vocation for hegemony—depending on their position vis-à-vis economic sectors and possibilities of market expansion. According to data collected in the early 1980s, they were very small.[18]

While this obviously entails a strong and closed (though not necessarily publicly ventilated) class identity for those on the top, the situation of those in the lower echelons was more complicated. It was not only deep exploitation that was at stake. Some, such as Touraine, do not think even that their class identity as such was ever properly developed, since they joined multiclass, national-popular, and so-called "populist" movements, to the detriment of their (imputed) interests. The main contentious issue in his characterization is given by a liberal concern with a division between public and private, state and society, especially in relation to identity creation and political mobilization. While in Europe the working classes were based on the private and civil society domains, in Latin America a sort of pathological blockage prevented this: Their identity was built in the public and state domains, with the workers' political limitations stemming from this distortion. In fact, in this connection Touraine basically reproduces a radically economicist Marxist view.[19] In addition, more than an echo of modernization theories and a narrative of "lack," rather than one that really comes to grip with what actually happens, can be found in this standpoint, as against a concrete and not foreclosed understanding of the specific Latin American reality. I will have more to say about the neo-Marxist or neo-Weberian tenets that underlie this view of social class below.

84 *Latin America and Contemporary Modernity*

Suffice for the moment to note that, contrary to such a view, strong working classes and, more generally, popular classes' movements were a crucial element of the political and social dynamics of Latin America especially during the twentieth century, in both urban and rural areas. The struggles that cut across that century and especially, more recently, the movement toward democratization that has changed the face of the subcontinent (as examined in Chapter 1) cannot begin to be understood without this class and popular dimension. But they did so not according to some sociologist's manual in which class identity had to be pure and conceptualized a-historically and in a de-contextualized manner. The actual and concrete development of conflicts, projects, and worldviews molded as much the working and popular classes—which in the case in point were highly *heterogeneous*—as they shaped ruling ones. Touraine himself narrates this almost in detail in his panoramic book, missing the elements of his own narrative out of a very biased and in my view totally mistaken conceptual construction of the social classes.[20]

Very common also in the politics of the Latin American popular classes was a phenomenon associated with the tertiarization of the economy and urbanization, as well as with its egregious informal labor markets, which was taken as a great novelty in 1970s–1980s. This refers to the so-called "communitarian" movements of the region. They had in fact an important role in the struggle against the military dictatorships and came to the fore in this period. But they were older across Latin America and, against much of a rather naïf view, were, again, rather heterogeneous and counted a lot on the presence of "external" actors for mobilization (Church, professionals, parties), regardless of their usual egalitarian ideology and anti-authoritarian phraseology.[21]

It was thus from this difficult, painful, but also highly creative interplay between distinct collective subjectivities that Latin America emerged and has since the nineteenth century modernized. All the imaginary elements and institutions we have hitherto considered in this book had their modernizing carriers in those collectivities during the first and the second as well as during the third phase of modernity. Our main task now is therefore to analyze more minutely how collective subjectivities have been shaping the latter. Before doing so, however, let us elaborate the theoretical framework necessary to account for such empirical phenomena.

INTERMEDIATE REFLECTIONS—COLLECTIVE SUBJECTIVITIES AND SITES OF SOLIDARITY

As pointed out in the Introduction, the concept of collective subjectivity is crucial for what we have been treating as modernizing moves. In terms of general theory, it has even greater implications. I originally put it forward refusing any view of "structures" as possessing any substantial character—they have merely a heuristic, descriptive utility, being crafted

Identities and Domination, Solidarity and Projects 85

by the researcher as a "snapshot" of a social formation, of whatever magnitude, at a given moment. But the theory of collective subjectivity aims at going beyond also an individualistic, reductive perspective. Social life is thus seen as woven certainly by the interaction between individuals as well as—and here lies the novelty of the conceptual construction—by the interaction between collective subjectivities. As individuals exert a causal impact upon each other, so do collectivities—through what I have called "collective causality." Collective subjectivities must not be seen as reproducing the traditional model of individual subjectivity. Instead, I propose to think of them as relatively *(de)centered,* that is, as enjoying distinct levels of identity and organization. This means that their "movement"—in terms of causally changing or maintaining any given social arrangement—is also variably intentional, depending on their level of centering. Such a concept does not suppose clear consciousness, in a Cartesian vein, of collectivities, although it may be that they are aware of themselves and of their impact as well as being organized enough to act in concert, either by the collaboration of individuals and subcollectivities or via hierarchical structures. It remains to be added that collective subjectivities have several dimensions, which we can analytically define as those of the hermeneutic fabric, of material belonging into nature, of power relations, and of space-time configuration.[22] Instead of trying to elaborate the theory in greater detail here, let us see how, in terms of the collective subjectivities dealt with in this chapter, we can unfold those basic ideas.

The logical place to start with this is the concept of social class. It has been by antonomasia the key issue in the conceptual history of collective subjectivity (alongside, in a lesser measure, state and nation). Marx is of course the main reference in this regard. For him classes and their struggle were the movers of history. Holding opposed interests, they clashed since humankind abandoned the original community. But some of them were capable of identifying their interests and acting on them, in a very Cartesian-Hegelian way, going from "class in itself" to "class for itself," while others did not. If the peasantry was totally incapable of achieving any level of class consciousness, and the bourgeoisie could do so only in a partial manner (otherwise it would transcend its own ideology—in any case it could act politically in a clear and organized way), the working classes were the collective subjectivities that could really accomplish that passage, produce a revolution, and inaugurate true human history with the establishment of communism. The first steps implied organization for the defense of material interests at the local level, the opening up for the national level and, eventually, the passage from narrowly defined material interests to political identity and struggle. Therefore, class existed in terms of economic structures and relations without any conscience in principle, which was achieved piecemeal, making recourse to the rational understanding of one's situation, to be then politicized. Ideologies and counter-ideologies emerged also in this process.[23] In terms of the theory of collective subjectivity put forward above, for Marx

86 *Latin America and Contemporary Modernity*

some classes, especially the working class, were capable of achieving a very high level of centering—hence of intentionality.

It is even more curious to note that Weber's theory reproduces some essential features of Marx's, despite his much more pluralist view of classes in the market, to which they take different resources. For him "class position" means the sharing of life chances as to the availability of goods, external life position, and internal life destiny, implying shared interests. "Social classes" arise from the foregoing, insofar as personal and generational situations are shared, and a certain level of class consciousness is thereby established. Thereupon "sociations" (*Vergesellschaftungen*) might develop, leading to the formation of class associations. Classes are no "community" as such; rather, they pose a possible basis for community formation and action. This appears, in his argument, in sharp contrast to "status positions," which hinge on specific valuations of honor and patterns of consumption and lifestyle. Classes belong to the economic order, status, to the social order (while parties are at home primarily at the sphere of power).[24] Thus, starting with a mere passive, unconscious, and so to speak structural situation (although Weber in principle had an individualistic view of social life) things may unfold in a way such that some sort of class consciousness arises and eventually, at times, class organization and common action develop. In contrast, "status" groups are from the very start self-aware and organized collectivities.

Poulantzas had already made some advancement in the Marxist theory of class, although the rhetoric that usually attributes all virtues and corrections to the founding father, in the case in matter through the supposed rejection of "historicism," clouded his own formulation as such. He correctly asserted that class situation and class consciousness cannot be separated (stating that Marx himself had relinquished this youthful, Hegelian view), but then reintroduces it via a structuralist (analytical) distinction between class structure, social relations, and class practices. In any case, he was right when he underscored that class is no mere economic phenomenon, instead belonging to all dimensions of social life.[25] But with reference to what we are discussing here, Giddens' formulations come closer to the mark by proposing the concept of "class structuration," the way "economic relationships" become "non-economic social structures" and lead to classes as "identifiable social groupings." "Proximate" elements propelling structuration are the division of labor and authority, patterns of consumption, community or neighborhood segregation; mobility chances—with greater or lesser identification between generations—work as "mediate" factors. More important is his distinction between "class awareness" and "class consciousness." The former implies the mere "common acceptance" of similar attitudes and beliefs, linked to a common lifestyle, without recognition of a particular "class affiliation"—meaning sometimes the denial of class existence (a usual phenomenon in the case of the middle classes). In turn, the latter is based on the recognition of classes (one's own and others), entailing perhaps, but

Identities and Domination, Solidarity and Projects   87

not necessarily, the identification of oppositions of interest, thus clarifying latent ideas. Class revolutionary consciousness is only a particular case of class consciousness.[26]

Before elaborating on the issue of collective subjectivity, let me just add to this a less controversial, substantive element of the theory of class, with which we will have no quarrel here either: The existence of middle classes is a key feature of previous periods of capitalism and the present one alike. Managers and experts as well as the old petty bourgeoisie, with varying degrees of power, rent appropriation, and loyalty to the upper classes, cannot be reduced either to the working classes or to the bourgeoisie. In turn, the so-called "managerial revolution" that was the focus of much debate in the 1960s did not imply changes in the actual control of property of corporate capitalism. It just made it more complex and mediated, by further delegating authority positions.[27]

The insights of Poulantzas, especially his understanding of classes as total social phenomena, and Giddens, in particular his view of a from the very beginning already present self-recognition of classes (even if this may ideologically imply denegation), lead us away from the curious mix, present in both Marx and Weber, of descriptive structuralism and, also more or less explicit in the two of them, a demiurgic sort of rationality that brings about consciousness and concerted action in a Cartesian-Hegelian way, most often in a utilitarist translation. The level of awareness of social classes varies therefore regarding all the dimensions in which they are part and parcel of social dynamics—economic, social, political, cultural, or whatever else one can propose. Of course, Poulantzas' defense of Marx has to be discarded as inappropriate; we must also go beyond Giddens' lingering debt to those both authors, when he thinks of a passage from economic to noneconomic social structures. We must leave behind those phasical presuppositions. Indeed, it is the varying levels of centering and distinct contents classes as collective subjectivities evince that are at stake here. In order to refine these ideas, I want to introduce a threefold distinction between practical, rationalized, and non-identitary reflexivity.

In social practices, especially in daily life, reflexivity operates often in an unsystematic way. People do take into account social settings, mobilize knowledge, draw upon memories and refashion them creatively, but without concentrated attention or sharp intentionality. A further development of this general and basic reflexivity stems from its rationalization. In other words, a second-level reflexivity—as "rational" thought—emerges from the application of concentrated attention and focused systematicity to oneself and others, to social action and interaction. Most theories of action take reflexivity as synonymous with rationality, but in the framework just proposed this equalization is not accepted. In addition, another, deeper sort of reflexivity, which is linked to the workings of the "it," in Freudian terms, and thus does not obey the logic of identity, must be accounted for in order that a complete picture is drawn (I cannot explore this theme at any length

88 *Latin America and Contemporary Modernity*

here, but it is worthwhile noting that this aspect of reflexivity is especially relevant for the workings of creativity). When Giddens differentiates awareness from consciousness, he is in fact implicitly introducing a distinction between practical and rationalized reflexivity (an issue he resumed later, in a flawed way, through the opposition between "practical consciousness" and "discursive consciousness").[28] We shall see in a moment the relevance of this distinction, especially when linked to the concept of collective subjectivity, when I propose a renewed view of classes, but also of gender, ethnicity, and race. Before doing so, I want to explore the main expressions of these sorts of collectivities such as they appear in the social sciences, something much less elaborate than has been the case with classes.

Let us start with ethnicity. Weber himself proposed a view that is somehow close to his own underlying perspective on classes. For him, ethnic groups have undefined bases, though these do exist. But, as they elaborate them, such bases must be "consciously mediated," implying beliefs in the commonality of blood, customs, language, religion, and culture. Some sort of political community (which would implicitly work as an organizing, rationalizing entity) facilitates the process. That is, passing from lived experience to systematically reflected-upon culture, especially if they can count on the propelling force of political power, ethnic groups might achieve a higher level of centering.[29] Other perspectives would place great explanatory weight either on the existence of primordial ties underlying any viable ethnicity—entailing deep emotional attachment by individual members—or on instrumental relations—in which case ethnicity means merely an asset to be mobilized in the search for other ends.[30] These theories are not incompatible with Weber's original perspective, but they do separate to the extreme a passive, unreflective (or practically reflective at best) ethnic belonging, with a variable degree of centering, from a highly rationalized and centered mobilization of ethnicity, in terms of both identity and organization. The problems of class theory, albeit perhaps mitigated, are reproduced in all these versions. The same may befall race analysis, which is even thinner conceptually (race has been shown to be not amenable to a final, bounded definition). It is pretty evident that "races" (pure or mixed) have no biological basis: They are social constructions closely connected to racism and its "labeling operations." But they are based on social interaction and usually on the identification of certain physical traces as symbolic marks as well as heredity so as to underpin ideologies, or "discourse" operations, plus biological and cultural distinctions.[31] Latent potentialities are then brought up, which are often already there and practically recognized, although the rationalization of such traces, irrespective of its highly arbitrary character, lends them a systematic appearance. If race comes up as intrinsically arbitrary, in the case of gender the biological substrate is just too strong to be ignored, which does not mean we should fall into any sort of biologism. Gender "consciousness" or, more neutrally, gender "discourse" (implying the construction of masculinities and femininities), arises from social interactions,

Identities and Domination, Solidarity and Projects   89

symbolic operations, and patterns of power distribution.[32] Yet, the definition of gender—a cultural category that gained ground in the early 1970s as opposed to sex as biologically given—begs the issue: Is there a woman or a man lying there that then becomes conscious or is it variably, in terms of content, discursively built? Or should we refuse this phasical perspective of the development of gendered collective subjectivity? The same could be said in relation to generational categories, biologically grounded of course, but socially and culturally constructed within a great range of variation and plasticity.[33]

I am now in a position to propose more explicitly and synthetically a renewed view of class, ethnicity, race, generation, and gender that, blending the theory of collective subjectivity with that threefold concept of reflexivity, is, I believe, capable of overcoming the shortcomings stressed above. Collective identities exist often as basically woven by practical reflexivity, shared memories, and practices in daily life, as well as by their daily reinvention. Many of them (such as class or gender) cut across several, or all, dimensions of social life. They may be rationalized, whereby their specific elements are reorganized, some aspects stressed, older memories recovered, while other elements are disregarded or even discarded.[34] Beyond that there may happen the politicization of collective subjectivity, which may acquire distinct contents (the revolutionary inclination being one among many possible others, never a necessary development). Organization and usually a social movement are needed to operate this passage. In all these forms, identities may intersect, overlap, inasmuch as they are not exclusive. The rationalization and politicization of collective subjectivities depends, however, on the *plausibility* of this reconstruction, which rests upon the practical-reflexive constitution of that more pervasive collective identity. To be sure, political and social power as well as the capacity to label people is crucial too, especially when the construction of collective subjectivity is a process steered from the outside and with negative orientations. We can grasp that easily in the case of socially constructed races, whose plausibility tends to be, out of itself, rather low, but are institutionalized due to the powerful interests that guide their imposition upon subaltern collectivities. Of course, external, negative labeling can and is often combined with self-definitions by collective subjectivities, sometimes defensively, as resistance or counteroffensively, consisting in an empirical issue how much the former impacts upon the latter.[35] Just as class, race, ethnicity, and gender cut across social dimensions, so too do the relations between different races, ethnic groups, and genders imply different access to material resources and exploitation, unequal power distribution and geographically distinct patterns of arrangement, cultural subordination and distinct hermeneutic views of social life, under the hegemony of the dominant collectivities in each relationship. It goes without saying that a view of identities according to an essentialist definition is totally incompatible with the conception put forward here.

90 Latin America and Contemporary Modernity

I must now introduce a further distinction, that between *quasi ascriptive* identities and *further optional* identities; this is related to the level of *plausibility* demanded of the new collective identities. The former refer to re-embeddings that depend to a great extent on already existing collectivities, demanding a high level of plausibility. The latter refer to freer constructions, which do not depend basically on pre-existing collectivities, notwithstanding the new ones making recourse to memories present in previous collectivities. In fact, it is a continuum that obtains, from strong ascription to radical choice. While the latter leaves greater room for creativity and the former delves deep into memory, both are traversed by these two elements.

Social (political, cultural, or religious) movements connect history and daily life—infusing the latter with meaning and linking the former to the quotidian activities of the people who are engaged in them, setting thereby the "horizon of possibilities" of a given social formation, beyond what is already given. When the social movements' identities must be rooted, due to the character of the movement, in already existing collectivities, often experienced through practical reflexivity, there is a natural demand for greater plausibility, whereas the opposite is true vis-à-vis movements whose make-up is more contingent and does not draw so heavily upon former collectivities. In any case, social movements usually evince a high level of centering, with strong identity and regardless of whether their steady organization hinges more or less on hierarchies or networks. In contemporary society, we can see the multiplication of social movements, the issues they deal with, the identities they craft, and the forms of organization whereby they arise and carry on. Issues that motivate people to establish ends and goals as well as coming together, plus propitious occasions for mobilization, are as important for their emergence as their capacity to mobilize external and internal resources and already existing, daily ties between people. Working-class movements remain important, indeed, assuming distinct forms, but are no longer *the* social movement of modernity. Others have emerged, and, while politics has not lost centrality for many of them, "culture"—even against, or with the back turned to, the political system—as well as religion has returned to the forefront of present-day social movements.[36]

Other collective subjectivities are thus added to the framework already outlined above, making social life more heterogeneous. The family and the nation—pristine sites of re-embedding especially in the first and second phases of modernity, along with classes—undergo strong mutations that are closely related to this pluralization of social life. The former itself becomes very pluralized and decentered, insofar as patriarchy relinquishes some of its grip and alternative forms of organization, due to the multiplication of marriages and unions, especially when they produce children, break away from the model of the unitary family cell. However, it keeps a reasonable level of centering, at least in relation to the units made up of parents (or one of them) and children—although separations, new informal unions, and even new marriages imply a centripetal push that inevitably lowers the level of centering of the family, in terms of organization but also of identity. The pluralization of re-embeddings cuts across moreover all other collective subjectivities such as class, gender, race, ethnicity, and generations, as well as family and nation—bringing up new forms and greater intensity to ethnic issues—plus social movements. The nation, in particular, as an "imagined community," becomes less homogeneous, due to internal processes of pluralization, as well as to external impacts of the deepening of globalization, which multiplies possible courses of life and types of individual and collective identity. This means also that the *emotional investments* of people, their attachment and commitment to encompassing subjectivities, becomes potentially pluralized, insofar as collective subjectivities are sites of *solidarity*.[37] We will examine this empirically in the following sections.

A theoretical examination of the state shall close the conceptual section of this chapter. Basically, I want to suggest a combination of the two main perspectives on the subject, a Marxist, but creative one, and another that, being original in many respects, owes a great deal to Weber.

Poulantzas proposes the key idea of power as "relational," whereby the state is understood as a "condensation of forces between classes and class fractions." Neither is it merely instrumental for social forces, nor does it hover above society. The state apparatuses are traversed by social struggles—political struggle is thus also internal, not absolutely external, to the state, and the classes are within it, in a differentiated manner in each of its apparatus. While Poulantzas does not deny the facticity of the state—especially pointing out that its apparatuses are "knots and fora of actual power" and that state personnel constitutes a "social category," with its own proper unity—those knots and fora, as much as the distinct layers of state personnel, are linked to classes in society. Moreover, the very division between state and society is not universal, nor does it mean, in capitalism, an exteriority with respect to the economy.[38] Mann, on the other hand, willing to go beyond the unilateral character of most state theories, affirms that states are both "places" and "actors," possessing varying degrees of cohesion (without final unity or consistency) and autonomy in relation to society, irrespective of the fact that they always respond to the pressure of capitalists and other major power actors. It has multiple facets, with "polymorphous crystallizations," centers of power, implying institutions, tasks, and constituencies. Within the state, we encounter distinct "elite" groups. Following Weber, he reckons that the state is a differentiated set of institutions and personnel, has a centre, covers a territorially demarcated area, enjoying legitimacy and organized physical force. In addition, its power over society has two facets: "despotic," exercised merely from the top down, and "infrastructural," which is mediated via society. Of course, relations, peaceful or otherwise, with other states are also crucial for its conformation.[39]

I want here merely to embrace most of Mann's view, with an emphasis taken from Poulantzas on the socially rooted character of the state, its shaping through power relations without as well as within itself. Capitalists and

92   *Latin America and Contemporary Modernity*

workers, races, genders, and ethnicities, as well as social movements and pressure groups, such as environmentalists, all contribute to the shaping of the state, which then shapes to a great extent society. But, beyond such a pluralization, a "historical bloc" (hegemonic and combining distinct collective subjectivities, implying political alliances and institutional arrangements, cultural politics and economic strategies and policies, and the possible and actual exercise of force) usually pulls the main strings, shaping and controlling the state, regardless of the influence exerted by collectivities at less relevant and decisive levels. In modernity, bourgeoisies and landed propertied classes, mostly white and male dominated (*pace* especially the changing character of the latter), have by and large ruled in connection with similar state-connected and -based collectivities, with which they usually have close ties, sometimes bringing the petty bourgeoisie or the middle classes, and even some fractions of the working classes, into the ruling scheme. Different "power blocs," in which one group or fraction predominates, cut across those more broadly conceived "historical blocs" (since they include "culture" in a general sense, beyond economic interests and political strategies, if they manage to achieve hegemony, alongside coercion, the two moments of the "enlarged state").[40] The state is therefore a collective subjectivity, which can, in its concrete workings, achieve a high level of centering, but has to grapple with internal tensions and centrifugal tendencies on a daily basis, being intertwined with other collective subjectivities. Generally speaking, the state does not enjoy emotional investments, unless seen as the concrete representation of the national community.

COLLECTIVE SUBJECTIVITIES AND MODERNIZING MOVES TODAY

As Latin America enters the changed configuration of the third phase of modernity, the collective subjectivities that have been carrying out such processes of modernization in connection with processes that unfold across other regions of the globe have been themselves modernized by those processes of modernization. A spiral of development obtains, insofar as every step reinforces the process as a whole, provision taken of the weight of the past and the limits faced in the subcontinent for some routes within the general unfolding of contemporary modernity. Due to the expansion and deepening of the processes of disembedding that have steadily figured in our analysis, identities have become much more pluralized in advanced—more specifically, in the third phase—of modernity. If citizenship remains its basic re-embedding, it is too thin to provide thorough solutions for identity building and social practices. The third phase of modernity is characterized by the deepening of processes of disembedding as well as by increasing complexity. Evolutionary complexification predates modernity, but carries on within it, thanks to the differentiation of social life in all its spheres and dimensions

Identities and Domination, Solidarity and Projects   93

(that is, not only in terms of the so-called "division of labor"). Hence a wider range of "choice" characterizes contemporary social formations.[41] Private processes of subjectivity constitution, on the one hand, and the organization of social, cultural, and religious movements, on the other, are at the basis of this pluralization, sometimes drawing upon collectivities that already exist, sometimes bringing into being collectivities that are almost entirely new. Such choices may indeed depend on rationalized reflexivity; but often they hinge on practical reflexivity, or on dislocations between these two aspects, as well as, of course, on the workings of non-identitary reflexivity and its decisive contribution to creativity.

Here I diverge in particular from García Canclini's main thesis is his well-known book.[42] For him (despite the elusive character of his formulations) we would be living in postmodernity, not exactly because we have superseded modernity, but due to the fact that the postmodern problematic has become pervasive. In other words, heterogeneity, pluralism, fragmentation, hybridism have come to stay and displaced the former concern of modernity with homogenization and a unilinear overcoming of the past (tradition), which now lingers on not as a remnant to be discarded, but rather as a lively element to be integrated without brushing its differential aspect aside. It is not by chance, indeed, that hybridism has been substituted for *mestizaje*, for instance. While the latter implied a tendency toward homogenization, the former may be thought of as giving rise to a new entity in which the components do not necessarily disappear; rather, they may live together in a state of creative tension.[43] Admittedly, some "societies" in Latin America today tend to fragmentation, partly because the nation-state has difficulty integrating plural identities and divergent aspirations, as well as because of internal strife and the state's low capacity to answer to it. But the main institutions of modernity, however transformed, remain in place, as much as their underlying collectivities. The changing aspects of the hermeneutic dimension of social life are not enough to define a new civilization, nor even the radical dislocation of modern concerns. In fact, I believe that it has been a deepening of some aspects of the modern problematic that has come about, along with its underlying evolutionary complexification, while others have not been so deeply altered in this third phase of modernity. In fact, it is a superposition and intertwinement of different traditions, including modern traditions, that takes place in these processes of disembeddings and re-embeddings.[44]

A different sort of criticism can be leveled against Tapia's view, concerned especially with Bolivia, which could be extended to at least some countries in the subcontinent with large original indigenous communities (such as Ecuador, Mexico, Guatemala). Drawing upon the work of his countryman René Zavaleta, he speaks of a "multisocietal," "multicultural," and "pluri-civilizational society." This derives from the fragmented (literally "abigarrado") character of that social formation, due to a sort of colonial domination that decapitated politically the former communities without

94 *Latin America and Contemporary Modernity*

fully integrating them within the dominant society, and which has never been totally overcome.[45] I think it is undeniable that such a fragmented outlook is typical of Bolivia and to some extent of those other countries, yet would also like to argue that those other civilizational elements have been reshaped and brought into the reach of modernity, an expansive civilization that is capable of dragging features from other civilizations into its own dominant dynamic—and even more so as more social integration is achieved. The discussions below will substantiate, I hope, this claim. More dramatic, and more arguable, is Zermeño's claim, according to which social fragmentation—beyond structural processes—derives from the neoliberal project and its deliberate effort to deconstruct collective identities. The Mexican neoliberal state would be playing a crucial role in this regard. The evanescence of the "social" emerges from this strategy.[46] Now, although there is a grain of truth especially for Mexico in his argument, the fact is that, as we will see, corporatism and the maintenance of (superficial) collective identities remains more central to the Mexican state than to other Latin American countries. Fragmentation is indeed related to problems of social solidarity, as I will argue below, stemming mainly from social complexification and the lack of social and political dynamics, as well as institutions, capable of answering to this challenge.

Individualism, moreover, has been a key element of modern liberal ide-ologies and is responsible to some extent for this break in the weaving of solidarity recently in Latin America. We can view this positively—if there are mechanisms to allow people to grapple productively with it—or nega-tively—especially when individualization befalls popular classes that are sinking into poverty, caught up in the whirlpool of neoliberal reforms and economic restructuration. Or else, may I suggest, we should see this as a contradictory process that can lead, depending on social conditions and political answers, to distinct outcomes. An ambivalent position should be taken in relation to them, in which disembeddings and pluralization are the propelling forces.[47]

Neither individualization and individualism, nor the identification of greater pluralism and complexity must, however, overshadow the para-mount importance of power distribution, as well as exploitation, in social life.[48] Dominant and subordinate collectivities are today a key factor in social dynamics as much as they used to be in prior phases of modernity. Classes in particular, as well as genders, races, and ethnicities, retain an enduring relevance as a structuring element of contemporary Latin America; they are crucial collectivities in the modernizing moves that have been enacted in this recent space-time configuration. The increased complexity of social life has, however, rendered unworkable the old arrangements—that is, cor-poratism—whereby their power and demands were channeled toward the state. The conjunction of the emergence of more plural popular classes with the ultimate internationalization of the ruling classes, vis-à-vis a state that has not as yet recovered from the crisis of developmentalism, has become

Identities and Domination, Solidarity and Projects   95

an issue that lies at the bottom of the region's disjointed development. We have already identified this in Chapters 1 and 2 especially in what refers to the contradictory dynamics of democratization and of the adaptation of the economy to the requirements of the third phase of modernity under the aegis of neoliberalism. Which sort of *complex solidarity* may be weaved by social agents in order to overcome this stalemate is an issue that, summing up, closing the chapter and lending it to some extent a programmatic direction, will be taken up toward its end.

Curiously enough, the most powerful collectivities extant today in Latin America have been the object of limited study. This is especially funny insofar as so many social scientists in the subcontinent explicitly espouse a "critical" perspective (albeit often vaguely defined), but have refrained from examining such relations of domination and exploitation. Besides mentioning the fact that the rich do "hide away" and the lack of interest of funding agencies and also of official global, regional, and national organisms on the issue (including for instance the Economic Commission for Latin America—ECLAC),[49] I shall draw upon the existing material and hope that, in a not too distant future, researchers will strive to systematically overcome such shortcomings. The role of very original and plural social movements will stand out throughout the exposition.[50]

Family, Genders, and Generations

Social and biological reproduction (including class, racial, and ethnic elements) has obviously been a crucial factor of social life in contemporary Latin America, the same as in other periods and elsewhere.[51] But families, genders, and generations have taken up specific characteristics in this concrete space-time, closely connected to the deeper disembeddings in course as well as to the pluralization of social life of which it is part and parcel. Let us examine each of them in turn, bearing in mind that family and generations have been crucial sites of solidarity and emotional attachment.

I have argued above that Latin America has already undergone a "demographic transition," implying the decrease of mortality and fecundity, as well as of family size, plus a longer, or much longer, duration of life. As aforementioned too, important authors suggest that a "second demographic transition" is under way, which partly overlaps with the former one; compared to the West, it still has supposedly to be completed. While the first transition rested on demographic aspects as such (what is usually called "transformations in demographic regimes"), the second is marked mainly by cultural and institutional changes. Among these some stand out: the diminishing control of institutions over individuals (i.e., further individualization), the greater acceptance of sexuality outside the wedlock plus more autonomy for the individuals and more symmetry of relations within the couple, meaning greater equality and the emancipation of women. The transformation of gender roles, growing divorce rates, as well as the control of reproduction and its decoupling from sexuality underpin such changes. Young people express these lifestyle changes, which unevenly cut across social classes, in a more straightforward manner. But let us note that whether the West is undergoing such a transition is open to controversy; whether this characterizes Latin America—especially account taken of the prevalence of informal unions—is even more arguable. Some would strongly disagree with such a thesis. In any case, greater diversity of family and cohabitation arrangements is a visible trait of Latin American sociability at present. In particular, as a phenomenon that is however very problematic, women have, due to male absenteeism or out of their own choice, often become head of families throughout the subcontinent, especially in the popular classes, with all the gain in autonomy as well as the emotional and material costs this implies.[52]

One must of course ask whether such an identification of tendencies would not be tantamount to a revival of modernization theory. Regardless of particularities, would the modernization of social life in general (urbanization and increased division of labor) per se imply demographic changes and the transformation of family structure? A study suggests that this is partly true, but not entirely. In fact, poorer and less developed countries lag behind in the demographic transition. A group comprising Bolivia and Haiti is more backward, followed by another one including El Salvador, Guatemala, Honduras, Nicaragua, and Paraguay. While Argentina, Chile, Cuba, and Uruguay, as well as some Caribbean countries, are at the forefront of demographic change, Brazil, Colombia, Ecuador, Mexico, Panama, Peru, the Dominican Republic, Venezuela, and other Caribbean countries are halfway into the process. The heterogeneity of situations and even social regimes is patent in this list, but modernization seems to be at least partly correlated to demographic changes.[53] Moreover, gender relations are connected to this in a complex manner: Whereas in some countries—Argentina, Uruguay, Brazil—changes can surely be spotted, albeit without a complete bouleversement of things, in others—such as Mexico, economically well-developed, according to Latin American standards—patriarchy seems to remain pretty strong. In fact, some even reject the idea that greater "reflexivity" would be emerging therein.[54]

To be sure, while men have been taking care of children more often, keeping the house tidy remains a woman's duty: They carry on with their double shift. Overall, the "traditional" nuclear family predominates—whether men are present or not—but a pluralization of family arrangements is evident: The nuclear family with a male breadwinner, a housewife, and children corresponds to only 36 percent of the total in contemporary Latin America.[55] In contrast, the formal labor force remains strongly masculine, while women take up more often informal jobs; rather than in industry they are employed more in the service sector (ranking there 60 percent, a high percentage in domestic employment, while constituting only 40 percent of the labor force). They receive lower wages than men. This happens irrespective of the level of education, which is roughly the same now across Latin America for

Identities and Domination, Solidarity and Projects 97

men and women. Data suggest too that, at the high managerial level, differences between men and women do not reproduce those found in the popular classes in what regards income.[56]

What can surely be said is that the family remains a crucial site of emotional investment, maintaining its role in biological and social reproduction. Inequalities and the rigidity of roles have decreased, but by no means disappeared, the same obtaining for patterns of income and gender inequality. Gender conflicts certainly became starker. This notwithstanding, the family has been the object of powerful modernizing moves. These are basically pushed in a rather decentered manner, since lifestyle politics in an explicit manner has not been particularly strong in Latin America (yet it did take part in the 1960s cultural revolution). The media plays a diffuse part in connection with such modernizing moves. Social change is related in all its aspects and processes of modernization are not an exception in this respect, which does not at any rate mean that there is a one-to-one correspondence between them. Instead uneven, combined, and contradictory developments are always a strong possibility. We will return to and elaborate on this point in the conclusion to this book. Hence, there is nothing strange in the association of variables such as demographic transition, urbanization, and economic development. The fact that there is no simple association between these variables tells us, however, that no mechanical and automatic links are to be found. Instead the mediation of individual and collective subjectivities is to be expected, played upon the ever stronger and more demanding processes of disembedding that unfold in the subcontinent, accompanied by increasing social differentiation. Social and moral plasticity results from this junction. In some countries, we can find modernizing moves that associate such crucial societal changes with "demographic transitions." In others, this is not true, or is less intense. By and large, in any case, modernizing moves are present across the subcontinent and gender roles, divorce, reproduction age, the relation between sexuality and reproduction, new identities, and so forth have been changing fast. Individuals try to further their interests and values, negotiate changes, accept the relative reinforcement of old patterns. Families as units also have their goals and social life modernizes according to them—the economic progress of the family unit may propel, given the appropriate conditions, economic growth overall, for instance.

But families have been themselves decentered too, since the split of many prior units and the succession of unions and marriages, with children from different couples living together or at least partly sharing home, is a natural consequence of the pluralization of family patterns and the spread of separations. The "traditional" pattern of informality in Latin America contributes to this, in that socially such sort of unions is more easily accepted and new family projects could draw upon old patterns. In addition, authority relations, whose hierarchy becomes fragmented thereby, assume distinct and plural contours. As mentioned above, the high number of families headed by women alone—meaning that they must support their

98   *Latin America and Contemporary Modernity*

offspring frequently single-handedly—are a specific and to some extent perverse aspect of such altered family and gender patterns in Latin America. Paradoxically, although it may represent poverty for women and children, independence from aggressive partners may imply greater personal freedom especially for the former, insofar as it allows them to avoid in particular domestic violence and the effects of patriarchy.

Emerging with particular force in the 1970s–1980s, under the military dictatorships, women's organized social movements have provided consistent and centered modernizing moves in relation to gender roles and power, helping to further those more decentered modernizing moves. They have been active in many domains, proposing all sorts of social changes. In fact, as part of an actual cultural revolution that points to a democratization of social life, feminist movements have had a great contribution to the changing face of Latin America "civil society," implying new power positions, practices, and identities, as well as novel tensions. New historical horizons have fast emerged from this, during the twentieth century and beyond; the social memories of gender roles have been obliged to re-mold themselves. Less auspiciously, although compatible with trends we can spot in other social movements, feminism has undergone a strong "organization" in the last decades, which impairs to some extent its capacity for mobilization, lending their modernizing moves a more professionalized outlook, while popular participation has decreased.[57]

Nowhere are these changes and the plasticity of demographic transformations shown more explicitly as in the shifting meaning especially of youth (a social concept whose meaning has expanded in terms of age cohorts, but diminishing in absolute terms, demographically) and, less glamorously, of old age (or "Third Age," as commonly said today, which increases as people live longer).[58] Maffesoli spoke of new "tribes," aesthetically defined and unstable, which above all the youth have created.[59] His perspective leans toward irrationalism, but he has a point indeed. It is one that we can discern all over Latin America. Some characteristics may be singled out in these modernizing moves, helping us go beyond the extremely large variation of empirical cases and identities—something that, out of itself, underscores the theoretical question of social pluralization. The velocity of symbolic change stands out in this regard and leads to the idea of "nomadism," in either a literal or a figurative sense; affective sociability plus multiple and shifting bonding and identities are crucial; deferred time, that is, the postponement of entrance in the labor market and "adult" life obtains too, especially for middle- and upper-class youngsters; vulnerability in what regards violence (as well as an inclination toward it at times) and unemployment in particular are key themes; rejection of institutional politics is usually found (in turn, "molecular" action, informal networks, and cultural movements are chosen as paths for some sort of participation, especially regarding new topics, such as the environment); the concentration on the present, whereby the closure of a utopian horizon comes to the fore, along with some sort of

Identities and Domination, Solidarity and Projects 99

rejection of the past, can also be detected; and, finally, the importance of the mass media, but also of a myriad of other electronic media of communication, is overwhelming.[60]

Once again disembeddings are present, which include the exposition to far-reaching global influences and new sources of memories for re-embeddings. New identities are therefore badly needed to supply for this practical and symbolic availability of socially defined youth. Music has played a particularly strong role in these new re-embeddings of young people, showing to which extent aesthetic sensibility is important for them, as well as how the multiplicity of " . . . musical tastes and preferences go together with the symbolic fragmentation . . . and the fragmentation of their own identity."[61] Modernizing moves are once again at the core of such re-embeddings, whereby individuals and very contingent collectivities redefine their presence in the world. Thus hip hop, rap, samba, cumbia villeja, all sorts of salsa, graffiti, new religious orientations, martial arts and football, symbolic interventions in the body, and an endless number of particularistic identity constructions are to be found in the development of youth "tribes."

One aspect must be emphasized in this connection: The new identities that emerge—and even the modernizing moves that underlie them—are often mediated by the market, albeit not always or necessarily (sometimes in fact a sharp rejection of this is systematically pursued). Post-Fordism, with its products tailored to answer to more varied needs, whose plurality it reinforces, as well as the adoption of imported fashions and fads, symbolic markers, bodily cult, and aesthetic lifestyles, in which by the way North American blackness is overwhelming, can be easily detected in this.[62] A key aspect of contemporary capitalism, consumerism, is thus ingrained here too, likewise it is in other dimensions of social life, entailing commodity of fetishism. It remains to be added that consumption today is as much homogenizing—in its fetishization—as heterogenizing—through market segmentation—and that consumerism is one aspect of more concrete forms of re-embedding insofar as it strongly differentiates people by lifestyles. These tend to become further pluralized and fragmented in this third phase of modernity and are, of course, starkly marked by class backgrounds.

Pluralism and the Nation

As previously seen, Latin American nations in the twentieth century were built having as an ideal end state their homogenization. While classes were placed in a more prominent and organized position in such projects, in particular due to corporatist ideology, this meant overall that racially, ethnically, and also religiously, such nations would lose their internal elements of differentiation. At present, this has become an impossible project. The pluralization of social life and the sharp processes of disembedding that unfolded in the last decades have opened room for a multiplication of social identities. The nation has therefore acquired unheard of characteristics.[63]

100 *Latin America and Contemporary Modernity*

We have seen that consumption and youth lifestyles were pluralized. Such modernizing moves draw a lot upon foreign influences. Globalization is here on the full. The same occurs with respect to the other moves we will study below, working as a further source of pluralization of social life, as a new reservoir of memories, of material influences as much as of frustration and absence, providing space for creativity.

Religion is one aspect of this. Catholicism was, at least officially, the devotion of Latin American populations. To be sure, pre-Colombian and African elements have always been pervasive in popular—and middle- and even upper-—class religiosity. It enjoyed a rather subordinate position, though. Moreover, other Christian cults were basically either not allowed or in any case commanded a small following. Things have changed very fast more recently:

> The close of the twentieth century witnessed radical changes in the religious field in Latin America. These changes have included the rise, crises, and rearticulation of liberation theology and Christian based communities, the rapid expansion of evangelical Protestantism, the growth of the Catholic Charismatic movement, the revival and re-Africanization of African-based religions . . . , and the emergence among the urban middle classes of 'New Age' religions. These processes demonstrate that the religious field in Latin America has become highly pluralistic . . . Moreover, despite claims of modernization and secularization, these processes point to the enduring role of religion in public life in the Americas.[64]

This is a field on which we must be careful to thread. Religious diversity, variations across denominations, the rationalization and politicization of African-based religions and of the indigenous peoples' religions, the role of Pentecostal sects (communities that believe in the Holy spirit) or of the Brazilian-born and expanding universal Church of God's Kingdom (with its Theology of Prosperity and personal advancement, with unambiguous "elective affinities" with neoliberalism): These are all specific elements to be taken into account when such a topic is tackled. But we must from the very start be careful especially when we talk about "secularization." Many believe and can mobilize data mainly from Europe that show that the influence of religion in social life decreases with modernity. This seems to be actually true, although not in an absolute sense: Religion becomes one form, among others, of identity-building. There is a sense in which the stress on secularization is, however, really misplaced, especially if we turn to Weber so as to develop our argument. Secularization, in a more restricted view, must be separated from the "disenchantment of the world," the shrinking role of *magic* in social life. Instead, while this may happen or not, entailing the decline or not—regardless of its specific magic content—of religion in social life overall, secularization would refer exclusively to the *separation*

Identities and Domination, Solidarity and Projects   101

between state and religion.[65] In this regard, in spite of some loose reference to God and the obvious role of religion in political movements and parties, the state in Latin America has long ago been secularized (basically since the turn of the nineteenth to the twentieth century at the latest).

Secularization in this precise sense has contributed to the pluralization of religious affiliation and to shifting patterns of allegiance over time. While Catholics are still the majority in Latin America—varying, according to country, from 75 to 90 percent—no one has to fear socially, and even less politically, for her commitment to other faiths any longer. Brazil in particular has a large number of Protestants—the fast-growing Christian faith, in a great deal of variations; they are very common in other countries too, often those with large indigenous populations, such as Guatemala, Bolivia, Ecuador, and Mexico. These are real social movements. Not only do they mobilize millions of people, they also imply changes in lifestyle, individualization, a search for personal dignity and advancement, as well as, often, collective mobilization, drawing upon local ties and taking advantage of social and political opportunities. Admittedly, it is frequently the case that the institutionalization of such religious movements and the deleterious role of their leadership, usually a self-appointed clergy, may have disastrous effects for the democratic character of the movement. Exploitation and political clientelism may easily derive from the control priests may exert over their destitute religious following. It is quite amazing to observe too how these sects operate as "electronic churches," providing for a true "cultural revolution" (and, for some, reintroducing magic in daily life), either in Chiapas, Mexico, or in the peripheries of Brazil and Argentina. More deeply yet, the worldview of the participants in such movements tends to change and such new or refashioned religions, in many different and sometimes contradictory ways, trigger actual changes in personal and collective behavior; and a search at least for "social cohesion"—or social solidarity—is unmistakably present in these religious movements.[66]

It is curious that the theory of social movements has not dealt with these sects or that its arsenal has not been mobilized to cope with their huge impact in social life. Neither Tarrow nor Melucci figure in the studies about religious movements in Latin America; nor did they lean over such phenomena. Social movements are deemed either up-to-date networks of free individuals or political structures that mobilize people and resources due to specific political conditions. Religion has no place therein, especially Protestantism, regarded moreover as politically conservative. But this is obviously a foul point; besides, was not Weber concerned especially with religious movements for the emergence of modernity?[67] This is perhaps more comprehensible if we briefly point to a comparison between evangelists and Kataristas in Bolivia, in the region of El Alto, close to La Paz. At first glance, they appear as "entirely distinct." However, closing in we can discern similar themes and membership, which they share sometimes consecutively, although the people who move especially from the former to the latter feel uncomfortable

102 *Latin America and Contemporary Modernity*

to bring this out. Both movements agree that there is a moral deficit at present; both seek to reinforce "pride, dignity and self-worth among Aymara indians." Protestants focus on culture and look to the future in order to find solutions, having side-effect political impacts; Kataristas (and their successors) are politically militant and reconstruct an idealized past. They are both answering to the challenges of modernity, social change, individualization, and the integration of indigenous people within the multiethnic national state of Bolivia.[68]

At this point, we move into a further element of pluralization of Latin American national "societies" and the conception of nation that used to obtain therein. While a reality of mixed elements can actually be discerned in such populations, culturally and politically we witness the emergence of new collective subjectivities. These have racial and ethnic features, aiming at projects that respond to issues arising from this condition. The plausibility of the religious movements focused on above did not hinge so much on previous traits, although there are obvious continuities with former religious practices. They are characterized, in any event, by what I have termed above "further optional" identities. The same obtains to some extent with the distinct identities crafted by generations today—within the hard limits posed after all by biological age. The interwoven collectivities we will analyze now, despite the various ways they may be constructed, are somewhat closer to the gender identities also discussed above. In a continuum, they are closer to "quasi ascriptive" identities, since their requirements of plausibility strongly imply former features that cannot be dispensed with.

The size of "Afro-descendants" (defined here to include blacks and mixed-race people) or "indigenous" population in Latin America varies a lot between countries (when self-definition is taken a whitening of such numbers occurs, in contrast to interviewers' perspective; in any case the assignment of such categories is of course rather complicated). Bolivia has 2.0 percent of the former and an astonishing 71.0 percent of the latter, Ecuador 10.0 and 38.0 percent, while Peru has 9.7 and 47.0, respectively. Brazil shows 44.7 and 0.4 percent of, respectively, Afro-descendants and indigenous population, Colombia having 20.5 and 1.8 percent of those. Whereas Nicaragua has 13.0 and 5.0 percent of Afro-descendants and indigenous people, Venezuela rates 10.0 and 0.9 in those counts. Mostly white, Argentina has no significant Afro-descendant population, and merely 1.0 percent of indigenous people. In turn, Chile contains 8.0, El Salvador 7.0, and Guatemala an amazing 66.0 percent of indigenous people, none showing an Afro-descendant population. The smallish countries of Uruguay and Costa Rica have both a small indigenous population—0.4 and 0.8 percent—but 5.9 and 2.0 percent of Afro-descendants. Paraguay evinces a similar pattern: 3.5 and 1.5 percent of Afro-descendants and indigenous population. Mexico and Honduras show an increase in such percentages: 0.5 and 14.0 for the former, and 5.0 and 15.0 for the latter. Cuba and the Dominican Republic have no indigenous population—early on massacred

Identities and Domination, Solidarity and Projects   103

by Spanish conquerors—but huge percentages of Afro-descendants, respectively 62.0 and 84.0. Panama maintains that percentage for Afro-descendants—73.5—and adds to it 10.0 of indigenous people. These data make patent the importance of distinct population and cultural heritages; a full breakdown of such categories brings out a high level of mixture—of *mestizage,* probably even among some indigenous groups. Other data (not necessarily consistent with those already listed) show this more clearly for Afro-descendants: Brazil has thus 4.9 of blacks and 40.1 percent of mixed people, Colombia 5.0 and 71.0, respectively, while Cuba shows 12.0 and 21.8 for those rubrics.[69] This is an actual fact of Latin American social life and not merely an ideology of the dominant white groups, which of course has not meant the absence of racism and similar discriminatory beliefs and practices.

But an analysis of data for race and ethnicity in Latin America also displays the inequalities associated with such definitions and population distribution. In fact, vis-à-vis income, differences between races and ethnic groups have greater impact than gender. In average, in Guatemala, Bolivia, Chile, Mexico, and Peru indigenous men and women earn 40 to 65 percent less than white men and women, whereas in Brazil a similar rate—48 percent—is found when Afro-descendants' income is compared to that of white people. These differences are moreover cumulative with gender, meaning that Afro-descendant and indigenous women are the worst-off group in the whole Latin American population.[70] But social mobilization by subordinate groups in what regards ethnicity and race has been recently quite powerful. This is particularly evident in the case of the "forth wave" of indian mobilization in the subcontinent, being true for Afro-descendants too.

Most indigenous populations of Latin America were, as already mentioned above, seen as peasants especially since the second half of the twentieth century. All of a sudden, this seems to have radically changed. There are many interpretations of this new wave of indian mobilization, but we must not, without detriment to the recognition of this aspect, lose from sight that many very practical and material elements remain at the core of the movements at stake: land, credit, education, plus, to be sure, autonomy, recognition (of one's particularity, beyond citizenship rights, to return to Honneth's category[71]), and so on. We have previously seen, when discussing collective subjectivities, that there are a number of general interpretations of ethnic identity in the social sciences literature. At times they have been present in the interpretation of Latin America. Nevertheless, more specific views have held the upper hand when explaining such phenomena recently in the subcontinent. They divide, with many variations, into basically two: one that stresses the adoption of neoliberal policies for the countryside in Latin America, meaning "the collapse of class identities;" and a second one, which sees it as "the involuntary outcome of the penetration of the indian world by alien actors," in close connection with the downfall of "real socialism." On the other hand, it is possible to recognize the role of former union

104 *Latin America and Contemporary Modernity*

structures (and of original ethnic structures, such as communitarian Aymara or Quéchua *ayllus,* which already underpinned rural unions) and the dwindling of the financing schemes of the developmental state as marginalizing peasants who then, bereft of class markers due to the general decline of such a perspective on the global political scene, make recourse to their older ethnic memories. To that we must add the role of churches, either Catholic or several Protestant variants, the adoption of multilinguistic education and the creation of an indian bilingual and sometimes middle-class leadership, the reforms that in the 1990s implied the decentralization of the state and the construction of autonomous administration and justice, as well as changes such as the modification of *ejido* law in Mexico and overall the failure or defeat of agrarian reform. The fact is that, slowly, banking on movements and organizations with a long history, in Guatemala, in Mexico, and especially in Ecuador and Bolivia, strong indigenous movements flourished at the turn of the last century, partly catalyzed by the passing of what they defined, against official celebrations, the "conquest of America."[72]

While it is plain to see that such identities are not fixed and should not be taken in an essentialist manner, this runs through much of the debate. Albó, one of the probably best-known authors on the subject, is capable of listing elements that were conducive to the upshot of ethnic identities, in Bolivia for instance. They were, he acknowledges, absent in Peru, which is characterized, instead, by the macrocephaly of Lima, its capital city, by the fact that people mingle there and do not entertain such strong ties with their families in the countryside, as well as by the specific political situation and form of the agrarian reform. Nonetheless, in his perplexity he cannot understand why indians in Peru have failed, *as yet,* to achieve a true ethnic consciousness.[73] Primordialism and echoes of Marxism go hand in hand here. In contrast, the real question is how and why distinct identities have developed in these countries. Although it was plausible indeed that ethnic identities strongly emerged in Peru, there is no reason to think they should, and that, if they did not, there has been some lack or pathology in this regard. In fact, even in the Ecuadorian, Bolivian, or Mexican cases, the identities of peasant and indian (or indigenous people as they rather call themselves now in many cases) are dependent on context and specific needs and strategies.[74] Anyway, the Movement toward Socialism (MAS), in Bolivia, the National Indian Confederation of Ecuador (CONAIE), or the Zapatista guerrilla and political movement in Chiapas give eloquent testimony of the fourth wave of indian mobilization in Latin America.

Black social movements have been on the rise too. This is true for Colombia, where civil rights movements and the Black Panthers organization initially, in the 1970s, had an imprint on black activities, which eventually turned to more Latin American symbols, such as "cimarrones," runaway slaves. This is true also above all in relation to Brazil. Since the struggle for the abolition of slavery, the issue has been somehow in the country's political agenda, but it has really started to acquire prominence in the 1930s,

Identities and Domination, Solidarity and Projects 105

with the Brazilian Black Front. It remained important henceforth, but has become an unavoidable issue since the 1970s, pushed by middle-class activists, popular organizations, in the midst of the struggle against the military regime, and, finally, by many nongovernmental organizations (NGOs) dedicated to fighting racism and discrimination. The issue in Brazil is compounded by the difficulty in separating blacks and mixed people, since the blend of "races" was real enough especially among the popular classes and the ideology of "racial democracy" laid deep roots, clouding the problem but offering too a *telos* for social democratization. Since that last period in particular, a tendency by black activists to look for a biracial pattern, mirroring the United States, has been firmly on the public sphere and been the object of fierce controversy, the same happening with affirmative policies to redress the inequalities derived from the past and racism at present. In fact, the movement seems to have become softer in this regard, broadening its conceptions to include Afro-descendants in a general way. But internally as well as abroad, resistance to the movements' stances has been stern, from right-wing spokespeople to others who stand on the left, such as Bourdieu and Wacquant, who accuse the Ford Foundation of imposing a foreign agenda and perspective through funding and cooptation. While this influence is not always positive, the debate is in this regard badly posed: It should not matter, in the end, who is funding what and whom, but rather the real outcomes of such policies. In any case, such political stance has helped bring the issue of racism strongly to the center of the political debate and to public policy. At the same time, the rise of black pride, the multiplication of identities related to blackness, and a general change, which is however very timid yet, seems to be impending in relation to such an issue in Brazil today. This shows that an identity that has "quasi-ascriptive" elements, albeit weaker and less convincing than ethnicity, may assume distinct political countenances and change over time.[75]

Not all the movements I have presented here are especially centered, and some aspects of such changes are rather decentered in daily life. All the same, they constitute powerful modernizing moves, of which often actual modernizing offensives are part and parcel. Latin American societies have become far more complex than ever, perhaps with the exception, in some degree and in a particular sense, of the colonial period.

The Overwhelming Presence of Classes

If in the past social classes were not well studied in Latin America, at present the situation is not at all brighter. A few contributions can help us trace the main contours of class systems of domination. An immediate drawback is that such accounts are basically cast in the form of a depiction of social stratification, and, furthermore, usually in terms of income distribution. Property underpinnings, relations to political power, and lifestyle are much less commonly treated. This means that classes as collective subjectivities

106   *Latin America and Contemporary Modernity*

that exercise a collective causality on each other and over social life as a whole are egregiously absent from such approaches. At most, in a useful albeit limited way, the influence of business associations on government and politics is accounted for.[76] Here we shall set out in our analysis with Portes and Kelly's contribution, the only encompassing view at present. One of their starting issues is the specificity of the working classes in Latin America insofar as they do not entirely belong to the regulated capitalist economy— large sectors are in the informal economy—and are thus not homogeneous as in "developed societies." Their classification of classes will depend, following this lead, on access to "assets," in a way such that ends up lending their view a rather Weberian flavor. Their data relate to 2000.

Capitalists would be the first class in their list: Owners of means of production and managers with shares of large or medium companies, they control capital and those means of production, an impersonal labor force bureaucratically organized, as well as subsidiary technico-administrative qualifications, counting on legal regulations. They are remunerated by profits and comprise 1.8 percent of the "economically active population" (EAP). Managers and bureaucrats in large and medium-size companies control almost the same as the former, except capital and the means of production. Moreover, they are remunerated with wages and dividends related to profits, amounting to 1.6 percent of the EAP. Elite workers, who comprise 1.6 percent of the EAP and are those waged workers with university formation in public and private administration, control almost the same as managers and bureaucrats, except a labor force, their income deriving from scarce knowledge. They work under legally covered relations. The petty bourgeoisie would comprise 8.5 percent of the EAP. Rather heterogeneous, it is made up of independent technicians and professionals as well as of small-business owners who personally supervise employees. It controls means of production and subsidiary techno-administrative qualifications, but not an impersonal labor force and only partially scarce and highly valued qualifications, the same being true vis-à-vis legal regulations. They are remunerated by profits. A non-manual formal proletariat comprises 12.4 percent of the EAP, possessing vocational, technical training. They possess nothing, nevertheless are legally covered, being waged workers. A second layer of workers is given by the 23.4 percent of the EAP who, specialized or not, are waged workers with contract, hence legally regulated. Finally, Porters and Kelly separate another group that would be waged workers without a contract, street sellers on their own account, with no legal regulations as to salary and irregular income from trade, amounting to an amazing 45.9 percent of the EAP (the informal-sector proletariat, that is). It is important to note that the two main trends that differentiate the 1980s from the 1990s are the increase of the petty bourgeoisie and especially of the informal proletariat (which of course derives from the economic restructurings we discussed in Chapter 2), as well as income concentration in the three upper layers. Argentina in particular tells a sad history of informalization and impoverishment.[77] On

Identities and Domination, Solidarity and Projects 107

the other hand, it is worth noting that, using distinct data and methodology, Pochmann and his co-workers got to the conclusion that the 5,000 richest families of Brazil (i.e., 0.001 percent of the total and based mostly in the state of São Paulo, above all in its capital city) concentrate 40 percent of the wealth (gross domestic product—GDP) annually produced as well as maintaining a high level of control over social life and politics.[78]

The Upper Classes

It is only for Argentina (in contrast to the more restricted character of the sources available for the reconstruction of its class stratification system) that an analysis in terms of lifestyle differentiation has been carried out. Drawing upon authors such as Basualdo and her own research, Svampa puts forward a general view of the Argentinean situation. One of the key elements of the period was the conformation of a "business community," including especially national economic groups and transnational corporations associated to the processes of privatization of state companies. A denationalization of capital is also easily detected. Socially and politically Argentina underwent a sort of process probably very peculiar if compared to its neighbors. While Peronism had always been a plebeian force and the ruling classes were disgusted by and inimical to it, the inflexion of that political and social force toward neoliberalism in the 1990s provided for an unforeseeable rapprochement between them. This meant that the nouveaux rich of privatizations, the new Peronist top politicians and officials, and the traditional ruling classes mingled as much as their symbolic markers mixed. A more supposedly iconoclast, but in fact rather cynical attitude stemmed from this: " . . . a lifestyle marked by conspicuous consumption, frivolity, excessive gestures, which embraced the whole of the Argentinean ruling class, in which not only successful businesspeople and exemplars of the political class, but also a great part of the most traditional elite embarked upon." This does not mean, however, that "distinction" marks were abandoned: Instead a "new rurality," away especially from Buenos Aires, new clubs, and private villas with strong security in the rich suburbs resulted from this effort to leave behind the increasingly numerous sectors of a decaying middle class and the rather impoverished working classes. The emptying out of the public spaces was crucial in these developments.[79]

Other studies show too that the internationalization of capital in Latin America has been very strong—which means that managers, many of them coming from abroad, have become a pillar of the subcontinent ruling classes. This is true for the service sector by and large (telecoms, energy, water, sanitation, roads—but, in many cases, also oil, etc).[80] In particular such is the case with the banking and the pension systems, strongholds of a major player in the recent model of accumulation: finance capital. They have been extensively denationalized. Bank assets in foreign hands have been estimated by Caputo (drawing upon data for 2000 from the

108 *Latin America and Contemporary Modernity*

Interamerican Development Bank—BID) as amounting to 76.5 percent in Mexico, 54.5 in Argentina, 53.8 in Peru, 43.7 in Chile, 42.3 in Venezuela, 30.6 in Brazil, and 21.4 in Colombia. Pension funds would belong in the following percentages to foreign capital: 73.6 in Argentina, 85.3 in Bolivia, 54.1 in Chile, 47.4 in Colombia, 66.6 in Mexico, 78.5 in Peru, and 29.5 in Uruguay.[81] Other authors propose similar and even more dramatic data, based for instance on information from the International Monetary Fund (IMF). From 1990 to 2001, the percentages of banking assets controlled by foreign banks in the region varied as follows: From 10 to 61 in Argentina, 6 to 49 in Brazil, 19 to 62 in Chile, 8 to 34 in Colombia, 0 to 90 in Mexico, 4 to 61 in Peru, and 1 to 59 in Venezuela.[82] Using data from ECLAC, amazing percentages may be pointed out in other areas of business too. As for the 200 main exporting companies in Latin America, a steady and fast increase in the presence of foreign capital stands out: According to Caputo, while in 1996 foreign capital controlled 76 of such companies, in 1997 it controlled already 92, reaching 97 in 1998 and, finally, 98 in 2000. As for investments in manufacturing companies, during the 1990–1992 period 48 belonged to foreign capital, with 53.2 percent of sales. In 1994–1996, this grew to 53 from 100, with sales reaching 59.3 percent of the total. Finally, in 1998–2000, they amounted to 59 out of 100, with sales increasing up to 61.7 percent.[83] Even in Brazil overall, a country with relatively greater autonomy and a reasonably differentiated economy, this has been the case:

> The extent of the denationalization of the economy via the privatization of state enterprises can be gauged from the degree of foreign ownership acquired by foreign capital in these forms. Between 1995 and 1998 FDI [Foreign Direct Investment] accounted for 42.1 percent of the accumulated value of privatizations. The figures would be even higher, if subsequent sales of shares by Brazilian partners were included . . . [. . .] Mergers and acquisitions of private firms have been equally central to the restructuring of the Brazilian economy promoted by [Fernando Henrique] Cardoso, and have operated as the other mechanism of denationalization. A recent study shows that between 1995 and 1999 there were 1,233 mergers and acquisitions in which multinational corporations acquired control or participation in Brazilian industries. . . .

This latter trend has been operative in many fields of the Brazilian economy. While it is true that a handful of big national groups have managed to survive and even become themselves transnational corporations (in a smaller scale and often associating with foreign capital) they are by far the exception rather than the rule in the displacement of national by foreign capital.[84]

A mixed outcome results from this sketch of class relations and behavior for the upper classes of Latin America. If more research is indeed necessary to substantiate more strongly such a contention, we may state, drawing

Identities and Domination, Solidarity and Projects 109

upon the studies already available, that a capitalist, concentrated, and internationalized class "structure" is in being therein; that its links with political power can and must be taken into account; and, if we take the liberty to extrapolate Svampa's findings and cross them with other fragmentary views we encounter here and there in the literature about the subcontinent (for instance, the correlation between increased inequality, high consumption for some sectors, and the spread of violence in the last decades[85]), that a very divided and even more polarized society has emerged since the lost decade of the 1980s began. In terms of social strategies and lifestyle, this is shown by studies of other cities of Latin America, with patterns of spatiality and seclusion similar to those of Buenos Aires, in, for instance, either Mexico City or Caracas.[86] In terms of the relation between politics and class, in particular in what regards the ruling classes of Latin America, we can take the studies about the crisis of corporatism to elaborate a bit more on the issue. In other words, we can work with strong suppositions, due to the data presented above, about the "practical reflexivity" of the ruling capitalist class in Latin America today, in which connections with foreign capital are strong, hence an intertwinement of people from both sides of capital, who mingle without further problems. Lifestyles evince a similar pattern and show a more concrete and colorful account of such class-practical behavior but also of a more rationalized pattern of social interaction and reproduction strategies. If we move a bit further and make recourse to studies where the rationalized and politicized behavior of the capitalist sectors was tackled, our depiction gains more precise contours.

A correlation, which is not univocal, can be traced between the greater capacity of business organizations in a given country to bring together the bourgeoisie, *qua* captains of industry, service, trade, or finance—especially at the top—and the facility with which neoliberal reforms were passed. Despite the limited character of such conclusions, they are rather useful for a reasoning aiming at placing the Latin American classes in relation to modernizing moves. One might think that neoliberal reforms would have a harder time where national business groups are organized; that is, that national associations of businesspeople would be more resistant to trade liberalization, to the opening of national markets to imported products, and to foreign competition. Of course, many branches of industry—and connected associations—are controlled by transnational corporations (for instance, automobiles and partly banks). Yet, that hypothesis could still apply. It does not, though. Why? First, the retreat of the state and the attack on the rights of labor have overall elicited sympathy from bourgeoisies across the subcontinent since the crisis of its developmental format. In addition, and fundamentally, only if we imagine that such internal business communities would have divergent interests in relation to foreign capital an opposite or even distinct correlation should be expected. In fact, strong business associations (in which foreign capital is often influential) were conducive to neoliberal reforms in the 1980s–1990s, generating consensus and perhaps the

110 *Latin America and Contemporary Modernity*

hegemony of one capitalist sector. This has happened without detriment to informal and direct linkages with top state personnel and politicians that especially big economic corporations enjoy.[87]

In addition, we may consider that the exhaustion of the developmental model, alongside rampant inflation, financial bankruptcy, and the lack of perspectives for most firms in the contest that immediately preceded the neoliberal reforms, has pushed such business associations and the bourgeois classes of Latin America as a whole—irrespective of size, relations with foreign capital, and position in the market—toward an acceptance of neoliberal reforms, even of a harsh type, similarly to what happened with most of the population.[88] The consequences were neither necessarily desired nor foreseen. Thereby a conjunction of factors had as an unintended consequence a far-reaching change in the upper-class structures and internal relations that reinforced and lent new meaning to patterns that were operative since at least the 1970s.

The basic fact, however, is that contradictions between internal capitalists and transnational corporations have not been crucial since Cardoso and Faletto pointed to the establishment of the pattern of "associated development" in the mid-1960s in some countries.[89] This remains so under a pattern of what might be called *associated underdevelopment* in most of them, due to lack of differentiation of the national economic structure (compared to central countries) and the return of primary products through agribusiness to the forefront of economic "growth," as already suggested in the final words of the previous chapter. Dependency is not a concern for most of the "national," in fact merely *internal,* bourgeoisies. Especially the fractions constituted by big capital, in industry, services, and agribusiness—a lot of it stemming from privatization processes—are at this point closely entwined, in a subordinate position, with the global capitalist classes based especially on the central countries of contemporary modernity. At most the sectors that cater for the popular classes could evince some deeper opposition, but have no strength for that, economically, socially, and politically. Besides, finance capital has been at the core of "power blocks" in Latin America, and even more so than in the United States or Europe. If contradictions here and there can be discerned in some situations and with respect to minor issues, by no means does this entail ruptures or the proposition of an alternative project—already difficult per se at present—or even of actual political will to reorient the economy and society. They rest content with a subordinate integration in the global economy as well as in the internal "power bloc."

In the end, along with the inclination toward a strategy nationally and privately rooted in economic reprimarization and the domination of finance capital, most internal business groups accept the restrictions to development and give up any further civilizatory project or process. Their modernizing moves and offensives shrink and appear as necessarily limited. This remains the same when businesspeople accept, but try sharply to narrow their

Identities and Domination, Solidarity and Projects 111

possibilities, governments in principle placed more on the left, most of which have had no strength or vision to break, in some reasonable degree, with the neoliberal way of coping with the requirements of the globalized third phase of modernity. In the limit, if politically incapable and without any actual national project besides subordinating economic policies to their immediate corporatist interests, such bourgeoisies may resort to domination merely at the local level, as in Ecuador. In other countries, such as Brazil, some feeble resistance and a search for minor shifts may be attempted. Overall, subjectively and objectively, it is a rather *passive adaptation* to neoliberal globalization that comes out of these limited strategies and projects.[90]

This is true also in what regards the rural sectors. Agrarian reforms were less than successful in the 1960s–1970s. Besides, they have been rolled back since neoliberalism became the dominant credo in economic and social police. Market-based reforms, land titling, credit reorientation, and export-orientated change to cash crops have further characterized the situation. While tenants have indeed become a minority in Latin America, with greater numbers of small peasants emerging from the reform, but always on the verge of collapsing, and a widespread proletarianization obtaining too, those who in the long run have benefited from the agrarian reform and especially from neoliberal policies were capitalist farmers, or *latifúndio* and *hacienda* owners turned capitalists. Capital, technical expertise, commercial and financial links, plus political influence are elements they control. In fact, powerful rural capitalists are a crucial element in the passive adaptation to neoliberal globalization.[91]

The Popular and the Middle Classes

We have seen already that a huge informal market has been typical of Latin America for a long time, and that this has been recently strengthened. This has also been a problem for the organization of unions in particular, but did not prevent it from happening; the other side of popular mobilization was, as pointed out above, communitarian movements. On top of that, however, firm restructuring, combined with changes in labor legislation, had disastrous effects on unions and organized labor. As the formal labor force shrunk, as job instability increased, and as unemployment became much worse, especially in countries that underwent also deep specific crisis (cf. Argentina), the organization of the popular classes changed. Communitarian movements, either of neighbors or of predominantly jobless people, bloomed in many countries. In some of them, almost insurrectional politics were played out. In a number of them, deeper political changes occurred; in others, this was at best partial. Elsewhere the political system resisted fiercely. We will examine such issues now. But we will also point to agrarian mobilization, another aspect of ethnic modernizing moves. This should be borne in mind, the same being true as for racial issues, as an element of popular classes' structure and movements, which have already been treated

112   *Latin America and Contemporary Modernity*

above. Religious movements, with their manifold character, must not be forgotten either.

Argentina and Bolivia have been the countries that, in the last ten years, have had the strongest waves of mobilization in the subcontinent. The former had its working class—once one of the main protagonists of an intensive, quasi-Fordist regime of accumulation—face a complete bouleversement of its insertion in the economy, of lifestyles, expectations, the weakening of unions, and the spread of unemployment. In the wake of the 2001 crisis and the financial debacle that befell the country, an enormous amount of movements emerged. Middle-class mobilization, the communitarian and somewhat more autonomous communitarian organization of the unemployed, and a change in the repertoire of protest have marked this period. The jobless *piqueteros*—cutting off roads and stopping traffic—have become the main expression of this. Peronism, however, managed to keep control of the political system and influence the main movements. Not by chance, the fragmentation of such movements has brought the phrase "social protest" to center stage, showing how goals and long-term strategies do not enjoy pride of place in them. Bolivia saw also communitarian movements ally with peasants *cum* ethnic identity and the remaining of the old powerful working class of the mines (destroyed by restructuring) consecutively oust governments until acceding to power. Mexico has seen far-reaching popular organization, but the establishment has managed to prevent real opposition from taking over the national government. In fact, while in other countries the corporatist structure has no longer been effective (in either rural Bolivia or urban Brazil and Argentina), in Mexico it still maintains a strong grip, though without being capable of representing workers, on unions. Some, however, tend to trace back the problem merely to neoliberal policies and bet on the continuous force of unionism, in Latin America as elsewhere, as in Brazil, in which social movements by and large declined in the 1990s.[92]

In the countryside, renewed landless worker or peasant movements have emerged. In Brazil, the Landless Workers Movement (MST) has been capable of mobilizing huge crowds. Whether it will have success or at least keep its momentum in a country that is predominantly urban, where agribusiness is very powerful and since its militancy is made up to a great extent of proletarians, is still to be seen. In many other areas, entangled or not with ethnic issues, agrarian struggles have not stopped to haunt Latin America, sometimes bringing together all the losers of neoliberal globalization, as in the case of Mexico and its large movement called El Barzón, in which peasants, medium-size farmers, and even large farmers have gathered trying to survive the politics of integration with the United States. In Bolivia in particular, especially among the *cocaleros* (coca planters of the Cochabamba region), the democratization of indigenous peoples' organizations—seen merely as "political instruments"—has been paramount and promises to reinvent the relation between leadership and popular following, a key theme.[93] Changes affect also the middle classes. Many social movements have had their bases

Identities and Domination, Solidarity and Projects   113

on these intermediate strata, either in environmental terms, in the process of democratization, in feminism, and in many other less "conventional" areas of social mobilization.[94] Nowhere, however, has the impact of the changes due to neoliberal policies and the country's debacle been more severe than in Argentina, where a polarization between upward and downward (the most traditional and linked to state welfare) sectors of the middle classes has been dramatic, leading them to a strong participation, at least up to a point, in protest, popular neighborhood assemblies, and social upheaval. But the "risk of impoverishment" has been generalized since the new model of accumulation set on in the 1990s.[95]

Two sets of questions have to be addressed now: first, whether these should be considered as "new social movements," and second, whether these movements have been or will be able to construct a new agenda and fight for "hegemony" in their specific countries, let alone build a subcontinental coalition.

It seems doubtless that more "traditional" movements, especially unions, still play a great role in contemporary politics. "Traditional" communitarian movements remain strongly on the scene too. Identity politics, democratization, lifestyle issues, gender change, and environmental concerns have all been, however, at the forefront of Latin American politics in the last decades. In a sense, as Santos notes, we cannot identify a break between interest politics and identity politics here.[96] To be sure, a sharp separation is already as such problematic—for what are "identities" and especially "interests" conceptually if not aspects of the same thing? But even if we take interests as referring to material desires and identities to symbolic constructions, it can hardly be said that in Latin America there has happened a severance between them, on the contrary. Even environmentalism in Latin America—the origin of many proponents of "sustainable development"—assumed the aspect of "socio-environmentalism." Nevertheless, the networked character of the emerging movements seems to be more easily detectable. Which are the features exhibited by such networks? Chalmers, Martin, and Piester suggest the following:

- First, the form of any single associative network is likely to be characterized by a diversity of organizations, individuals, and other participants.

- Second, any particular network is likely to be reconfigured over time as issues, decision-making rules, participants, and opportunities change.

- Third, the associative network entails strong emphasis on what we have called cognitive politics, involving debate and discussion of preferences, understandings, and claims, in addition to—and potentially transforming—more conventional bargaining over demands and interests.

114 *Latin America and Contemporary Modernity*

- Finally, while associative networks can and often involve actors with sharply unequal resources, there are typically more chances to escape or shift the ground to avoid a direct test of strength with an unequal competitor.[97]

Two issues are in order here. They hark back to our former discussions. First, *networks* tend to become more present when complexity is increasing. This is precisely what is happening across Latin American social life, and the popular sectors could not help being affected by this, implying greater pluralism, new identities, divergences of interest, distinct hierarchizations of goals, as well as different histories, memories, and projects. But we must recall a second issue, addressed more than once in Chapters 1 and 2: The concept of network should be seen as an *analytical* device, not substantially. This means that such movements, although counting a lot on network coordination, that is, on *voluntary collaboration,* have traits linked to hierarchy—another key mechanism of coordination, based on *command.*[98] The novelty is that the former rises to prominence, or at least gains more room. Thus internally the network mechanism has been crucial for the articulation of the new Latin American social movements, albeit not alone. Such movement has allowed them at times, as in the case of the Zapatistas, to develop and move further, building truly global networks.[99] This is also very important in the alliances between them, since no movement can any longer impose itself as the almighty one for ideological or practical reasons, and to their links with the political system and the state. That is precisely what we shall see in the two following sections, where the issue of a popular project of hegemony will also be addressed. In any case, while progress has been difficult and the mobilization of popular classes is never without high costs, new utopian horizons and new historical possibilities have been suggested by the very fact that it has been not inertia and apathy that has necessarily accompanied the emergence of the third phase of modernity and the implementation of neoliberal policies.

Political Parties and the Media

Political parties were born as instruments at the service of groups of "notables." In the course of the nineteenth century in Europe but mainly in the twentieth all over the world, they became instruments for the participation of the masses and their incorporation into the polity. A negative development of that was the emergence of what Michels called the "iron law of oligarchy": A few members, either bureaucrats or people in alliance with them, ended up controlling parties, whereby their democratic character was gone or twisted. For some, the twentieth century was indeed "Michels' century" in Latin America. And, in fact, it is not difficult to identify many elements of stiffness and lack of participation in Latin American contemporary political parties, similarly to what happens in other quarters of the world.

Identities and Domination, Solidarity and Projects 115

As already mentioned, originally Latin American parties can be divided into two groups: those that had corporatism as an important element in their constitution—in Mexico, Argentina, and Brazil—and those that organized oligarchic power through popular clienteles—Venezuela and Colombia—while Chile was an exception, building a partisan party system. Bolivia approached a clear-cut party system somehow, in which the National Revolutionary Movement (MNR) was central, although the Bolivian Workers Confederation (COB) remained external to it; Peru never achieved a proper party system. Today analysts recognize a profound crisis of representation of parties in Latin America, irrespective of how recent many of them are and of the renewal many of them underwent since the democratic transitions of the 1980s, and of the almost *de facto* monopoly enjoyed by the Justicialista Party (PJ), the present name of Peronism. Other parties emerged afterward, sometimes with rather distinct projects and trying to operate as movement parties. Remarkable was the breakdown of traditional "partidocracies" in Venezuela and Colombia, but also Ecuador. In Mexico, the Institutional Revolutionary Party (PRI) has managed, in alliance with the National Action Party (PAN), to block (through repeated fraud) a deeper power change toward the Party of the Democratic Revolution (PRD); in Brazil, new parties emerged—the Workers' Party (PT) intended to consist in a new type of organization, without actually being able to break clean with the past. Many parties, which include the Party of the Brazilian Democratic Movement (PMDB), the Party of Brazilian Social Democracy (PSDB), and the Party of the Liberal Front (PFL), compose the system. Chile seems to offer a particularly stable and traditional party system, with especially Christian Democracy and the Socialist Party (PS) reviving, with the addition of the Democracy Party (PD). In other places, new organizations emerged (see below). Peru and Ecuador retain unstable party systems.[100]

A further problem here seems to consist of some salient features of Latin American party systems, with opinions divided vis-à-vis the issue. For Mainwaring, Latin America suffers from institutional instability due to the "explosive" combination of presidential regime, an often fragmented multiparty system and proportional representation. Others see more virtues in the system, although a trade-off between stability and accountability is identified.[101] Basically, however, systems work and there have been no breakdowns in political democracy in Latin America, despite the fact that right-wing sectors often maintain an inclination to look for coups d'état, which were defeated on occasion or had no room even to be tried. More complicated has been the capacity of political parties to bring the masses into the political system since the end of corporatism (protracted in Mexico, let me underline). The left has achieved this at times, originally with the PT in Brazil—which paid the price of having grown oligarchies inside itself—or in Uruguay, with the Broad Front (FA), for instance. It has achieved even more in Bolivia with the MAS, while in Mexico things are more mixed within the PRD and in Venezuela organization subordinated to what might be deemed

116 *Latin America and Contemporary Modernity*

"progressive cesarist" emerged with Hugo Chávez and his Bolivarian party. In most cases of success, a subtle combination of network construction to form movements and parties seems to have been present, while, on the other hand, the vitality of such sociopolitical coalitions is probably greater when movements maintain a reasonable degree of autonomy.[102] This happens possibly also because changes in the state apparatus, leading toward the dispersion of decision making and local-level politics, increase complexity and require more flexible political organizations. In the less democratized cases, clientelism is not entirely eschewed, as shown by the Argentinean and the Mexican situations (but the multiplication of state philanthropy by the left is not far from this).[103] A limited capacity for society-state mediation and citizen representation, a tendency to self-centeredness and bureaucratization, as well as recourse to "traditional" clientelistic practices and little commitment to their own programs: These are aspects that are at the core of much of party politics in Latin America. But others are more optimistic at least with respect to their own experience and believe that political processes such as the one unfolding in Bolivia will be able to create a new "national-popular" collective will and initiate a breakthrough in the stalled Latin American political process under the leadership of Evo Morales.[104]

The mass media—television, radio, large newspapers, the editorial industry—must be taken as another pillar of power and mediation between society and politics, across the globe and in particular in Latin America, where it commands huge resources. Especially television networks have been privatized, concentrated, and at times denationalized. The Globo network, in Brazil, and Televisa, in Mexico, appear as the most powerful Latin American corporations in this area, along with Cisneros in Venezuela and Telefe in Argentina; the latter appears, as usual in this country's case, as a paradigm of denationalized television system. Editorial business was greatly denationalized in Spanish-speaking countries, albeit not in Brazil, whereas radio remains to a great extent a national preserve. The results of that are not clear yet. In contrast, we can confidently state that the worsening and denationalization of content are ongoing processes in television. More problematic, of course, is that communication corporations, which are basically not submitted to any kind of state regulation, maintain close links with and a huge influence over politicians. The power of television networks is even greater in Latin America than in other regions of the world; they are at the kernel of present power blocks and of neoliberal modernizing moves.[105]

The State and the Nation

We have already seen how decisively the substance of nations has changed in the subcontinent. I will deal now with two features of the state-society relation in contemporary Latin America: its weak infrastructural power and the reforms that have been tried out in order to modernize its machinery;

Identities and Domination, Solidarity and Projects   117

and its reduced capacity to mediate and organize society and a general national project.

I have insisted on the very first of them at several points in this book. Here I will basically reinstate the issue. Unfortunately, things have not actually changed. To be sure, social density, the need to monitor social policies in many cases, under the influence of international organisms, and the integration of the national territory have all conspired to deepen the infrastructural power of the state. On the other hand, populations no longer rest content with its despotic power. Transitions to democracy and the struggle for rights, as seen in Chapter 1, are a firm indication of that. Yet, states in Latin America remain relatively weak. Arms and drug trafficking, the permanence of vast territorial spaces that remain almost "no man's land," and even the perennial or new character of some guerrilla forces in a few countries, express this sharply. Colombia is the paramount example of that, with large swaths of the country controlled by drug dealers, left-wing guerrillas, and right-wing paramilitary forces; but in its own radical way, it merely takes to extremes what is more or less widespread in the subcontinent.[106]

The connection with society has been tackled more recently within the imported North American frame of "social policy" studies. Social knowledge and technical expertise are at the core of such an approach.[107] The bureaucratic aspects of the state have been once again the object of a few attempts at reform. Overall, cutting back has been the key concern, within the neoliberal frame of mind. In Argentina, this held pride of place in the first phase of the 1990s reforms, although strengthening tax collection and restructuring the central bank were also important strategies. Later on adjustments were made that slightly reversed the dismissal of public officials, yet maintained the decentralization of services to the provinces and underfunding from the center. In Chile, the same was true under the military dictatorship. Democracy inherited a weakened state but strengthened decision-making nuclei and agencies for social policy; it deepened and democratized municipalization, with more resources available. The rationalization of the state, with unsteady steps, was taken via managerialism, according to which citizens should be treated basically as consumers (a step ventilated but basically absent in the Argentinean case). Curiously enough, much of this reform was pushed by endogenous bureaucratic elements, usually said to be recalcitrant. In Mexico, in contradistinction, reforms fell short of even being initiated, in a state that has no civil service career, *pace* the impossibility of firing low-level employees (who are strongly unionized), while high-level officials are all political appointees, hence inherently unstable. In Brazil reforms went further, with Bresser Pereira's managerial schemes (thought out however within what he considers to be a rather republican and not consumer-oriented perspective) being to a good extent implemented. Flexibility, responsibility, and outcomes, rather than bureaucratic methods, were envisioned.[108]

118 *Latin America and Contemporary Modernity*

Thus, state personnel in Latin America, with in some measure the exception of Brazil, has not been really transformed in terms of methods and practices more recently. In themselves these would be modernizing moves that intended to prepare state machinery and refashion its links with society in a way such that it could relaunch its own modernizing offensives. The processes of creation of regulatory agencies were usually not, as seen in Chapter 2, very successful either. Great transformations and a change in the role of the state derived really from privatization and the subordination of the state to the new patterns of financial accumulation and the passive adaptation to neoliberal globalization that we have also been discussing in this book. The fact is that the exhaustion and dismantling of the developmental state was not followed by a true reconstruction. Instead, a relatively feebler state has substituted for it. Whereas in other regions (North America and Europe, predominantly but not exclusively) the passage from the second to the third phase of modernity has implied an actual reconstruction of the state toward what may be called a "Schumpeterian Workfare Competition State" (which may or may not include generous social welfare),[109] in Latin America it is a sluggish, inefficient, and underfunded state that has been charged at times with duties it cannot fulfill, if even the perspective of advancement of Latin American societies is placed on the agenda beyond easy rhetoric.

If this is so, and conditions remained unaltered, can the state resume its former place—with its relative quasi-Weberian autonomy—in the processes of development and vertebration of Latin American societies? Can it propel the economy beyond such a passive adaptation at the same time that it generates and organizes social solidarity? This is a problem that afflicts the main theoretician of the so-called "network society." Castells departs from an analysis of contemporary Chile, stating that its main challenges are to reform its state and achieve greater productivity. He does not question the agrarian character of the country nor, to the reader's surprise, brings in the necessity of building networks within the Chilean economy. Sorting out the problem of the incorporation of the indigenous Mapuche was important, but the same is actually not true as to change in economic policy. Castells recognizes that during the 1990s the state became an agent of globalization, whereby it " . . . moved away from its traditional social basis," a derivation that led to "a crisis of the national identity as a principle of social cohesion." But he thinks that, based on the more inclusive model developed by the democratic, post-dictatorship Chilean governments, a new "identity-project" can be launched so as to achieve social development and technological advancement. Implicitly, he suggests that this might be extrapolated to the whole of the subcontinent.[110]

Should we take into account what has been said about the state above, his proposal would sound nonetheless as fanciful or at least very unlikely to come about. Neither such projects seem to be on the agenda, nor has the state a machinery to pursue them; even worse, there seems to be no, or at least only a few, collectivities that might bet on such changes and perspectives.

Identities and Domination, Solidarity and Projects 119

For, in order to accomplish such a radical transformation of present-day Latin American societies in the direction of development and to rebuild social solidarity, a new *historical block* would have to be formed. Is that possible? Could such a move come about that would work as the basis for even more far-reaching modernizing moves? The situation indeed begs the question.

PARTIAL CONCLUSIONS: MODERNIZING MOVES, TRANSFORMISM, AND MOLECULAR CHANGE

In the former two chapters, we have constructed a horizontal analysis of contemporary Latin America, dealing with specific imaginary and institutional aspects of modernity, in their multidimensionality. The dynamic element of social change was surely present there, but in a more limited sense. In this chapter, we have carried out a perpendicular analysis, cutting across those imaginary and institutional elements by bringing collective subjectivities to the fore. While modernizing moves referred to these elements in the foregoing chapters, in the present one it was the very producers and carriers of such modernizing moves that stood out. Class, race, ethnicity, gender exploitation, as well as parties and states were key issues in the chapter, along with others in which collectivities such as the family and generations were both patient and agent in such modernizing moves, as they all are.

We have in any case dealt in some detail with the collective subjectivities that underlie the struggle for law, rights, and justice, with those who are the bearers of the three possible societal projects we singled out as authoritarian, neoliberal, and progressive vis-à-vis the construction of democracy today. We have also discussed those that support the neoliberal commodification of most dimensions of social life, economic globalization, and firms restructuring, as well as others that challenge, albeit with less power, their implementation. The popular classes have been in the forefront of that democratic project as carriers of citizenship in its dialectical instituting moment. As we have seen, their networks and movements have pushed the process of democratization and establishment of rights to a higher level, while bourgeois groups and foreign capital, dominant state officials and politicians, have been at the basis of more limited democratic moves, insisting precisely on policies that, although usually maintaining the liberal democratic system and citizenship as a real abstraction confined to the civil and political systems, are assisted by clientelism, media power, and new state-based philanthropic moves and targeted social policies.

Two issues must be explored here in this connection. First, we need to explore the relation between the economic and political projects, and how collective subjectivities are positioned in relation to them, especially in what regards hegemony and the so-called historical bloc. Secondly, we must ask about the possibility and shape of a reconstructed solidarity adjusted to the third phase of modernity.

120 *Latin America and Contemporary Modernity*

Let us start with a very severe assessment of the bourgeois—industrial and agrarian—perspectives and practices at present in Latin America. Basualdo and Arceo suggest that the immediate subordination of the state to their interests and the mere prevention of the emergence of alternative popular projects is all that Latin American bourgeoisies strive for today.[111] In order to judge the correction of their view, it is necessary to go into greater detail about Gramsci's own perspective. According to him "transformism" implied, during the Italian *Risorgimento* in particular, very limited changes, with the leadership of the subaltern collectivities being coopted by conservatism throughout the process, without the beheaded classes they expressed benefiting from this. Overall the progress of Italy was coy, insofar as the ruling classes had as a goal mainly the avoidance of a democratization of social life that would lend centrality to the issue of hegemony (consensus and really the construction of a new historical block), in detriment to the moment of sheer domination. In order to deal with this new situation, the ruling classes, in which there was no strong bourgeoisie, had to weave a "balance of compromise." For this to be possible, those on the top had to take into account the interests and tendencies of those from below, something that they refused in the case in point. "Passive revolution" ("revolution-restoration") and a mere "molecular change" derived from this.[112] In what follows, however, transformism and passive revolution will be clearly, analytically distinguished from molecular change, which will be seen as rather active and at times transformative in a radical way, though not in the highly centralized manner that underlies Gramsci's negative definition of the theme (that is, the absence of a leading "party" and actual revolution).

We see therefore that Basualdo and Arceo's argument has to be very much refined and changed. On the one hand, it is clear that a far-reaching transformation swept through Latin America. It is true that it implied in great measure a reinstatement of the subcontinent position in the global order once again as an underdeveloped region, as seen in Chapter 2. However, economically it was by no means a "molecular" process that took shape. At its start, in addition, it seemed capable of building a new genuine historical block based on liberal democracy and liberalized markets, hence opening a period of hegemony for the new power block commanded by transnational corporations, agribusiness, and, last but by no means least, finance capital, on the one hand, alongside, on the other, top state officials and politicians, the IMF and the World Bank. This was exhausted a few years ago, since it became obvious that, beyond relatively short moments of well-being (the dollar-peso parity in Argentina, the Real Plan in Brazil), and despite even the painful "side-effects" of "adjustment programs" for the popular classes, and even large swaths of the middle classes, the passive adaptation to neoliberal globalization meant, in the long run, a future without much hope. We can say, therefore, that *the moment of domination, in which the state and coercion have such a central part to perform, has become predominant for the power block* in the recent developments of

Identities and Domination, Solidarity and Projects 121

Latin American societies. Furthermore, no alternative has as yet emerged. However, culturally and politically, in terms of modernizing offensives toward greater democracy, especially after the main steps of transitions from dictatorships were completed, it has been indeed a "molecular," rather decentered but very active process that has unfolded, with popular struggles, professional commitments (in the judicial system, at times in NGOs), and specific realizations coming about in different junctures and through distinct collectivities and moves. It has been in the long *duration*, rather than on impacts on the short-term of history, that its influence must be identified.[113]

Could Brazil under the Workers' Party government be considered a typical case of transformism? This seems not to be the case, really. Moving within very strict bounds in terms of economic policies, media regulation, democratization, social policy, and so on, Luís Inácio Lula da Silva and his co-workers have not been by any means assimilated by the upper echelons of the Brazilian society. Even there the moment of coercion seems to carry more weight than the construction of consensus—they have been blackmailed to maintain basically the pillars of neoliberalism.[114] Will we say the same in relation, for instance, to Uruguay's FA in the future? It is quite likely. In this regard the Bolivian process may go further, but hardly holds a greater promise for the most complex countries of the region, while Venezuela' cesarist process cannot be taken as a beacon for democratic and real social change.

Could the state demiurgically do such a job? That does not seem to be the case either, regardless of the reasonable degree of autonomy we can attribute to it, which I think is greater than Marxist analyses permit. But in Latin America lately, an already weak state was rolled back to even smaller capabilities and there is no project that can at present make it move in a new direction. In order to do so, it would have to face up, at the same time, to the question of social solidarity in order to gain legitimacy for a new national project. I have argued elsewhere that in the first phase of modernity rights and an overseeing state responded for social solidarity, with responsibility being trusted basically to individuals. The second phase of modernity, having the state far more at its center, brought such responsibility onto it and gave pride of place to social citizenship in the crafting of social solidarity. In both cases, a homogenization of society was a starting point; it was also deemed possible and necessary. In this third phase of modernity, with greater social pluralism and the freedom of individuals and collectivities augmented by deepened disembedding processes, resulting in a much more complex society, in which moreover participation has become a vital necessity, only a *complex form of solidarity* could yield social integration (that is, a real sense of belonging and practical connections) to an extent comparable to what happened during those former phases.[115] The elements of liberal democracy would be preserved, but so would the lessons of corporatism and the need to grapple with collectivities, allowing for their concerted participation, in a

122 *Latin America and Contemporary Modernity*

post-corporatist and rather plural setting. This has been rehearsed in some constitutional provisions and in other popular inventions (councils, new judiciary designs, direct democracy, networks, etc.) we have analyzed in Chapter 1 and above in this chapter, but is far from accomplished or even truly outlined. In fact it would imply demands from the popular classes and the need to respond to them in terms of a "balance of compromise," with development and citizenship. This is unlikely, or at least very difficult in this precise moment. It would depend on an enormous change in the present correlation of forces and political tendencies would have to bear this really in mind, which is far from being the case. At this stage, it is mostly within a few state "crystallizations" that disputes seem to obtain any success (central banks and finance ministries are, however, usually out of question). Besides, it may be that an absolute contradiction exists between the sort of "model of development" in being now and the demands for rights and a radicalized form of democracy such complex solidarity would require. I will return to this in the book's general conclusion.

If the lack of alternative programs remains a problem, so do collective subjectivities. Apparently we have not advanced in relation to the time when Touraine spoke of the search for "actors" that could transform Latin America.[116] After the analysis carried out in this chapter, I think we can say without further doubt that modernizing moves in a more decentered sense and modernizing offensives too have been carried out intensely in Latin America. Advances notwithstanding, they do not seem really to be capable of establishing a progressive historical block that might do justice to the historical problems the population of this multifaceted region has endured and open wide the horizons of its contemporary modernity.

Conclusion

The bulk of the argument of this book is contained in its chapters. It would be pointless going over all topics and themes in detail in this conclusion. Instead, I shall briefly recapitulate the main issues treated in each chapter and then move on to a discussion that will place those elements within a more general theory of modernity as a civilization, especially at present. This section will introduce new issues or treat in a more systematic manner themes that were present in the foregoing pages. Finally, I will have a few words to say about the subcontinent's present condition and future possibilities.

A RECAPITULATION OF BASIC ISSUES

1. We analyzed in Chapter 1 the multifaceted struggle for rights and justice in the subcontinent especially since the 1980s, the workings of instituting citizenship. Manifold, decentered, as well as centered modernizing moves were seen at the core of such creative endeavor, in which the popular classes, indigenous people, blacks, and women have striven to advance modern civilization in a democratic direction, realizing therefore some of the key elements of its imaginary. There is a systematic advance of law and citizenship in its instituted moment, which finds expression especially in real abstractions, which thus embody a universalist perspective. I have, in the partial conclusions to Chapter 3, suggested that to some extent this whole movement may be deemed a molecular democratic revolution (with here and there more potent and centered moves being launched, sometimes with true offensives being carried out by social movements, political parties, or "instruments"). But we have also seen that there are other modernizing moves that are carried out by neoliberal forces, with the more modern authoritarian alternative in a defensive position at present. In addition, we have noted that citizenship has had to come to grips with plurality, whereby real abstractions have had to open up, without by any means dissolving themselves, to particularities and concreteness. Basically, although it is part of a larger movement of democratization of modernity in the twentieth

124 Latin America and Contemporary Modernity

century and especially since the 1980s, its propelling forces are basically internal. Social rights have not advanced that much, despite the increase of social expenditure.

2. In Chapter 2, the processes of economic restructuring, the changes of capitalism in a globalized and high-tech direction, were focused on, worldwide but in particular in Latin America. The other crucial aspect of recent global and regional developments we dwelt on was the role played now by finance capital. Overall, modernizing moves and offensives, by large firms, international financial organizations, and national governments were based on the neoliberal standpoint. Workers and even small and medium-size firms were smashed in this process of radical transformation. In this regard, while we cannot really speak of a truly hegemonic project, especially because neoliberalism soon proved to be a failed alternative, we cannot see the process as a "passive" revolution. In fact, the moment of coercion has come to prevail—alternatives have been violently ruled out by international organizations and the "risk assessment" agencies of global capitalism. A passive adaptation to globalized capitalism, entailing even reprimarization, and the reinforcement of underdevelopment have been at the core of the mode of development (accumulation plus regulation) in all countries as the overall result of modernizing moves and offensives in Latin America. Whether in the future a cooptation of popular leadership will take place is uncertain, but unlikely, insofar as this would require that the upper classes let go of some of their profits in favor of the subaltern classes.

3. A pluralization of social life has been shot through Latin American societies as a result of evolutionary tendencies that multiply all sorts of activities in all dimensions. Deep processes of disembedding, connected to capitalism, citizenship, and globalization, and the subsequent processes of re-embedding they impose, have entailed new and multifarious identities, which may then assume that plural countenance. A complexification of social life results from this combination and is patent in Latin America today, with freer individual subjects and collective subjectivities having emerged to social and political life, even if they eek out in a situation of social "risk" and destitution. This is the underlying basis of democratizing moves in Latin America and the molecular democratic revolution unfolding now. Class, ethnic, racial, and gender divisions remain, however, profound and influence decisively economic, cultural, and political life. Social movements connected to such divisions, as well as others that have a more contingent constitution (religious movements in particular), launch at times powerful modernizing offensives. Mostly their reproduction as well as change—which, if it happens, does so only in a minor degree—is carried out through more decentered modernizing moves. They are also patient and agent of modernization. I have argued too that, in view of the radical pluralization of social life and the ensuing changes in the very idea of the nation, a change in social integration toward a form of complex solidarity is necessary.

Conclusion   125

4. I have identified a contradiction between the democratic evolution of the subcontinent and the neoliberal project that has been absolutely dominant in the economic dimension. I suggested that they are at odds with each other, although I have not elaborated on the issue. I have also argued that a reconstruction of the state that would then have at its core a new historical block, which might resume development in tandem with democratization, is also unlikely. A solution for that contradictory clash of modernizing tendencies through the state as such is thus a mirage, irrespective of the relative autonomy it does enjoy as a collective subjectivity. It is time, therefore, to expand on this theme, drawing upon the points summarized above and introducing a few conceptual precisions. This will be done within the framework of a civilizational theory of modernity.

MODERNIZATION, CIVILIZATION, AND DEVELOPMENT

America—including its southern regions—has a clear beginning, different from most areas in history: 1492, the year of its "discovery"—or "conquest," from another angle, and of course "invention," as any social phenomena—by the Spanish crown, to be formally completed by the Portuguese in 1500. At that point, modernity was slowly opening its wings in Europe and the expansion toward the "New World" played a key role in the take-off of the process, which cannot be understood merely in the narrow terms of "nationalist" methodology, which confines it to the limited space-time configuration of the nation-states that were being forged in Europe in the sixteenth and seventeenth centuries. That is, the "episodic" (contingent and not necessary in evolutionary terms) emergence of modernity has to be placed within larger global processes, in which Portugal and Spain were eventually sidelined. This is not by any means tantamount to affirming that the origins of modernity lay fundamentally in the colonial systems of the Americas, that Western "rationality" was born therein, in the construction of administrative machines to oversee the Iberian colonial areas as well as in the "ego conquiro" that could be seen as predating the "ego cogito," even when such statements may be tempered by an acknowledgement of pristine processes internal to Europe.[1] If a specific variant of so to speak "proto"-modernity, of Iberian origins, did develop in the Americas, it stemmed from Europe, in its encounter with the other, varied civilizations previously existing in the "New World" and in Africa. The dynamic center of the global system lay in the West—and it remains so to this day to a great extent, with the United States substituting the European countries as the world hegemon, although a number of modernizing moves and dynamic processes, especially if emancipatory, often emerge in the periphery, as I shall argue below in relation to Latin America. Until then a peripheral region in the Islamic-dominated Mediterranean, Europe was undergoing manifold internal transformations (economic, political, and cultural) that also pivotally increased its

126 *Latin America and Contemporary Modernity*

power in relation to the world at large (and allowed for the successful "discovery" and colonization of America). This entailed "forms of consciousness," institutions, an imaginary, which had as protagonists individuals and collectivities that eventually became responsible for the first actual modernizing moves in history. Those changes and such agents were certainly influenced by and drew upon processes taking place on the eastern shores of the Atlantic—and from other areas that were dragged into the emerging global system; but while the former were elaborated and unfolded at the center of the rising global modern civilization, it was precisely in the space-time of Europe that the latter enacted their main moves. To be sure, the exclusive focus on the "old continent" vis-à-vis the inception of modernity must be criticized and reversed; there is no reason, however, to overlook the colossal pile of literature on the topic, which has been continuously renewed. Only later on were the emerging countries of Latin America the object of truly modernizing moves, weaving an imaginary, erecting institutions, establishing practices, and fashioning "forms of consciousness" that were typically as well as regionally modern, connected, and at once distinct from those in the West, even though societal continuities and the unfolding of that pristine encounter of civilizations could and can still be observed across the subcontinent.[2] Modernization theory and its "Westcentrism" offer indeed bad evolutionist advice. To embrace a *quasi* inverted position is not helpful, though. It is on the *episodic modernizing moves* carried out in the subcontinent, in connection with global modernity, that we must concentrate, theoretically and methodologically. That is what we did in the former chapters, for the first two and especially the third phase of modernity. At the same time, we must go beyond the reification of modernity from an a-critical position, as common in sociological theory as it has been in Latin America overall and its yearning to modernize.[3] We must see it in a more contingent way, as a relatively open-ended process, in which however some themes are played out, institutions persist in some basic ways, and the imaginary retains a number of characteristics that define whether a social formation falls within the bounds of modernity—concretely or at least as an aspiration and as its subjective teleological horizon. It was so in the past, since the nineteenth century when, as I have argued in all the foregoing chapters, modernity slowly set in in Latin America; it is so now, when the staggering challenges of the third phase of modernity are there to be faced.

We may thereby outflank what may be called, drawing upon Marx,[4] the "fetishism of modernity." That is, its transformation in a thing-like entity, supposedly homogenous and universally ready-made, which would be in being in the West (Europe and North America) and imperfectly realized in Latin America. That is of course, as argued in the Introduction and the chapters of this book too, the approach of modernization theory, but often Marxism reproduced the same perspective. Instead, with episodic and variably centered modernizing moves, having at their bases collective subjectivities, modernity becomes historical, more complex, and multiple; its

Conclusion 127

relations with other traditions and heritages become far more unpredictable and entangled; and agency is reintroduced into the fray, without detriment to the existence of some key institutional and imaginary elements that have a powerful steering force.

Moreover, other elements, which stem from other civilizational constellations, have been brought into the sphere of modernity. This happened thanks to civilizational encounters as well as due to modernity's capacity of putting everything at its service, even if often in a destructive way—against which only recourse to modern means or the modernization of former traditions are efficient answers—and also to the underlying social processes it unleashes. Last but not least, this happens as a consequence of its power of attraction, since its promises and at least some of its emancipatory realizations (centred around equal freedom, also at the collective level) have furnished a seductive horizon to populations that might in principle try to resist its appeal (what on occasion they have in fact done).[5] While other cosmologies, what some call "border thinking" (and I would frame as being within as well as without or belonging unwillingly and in an ambivalent way, with moreover other emotional and intellectual resources, other traditions and memories), different ways of understanding social life and nature, do arise from such other civilizational influences, they are already in dialogue as well as to a great extent articulated by the imaginary of modernity and its institutions.[6] And, if they can effectively suggest new—local or more general—horizons to modernity—or even beyond its presuppositions—it is within it today that they must be practically played out. No dualisms must be accepted here. In turn, the issues of "recognition" and "interculturality" (implying a true two-way dialogue) are surely central to this discussion. However, we must also be weary of the possibility that, based on social fragmentation and separations between popular subjectivities, other forms of domination may be thereby introduced (postmodern, some would say; typical of the heterogeneous third phase of modernity, I would rather argue).[7]

To put in a slightly different manner what I have already stated in former passages, we may say that, in a sense, while the expansion of modernity has meant that it engulfed and subdued even large social formations of a different civilizational origin, it has also implied that the modern imaginary and its utopian elements were then built into the horizon of these newly encompassed areas. In Latin America, these were usually rooted in pre-Colombian times and traditions, featuring indian populations. That is to say that what has been conceptualized by some authors as a form of "internal colonialism" (in an unspecific and dualistic way, and as an analogy) after the nineteenth-century independences,[8] entailed that modernization brought about the dynamic of further modernization. This had then to be carried out in an integrative and democratic direction, toward full inclusion and recognition, although tensions are inevitable and ruling collectivities often resist this move. Things happened this way in the first two phases of modernity; they are bound to happen likewise in the course of this third phase.

128 *Latin America and Contemporary Modernity*

The difference is that very little, if anything, is at this stage still left out of modernity, without detriment to the irreducibility of social formations and collectivities, in their particularity. The problems generated by those resistances are notorious, but we witness great changes today in this regard, pushed through of course by the molecular democratic revolution. Besides, in fact the present phase of modernity has much less trouble to incorporate difference, that which is heterogeneous, notwithstanding remaining problems such as racism and exploitation.

Civilizational theory has enjoyed a revival in the last years, especially with the works of Eisenstadt and Arnason. They have suggested interesting ways to face long-term historical processes. Some of their main shortcomings are, however, associated with a definition of civilization that reproduces the "nationalist methodology" of traditional sociology. This is true in particular with world religions that become, in the writings of Eisenstadt, something similar to national or in any case closed cultures. This in turn becomes a problem insofar as this operation compels him to multiply modernities, which might in fact get down to regions, cities, and so on, should we take the argument to its radical implications.[9] Here I shall reject this standpoint and, refusing also the ideas of "multiple," "alternative," or "entangled" modernities, grasp *modernity as a heterogeneous global civilization,* which has brought into itself, transforming them, other civilizations, or civilizational elements, thanks to its greater power and power of attraction.[10] But, while this global character has to be accentuated here—and we have seen how this works for Latin America throughout this book—we must also come to terms with its heterogeneous expansion.

An important concept to be introduced at this stage is that of "uneven and combined development." Trotsky originally formulated it to grapple with Russia's path onto capitalist civilization, integrated to the world market but at the same time as much internally heterogeneous as it was vis-à-vis Western capitalism. I have, implicitly, supposed it throughout this book, in relation to Latin America's position in the world, to its uneven internal—both national and infra-national—developments and in what concerns the several dimensions of its social life. The uneven development of modernity must be accounted for with respect to what happens in the West and elsewhere, but also regarding countries and regions, as well as between the dimensions of social life. Trotsky used the concept to show that regional or national particular developments of capitalism in a backward country such as Russia not only evinced that "primitiveness"; they yielded more advanced structures and actors as well (especially, for his historical narrative, implying the political impotence of the country's bourgeoisie and the fresh and advanced character of its proletariat). There laid the roots of many Russian paradoxes and of the revolutionary process led by the bolcheviques in 1917.[11]

The uneven and combined development of modernity is the other side of the unification of human history that this civilization has achieved. This was

Conclusion 129

carried out through very concrete processes that have nothing to do with Hegel's view of "Universal History." This is to say that there is not a homogeneous space-time configuration of global social life and of evolution. On the contrary, there are several regionalized space-time constructions, with their own rhythms, configurations, densities, processes of exchange with nature, power relations, and symbolic-hermeneutic patterns, in a multilinear process of social evolution, wherein collective subjectivities exert their creativity. Those space-time configurations may even remain in tension with one another, but are now irremediably entangled and subordinated overall to dynamic centers that spur modernity. Latin America is one of such space-time constructions—traversed itself by heterogeneity and creativity from its inception.[12]

Carrying the argument further, I want to add to the phrase "uneven and combined development" the further term *contradictory*. The position of Latin America, formerly and today, in the global system, as well as the disparity of regional configurations across the subcontinent, patently agrees with Trotsky's use of the concept (although his optimism would probably be misplaced now). The way the third phase of modernity has unfolded in Latin America, with specific characteristics and in a subordinate manner in many respects, plus the changes in different regions, which develop with specific and even opposite features, and which are sometimes connected rather directly to "exogenous" systems, surely fit well into his categorization, as we have seen throughout this book. But that further point may have also a special relevance here. In fact, between the several dimensions of contemporary social life we can detect strong tensions and oppositions, contradictions, which entail serious problems and possibilities of breakdown—in this region or elsewhere. For Germani, a key interpreter of Latin America, they resulted from misfits between the "parts" (and groups) of the social system and would eventually fall together harmoniously once the transition from ascriptive to modern society was fully achieved there or wherever. This time lag, expressed in what he called the "asynchrony of social change," was bound to be overcome in strong and mechanical teleological terms.[13] But this was a functionalist argument that was plausible at that time, but is, at this point, not sustainable at all, *pace* the recent stark ideological comeback of even blunter versions of modernization theory. There is no reason to think that harmony will come about in specific social process, and even less so in Latin America. Nonetheless, there is no reason either to suppose that contradictions between social dimensions and collective subjectivities, as carriers of opposing modernizing moves shaping those dimensions, must lead to any sort of resolution, whether catastrophic, neutral, or benign.

I have indeed underscored a contradiction between democratizing modernizing moves, which aim at the core elements of modernity's imaginary, and the neoliberal sort of project that has been thus far predominant in this third phase of modernity in the subcontinent. I tried to substantiate this thesis with the detailed analysis of a large body of literature. Others did

130   *Latin America and Contemporary Modernity*

something similar, albeit in a much briefer way and with a more catastrophic view, almost predicting a demise of democracy and the defeat of popular movements in case they were not capable of reversing those economic trends and directives of social policy—or else it was the rise of such movements that would win over capitalist impositions. Too often it is only one aspect of this twofold development that is indicated. Even more common has been the recognition of the damaging effects of neoliberalism to democracy and the high price paid by elected governments on an anti-neoliberal platform that then either give up or prove unable to implement changes as to economic policies (cf. Argentina and Ecuador).[14] But the process is complex and all outcomes are indeed possible. Things can go either way and we may also be witness to a protracted social process in which such modernizing tendencies linger on side by side, without any resolution of their contradiction. Thus, accommodations may set in and popular energy may wither away; or it may be enough to defeat neoliberalism, gathering momentum at some stage. More likely, due to the strength of both currents of modernizing moves, is that a *tense dialectic* permeates social life. The contradictions between those tendencies would be reiterated, insofar as no alternatives emerge, with the moment of coercion predominating from the top down, accommodations perhaps accepted by ruling classes notwithstanding, while the search for law, rights, and justice carries on relentlessly, despite the tides that may come and go in this regard.

This is in a sense the perennial dynamic of modernity, in which freedom and domination, equality and inequality, solidarity and social fragmentation are always at odds with each other in a dialectical relation. This dynamic finds its particular expression and is re-elaborated concretely in the democratizing and creative processes spurned by the modernizing moves of popular masses and some middle-class sectors, on the one hand, and the liberal-conservative projects advanced by ruling collective subjectivities, who have their own modernizing moves, on the other. A peculiarity to take into account refers to the fact that such a tension is so great in contemporary Latin America that the inconsistency of social practices and institutions is very visible—hence the concept of combined, uneven, and contradictory development.

SHORTCOMINGS OF THE PRESENT, POSSIBILITIES OF THE FUTURE

The third phase of modern civilization in Latin America develops, therefore, within such a frame. It draws upon more advanced achievements from elsewhere, is combined with them, and combines them with elements prior to modernity as well as with processes internally generated or that were absorbed formerly; it offers creative advances within the frame of modernity and is partly at odds with itself, as to dimensions and moves, in a tense

Conclusion 131

dialectical spiral. A permanent dispute marks it as much as it has marked the other phases of modernity, in the subcontinent and elsewhere. If a path dependency can be identified and must be reckoned with in the directions of development and the collectivities that originate and are transformed as well as reinforced by them, the ruptures social creativity may bring to such conditions, hence deflecting the direction of social development even in a radical way, have also to be recognized and, I believe, celebrated. While the Latin American countries, as argued in Chapter 2, should be seen a part of the periphery or the semiperiphery of the modern civilization in economic terms, with respect to democracy and justice this is not exactly the case.

I do not want to resuscitate the idea of "advantages of backwardness," which is indeed present in Trotsky's original formulation and has also made fortune across the planet. However, insofar as there is no necessary and, in the case in point, no actual fit between the dimensions of social life, we can suggest that the political and cultural dynamics of modernity in Latin America, which are fraught with creative possibilities, dislocate it to a more favorable and active position on the global scene. It would be too much to propose that Latin America stands in this regard at the center of the global system since institutionalized power remains in the hands of neo-liberal forces oriented toward modes of low-intensity democracy and the passive adaptation to the new underdevelopment of the region. Besides, the region's states evince many shortcomings. But, in terms of emancipatory movements, it is on a par with other regions, especially Europe, or rather at the forefront of modern civilization. The imaginary of modernity finds here creative forms that, as to internal institutional arrangements, as well as in what concerns the very peripheral insertion of Latin America globally, move forward in the direction of broadening and updating its axiological and normative horizons, toward emancipation, in the largest possible sense, individually and collectively.

That said, a further reflection is necessary, since Latin America has been the object of much hope due to its creative social movements and cultural ebullition, the appearance of the World Social Forum in its soil, and a tradition of struggle against foreign domination that has never died out.[15] Are such hopes justified, especially in the view of the argument about emancipatory movements just advanced above? It is not the case to end this book with a pessimistic note. Yet, a positive answer is not easy. The reasons for being cautious, along with the theoretical points about the possibly disjointed structure of social life, are political and intellectual. The correlation of forces is not favorable today, despite real advances, and the possibilities for the development of alternatives, economic, political, or cultural, are at least doubtful, beyond molecular change. The horizon for the assumption of state power by really transformative forces, beyond transformism, seems especially remote, *pace* the recent Bolivian process. The internal bourgeoisies are no longer to be seen—if they ever were—as partners in a movement of emancipation, in the implementation of equal freedom and in the search

132 *Latin America and Contemporary Modernity*

for a more beneficial position in the global system. Nor do the popular classes look capable of gathering strength, though, to craft a political program and mobilize themselves and other collectivities to develop in practice a hegemonic alternative that would allow them to build a complex solidarity and refashion the state to operate as a machine oriented toward the overcoming of the passive adaptation to globalization. This limitation may persist irrespective of the continuing importance of the molecular democratic revolution unfolding. To be sure, this is not an exclusively Latin American shortcoming.

Nowhere has the neoliberal direction of the third phase of modernity been faced with a true challenge, especially one at whose core lies emancipation in a broad sense[16]—nationally, with respect to class, and individually. Let us hope, however, that the creativity of the steadfast molecular revolution triggered by popular forces especially since the 1980s will eventually produce a spate of political organizations that will not give up their original ideas once close to state power and will become capable of accomplishing a real breakthrough.[17] Contemporary modernity could thereby move onto a new path. There the emancipatory imaginary elements of modernity— equal freedom, solidarity, and new forms of collective responsibility, in their opposition to domination, inequality, and a merely self-interested conception of responsibility—might then win over institutions and modernizing moves that betray what surged as one of the greatest inventions of humanity in its rich and tormented history thus far. Latin America does seem to have a particular role to play in this process.

Notes

NOTES TO THE INTRODUCTION

1. See Ricardo Bielschowsly (ed.), *Cinqüenta anos de pensamento na CEPAL*, vols. 1 and 2 (Rio de Janeiro: Record, Cepal, and Cofecon, 2000). For another, more recent view, see Immanuel Wallerstein, *The Politics of the World-Economy: The States, the Movements and the Civilizations* (Cambridge: Cambridge University Press; and Paris: Editions de la Maison des Sciences de l'Homme, 1984), pp. 14–17. He prefers to speak of core, peripheral, and semiperipheral *states,* something that seems too reductive for me.
2. See, respectively and especially, Martin S. Lipset and Aldo Solari (eds.), *Elites in Latin America* (New York: Oxford University Press, 1967); Jacques Lambert, *Amérique Latine: Structures sociales et institutions politiques* (Paris: Presses Universitaires de France, 1963); and Fernando Henrique Cardoso and Enzo Faletto, *Dependência e desenvolvimento na América Latina* (Rio de Janeiro: Zahar, [1970] 1979). For analytical discussions, see Wolfgang Knöbl, *Spielräume der Modernisierung: Das Ende der Eindeutigkeit* (Weilerwist: Velbrück, 2001), chaps. 2–4; and João Feres Jr., *A história do conceito de América Latina nos Estados Unidos* (Bauru: EDUSC/ANPOCS, 2005).
3. José Maurício Domingues, *Modernity Reconstructed* (Cardiff: University of Wales Press, 2006); and, for an initial application of the theses to Latin America, see my "A sociologia brasileira, a América Latina e a terceira fase da modernidade" (2005), in J. M. Domingues and María Maneiro (eds.), *América Latina hoje: Conceitos e interpretações* (Rio de Janeiro: Civilização Brasileira, 2006). The idea of a third phase of modernity applies also to Cuba. Authoritarianism, increasing social pluralism, and economic reforms combining strong state presence with rampant informality conform some of the main characteristics of the country today. Cuba took a radical route into the second phase of modernity, which was also a desperate attempt to resist the pressures of the United States and produce a rupture with capitalism, hence with modernity. It offered a variant of the Soviet model. Much has changed there, and many elements of social life today are common to the other countries of Latin America—including economic backwardness—but its path differs from them inasmuch as state officials and party leadership try not to give in to democracy (with justified fears of a North American takeover and a radical counter-revolution) and merely adjust to the situation that arose from the demise of the Soviet Union, by de facto flexibilizing the state-centered model. For an overview, see Velia Cecilia Bobes, *Los laberintos de la imaginación: Repertorio simbólico, identidades y actores del cambio social en Cuba* (Mexico: El Colegio de México, 2000).

134 Notes

4. The issue is particularly well elaborated in Anthony Giddens, *The Nation State and Violence* (Cambridge: Polity Press, 1985).
5. In my view, Roland Robertson's perspectives on the subject are precise on this point. See his *Globalization: Social Theory and Global Culture* (London: Sage, 1992) and R. Robertson, Scott Lash, and Mike Featherstone (eds.), *Global Modernities* (London: Sage, 1995).
6. For instance, Wallerstein, *op. cit.*, and Enrique Dussel, *1492: El encubrimineto del Otro: Hacia el origen del "mito de la modernidad"* (La Paz: Plural Editores, Universidad Mayor de San Andrés, 1994).
7. See, for a full exposition of the concepts put forward below, J. M. Domingues, *Sociological Theory and Collective Subjectivity* (London: Macmillan; and New York: St. Martin's Press, 1995); *Social Creativity, Collective Subjectivity and Contemporary Modernity* (London: Macmillan; and New York: St. Martin's Press, 2000); and *Modernity Reconstructed*.
8. Aníbal Quijano, "Coloniality and modernity/rationality," *Cultural Studies,* Vol. 21 ([1989] 2007).
9. For some aspects of this discussion, see Domingues, *Social Creativity, Collective Subjectivity and Contemporary Modernity,* chap. 2.
10. See Cristina Reigadas, "Modernización e identidad en el pensamiento argentino contemporáneo: revisando el argumento de la inferioridad," *Revista latinoamericana de filosofía y ciencias sociales,* segunda época, año XXV, no. 22 (2000); Sérgio Costa, "Desprovincializando a teoria sociológica: a contribuição pós-colonial," *Revista brasileira de ciências sociais,* vol. 21, no. 60 (2006). To be sure, their efforts are warranted insofar as North American Latin American studies still often hold a much distorted (close to modernization theory) vision of the "other."
11. I cannot fully engage with their views here, but a summary where this is expressed in very straightforward terms is found in Arturo Escobar, "The Latin American Modernity/Coloniality Research Program," in Guillermo O'Donnell et al., *Cruzando fronteras en América Latina* (Amsterdan: CEDLA, 2003). In any case, I shall return to some of these themes in the Conclusion to this book.
12. See Domingues, *Modernity Reconstructed,* chap. 9.

NOTES TO CHAPTER 1

1. Jonathan Hartlyn, "Democracy in Latin America since 1930," in Leslie Bethel (ed.), *The Cambridge History of Latin America,* vol. VI, Part II (Cambridge: Cambridge University Press, 1994), p. 99.
2. José Maurício Domingues, *Modernity Reconstructed* (Cardiff: University of Wales Press, 2006), especially chap. 2.
3. Robert E. Scott, "Political elites and political modernization: The crisis of transition," in Martin S. Lipset and Aldo Solari (eds.), *Elites in Latin America* (New York: Oxford University Press, 1967).
4. Talcott Parsons, "Evolutionary universals in society" (1964), in *Sociological Theory and Modern Society* (New York: Free Press, 1967). See also his *The System of Modern Society* (Englewood Cliffs, NJ: Prentice-Hall, 1971).
5. See Jürgen Habermas, *Theorie des kommunikativen Handelns,* vols. 1–2 (Frankfurt am Main: Suhrkamp, 1981), as well as *Fakzität und Geltung* (Frankfurt am Main: Suhrkamp, 1992). For a view that could be taken as somewhat more contingent, since modernity might be seen a basically implying a "project," see his "Die Moderne—ein unvollendetes Projekt" (1981), in *Kleine politische Schriften I–IV* (Frankfurt am Main: Suhrkamp,

Notes 135

1981). I believe that an evolutionary standpoint is present even if the hypothesis is advanced that only the systemic aspects of modernity were transferred to the periphery, and not the features of its life-world: In the end it is toward that evolutionary end point that we are (or ought to be) moving. For this last Habermasian standpoint, check Leonardo Avritzer, *A moralidade da democracia* (São Paulo: Perspectiva; Belo Horizonte: Editora UFMG, 1996).

6. Peter Wagner, *A Sociology of Modernity: Liberty and Discipline* (London: Routledge, 1994); J. M. Domingues, *Social Creativity, Collective Subjectivity and Contemporary Modernity* (London: Macmillan; and New York: St. Martin's Press, 2000), chap. 7; *Modernity Reconstructed*, chaps. 3 and 8.

7. Florestan Fernandes, *A revolução burguesa no Brasil* (Rio de Janeiro: Zahar, 1975), chap. 2.

8. Idem, p. 33.

9. For general historical information about this period, see Leslie Bethell (ed.), *The Cambridge History of Latin America*, vol. II (Cambridge: Cambridge University Press, 1984–1991); Tulio Halperin Donghi, *Historia contemporánea de América Latina* (Madrid: Alianza, [1969] 1993). Of course, historians and sociologists have proposed much more detailed reconstructions for each of these countries. See especially Carlos A. Forment, *Democracy in Latin America, 1760–1900*, vol. 1 (Chicago: University of Chicago Press, 2003). His main thesis is that the white and male citizens of Latin America were extremely active in creating associations of the sort de Tocqueville found in the United States in the period I have defined as the first phase of modernity. Their language was given by "Civic Catholicism" and they basically wanted to protect themselves from the authoritarian view of the groups that controlled the state.

10. Piet Strydom, *Discourse and Knowledge: The Making of Enlightenment Sociology* (Liverpool: Liverpool University Press, 2000).

11. Cf. Reinhard Bendix, *Kings or People: Power and the Mandate to Rule* (Berkeley: University of California Press, 1978). For a classical contrast, see José Medina Echevarría, *Consideraciones sociológicas sobre el desarrollo económico de América Latina* (Buenos Aires: Solar and Hachette, 1964).

12. See Donghi, *op. cit.*, chaps. IV–VI.

13. Carvalho argues, in relation to Brazil and with reference to Marshall's classical view of the development of citizenship, that social rights were prior to civil rights in their actual implementation. Although his point is not totally mistaken, he takes it too far, since it has been a faint and incomplete implementation of both civil and social rights—though by now political rights are much more secure than ever—that has obtained in Brazil and in many of the Latin American countries, which does not mean they are not in place (take just the notion of *private property* . . .). See José Murilo de Carvalho, *Desenvolvimiento de la ciudadania en Brasil* (Mexico: Fondo de Cultura Económica, 1995). Similar problems come up in Juan Méndez, Guillermo O'Donnell, and Paulo Sérgio Pinheiro (eds.), *La (in)efectividad da ley y la exclusión en América Latina* (Buenos Aires: Paidós, [1997] 2003); and G. O'Donnell, "Notas sobre la democracia en América Latina," in G. O'Donnell et al., *La democracia en América Latina: Hacia una democracia de ciudadanos y ciudadanas: El debate conceptual sobre la democracia* (PNUD, 2004). The ambiguous character of civil rights, in particular, must be borne in mind when the topic is discussed—not only freedom, but domination too, is connected to them. Marshall's theory will be mentioned below. Of course trajectories are varied and contingent; however, I think that it does not make sense speaking of reversal of sequence for no case.

136 Notes

14. Philippe C. Schmitter, "Still the century of corporatism?," *Review of Political Studies*, vol. 36 (1974); Hobart Spalding Jr., *Organized Labor in Latin America* (New York: Harper & Row, 1987); Claus Offe, "The attribution of public status to interest groups," in *Disorganised Capitalism: Contemporary Transformations of Work and Politics* (Cambridge: Polity, 1985).
15. Richard Morse, *El espejo de Próspero* (Mexico: Siglo XXI, 1982).
16. Domingues, *Modernity Reconstructed*. A great many insights in this respect, although he was a key proponent of the "populist" interpretation (see Chapter 3), are to be found in Gino Germani, *Política y sociedad en una época de transición* (Buenos Aires: Paidós, 1965), pp. 161, 234, 240–44. And, in fact, Argentina is the country in Latin America where social rights and social policy came closer to something similar to social democracy, in a corporatist mould. See Ruben Lo Vuolo "¿Una nueva oscuridad? Estado de bienestar, crisis de integración social y democracia," in R. Lo Vuolo and Alberto Barbeito, *La nueva oscuridad: Del estado populista al neoconservador* (Buenos Aires: Miño y Dávila, 1998).
17. Spalding, *op. cit.*; Domingues, *Social Creativity, Collective Subjectivity and Contemporary Modernity*, chap. 7. The argument against a corporatist model being in place in Brazil after the end of the Vargas' dictatorship was recently put forward by Adalberto Moreira Cardoso, "Direito do trabalho e relações de classe no Brasil," in Luiz Werneck Vianna (ed.), *A democracia e os três poderes no Brasil* (Belo Horizonte: UFMG, 2002).
18. Bruno Lautier, "Les politiques sociales au Mexique et au Brèsil: l'assurance, l'assistance, l'absence," in B. Lautier and Jaime Marques Pereira (eds.), *Brèsil, Mexique: Deux trajectoires dans la mondialisation* (Paris: Karthala, 2004), pp. 168–69; Germani, *op. cit.*, chaps. 3–5 and 9; Alain Touraine, *La Parole et le sang* (Paris: Odile Jacob, 1988), Part III.
19. Armando Barrientos, "Latin America: Towards a liberal-informal welfare regime," in Ian Gough and Geof Wood (eds.), *Insecurity and Welfare Regimes in Asia, Africa and Latin America* (Cambridge: Cambridge University Press, 2004). This has in any case fallen absolutely short of the "de-commodification" of the labor force in advanced European social democracy. Cf. Goran Esping-Andersen, *Politics against Markets. The Social-Democratic Road to Power* (Princeton, NJ: Princeton University Press, 1985).
20. Michael Mann, "La crisis del Estado-nación en América Latina," *Desarrollo económico*, vol. 44, no. 174 (2004)—also in J. M. Domingues and María Maneiro (eds.), *América Latina hoje. Conceitos e interpretações* (Rio de Janeiro: Civilização Brasileira, 2006).
21. For a review of the literature on the military dictatorships, see José Luis Fiori, "Para uma crítica da teoria latino-americana do Estado," in *Em busca do dissenso perdido* (Rio de Janeiro: Insight, 1995). I will return to that in Chapter 3.
22. For a full discussion vis-à-vis Europe, see Offe, *op. cit.*
23. L. Avritzer, *Democracy and the Public Space in Latin America* (Princeton, NJ: Princeton University Press 2002), pp. 29–35, chap. 2 (quotation on p. 98); Frances Hagopian and Scott P. Mainwaring (eds.), *The Third Wave of Democratization in Latin America: Advancements and Setbacks* (Cambridge: Cambridge University Press, 2005). See also G. O'Donnell, P. C. Schmitter, and Laurence Whitehead (eds.), *Transitions from Authoritarian Rule* (Baltimore, MD: Johns Hopkins University Press, 1986). "Poliarchy" was used above in the sense of Robert Dahl, *Poliarchy: Participation and Opposition* (New Haven, CT: Yale University Press, 1971).
24. Mann, *op. cit.*; J. M. Domingues, "Nationalism in Central and South America," in G. Delanty and Kris Kumar (eds.), *Handbook of Nationalism* (New

Notes 137

York: Sage, 2006); also in *Aproximações à América Latina* (Rio de Janeiro: Civilização Brasileira, 2007).

25. Domingues, *Social Creativity, Collective Subjectivity and Contemporary Modernity*, chap. 7; *Modernity Reconstructed*, chaps. 1, 3, and 11.

26. We should not speak here, vis-à-vis the nineteenth and the twentieth centuries, of a mere "positivization" of rights, but rather of the social creation of rights and citizens, something that goes far beyond the importation of values that would have to be turned into norms legally guaranteed.

27. Jorge Castañeda, *Unarmed Utopia: The Latin American Left after the Cold War* (New York: Vintage, 1993); Evelina Dagnino, "Culture, citizenship, and democracy: Changing discourses and practices of the Latin American left," in Sonia E. Alvarez, E. Dagnino, and Arturo Escobar (eds.), *Cultures of Politics, Politics of Culture: Re-envisioning Latin American Social Movements* (Boulder, CO: Westview, 1998).

28. John Henry Merryman, *The Civil Law Tradition. An Introduction to the Legal Systems of Western Europe and Latin America* (Stanford, CA: Stanford University Press, 1985, 2nd ed.); Rogelio Pérez-Perdomo and Lawrence Friedman, "Latin legal cultures in the age of globalization," in R. Pérez-Perdomo and L. Friedman (eds.), *Legal Culture in the Age of Globalization: Latin America and Latin Europe* (Stanford: Stanford University Press, 2003).

29. Enrique Peruzzotti, "Modernization and juridification in Latin America: A reassessment of the Latin American developmental path," *Thesis Eleven*, vol. 58 (1999). I shall return to this later.

30. Karl Marx, *Zur Judenfrage* (1847) in Marx & Engels, *Werke,* vol. 1 (Berlin: Dietz, 1956).

31. Habermas, *Theorie des kommunikativen Handelns*, vols. 1–2; *Fakzität und Geltung.*

32. Domingues, *Modernity Reconstructed*, chaps. 1–2 and 4.

33. T. H. Marshall, "Citizenship and social class" (1950), in *Class, Citizenship and Social Development* (Garden City, NY: Doubleday & Co, 1964).

34. Domingues, *Modernity Reconstructed*, chaps. 3–4.

35. Anthony Giddens, *The Consequences of Modernity* (Cambridge: Polity, 1990); K. Marx and Friedrich Engels, "Manifest der kommunistischen Partei" (1848), in *Werke,* vol. 4 (Berlin: Dietz, 1939).

36. Theodor W. Adorno, *Minima Moralia* (Frankfurt am Main: Suhrkamp, [1945–1947] 1997), pp. 23, 130.

37. Gyorg Lukács, *Geschichte und Klassenbewusstsein* (Berlin: Herman Luchterhand, [1923] 1977), pp. 271ff.

38. See Robert R. Kaufman and Stephan Haggard (eds.), *The Politics of Economic Adjustment: International Constraints, Distributive Conflicts, and the State* (Princeton, NJ: Princeton University Press, 1992); Atílio Borón, *Estado, capitalismo y democracia en América Latina* (Buenos Aires: CLACSO, 2003); plus Néstor Garcia Canclini, *Consumidores e cidadãos: Conflitos multiculturais da globalização* (Rio de Janeiro: Editora UFRJ, 1995), who looks for a democratic solution to this problem.

39. E. Dagnino, Alberto J. Olvera, and Aldo Panfichi, "Para uma outra leitura da disputa pela construção democrática na América Latina," in E. Dagnino, A.J. Olvera, and A. Panfichi (eds.), *A disputa pela construção democrática na América Latina* (São Paulo: Paz e Terra, 2005).

40. Jorge Bengoa, "25 años de estudios rurales," *Sociologias,* no. 10 (2003).

41. J. M. Domingues, "A dialética da modernização conservadora e a nova história do Brasil" (2002), in *Estudos de sociologia* (Belo Horizonte: Editora UFMG, 2004); Afrânio Garcia, "A sociologia rural no Brasil: entre escravos do passado e parceiros do futuro," *Sociologias,* no. 10 (2004).

138 Notes

42. Mann, *op. cit.*
43. Manuel Castells, *End of Millenium* (Oxford: Blackwell, 1998), p. 205.
44. Loic Wacquant, *As prisões da miséria* (Rio de Janeiro: Zahar, 2001).
45. See, for a general discussion, M. Maneiro, "Os movimentos sociais na América Latina: Uma perspectiva a partir das relações do Estado com a sociedade civil," in Domingues and Maneiro, *op. cit.*
46. Diniz has perceptively discussed the issue some years ago. Cf. Eli Diniz, *Voto e máquina política: Patronagem e clientelismo no Rio de Janeiro* (Rio de Janeiro: Paz e Terra, 1982).
47. G. O'Donnell, "Delegative democracy," *Journal of Democracy,* vol. 5 (1994) and "Illusions about consolidation," *Journal of Democracy,* vol. 7 (1996).
48. For Argentina, see Javier Auyero, *La política de los pobres: Las prácticas clientelistas del peronismo* (Buenos Aires: Manantial, 2001), and Pablo Torres, *Votos, chapas y fideos: Clientelismo y ayuda social* (La Plata: de la campana, 2002); for Mexico, see Jonathan Fox, "The difficult transition from clientelism to citizenship: Lessons from Mexico," in Douglas A. Chalmers et al. (eds.), *The New Politics of Inequality in Latin America: Rethinking Participation and Representation* (Oxford: Oxford University Press, 1997), and Fernando I. Salmerón Castro, "Modernidad y prácticas políticas: democracia, eslabonamientos y mediaciones en la sociedad civil," *Revista mexicana de sociología,* vol. 1 (2002); Marcus J. Kurtz, "Understanding the Third World Welfare State after neoliberalism," *Comparative Politics,* vol. 24 (2002)—which includes a discussion of the Chilean case; Jaime Ornelas Delgado, "La política de combate a la pobreza en México, 1982–2005," *Papeles de población,* no. 47 (2006). For Mexico too, but from a more general angle, see B. Lautier, op. cit., pp. 181–82, 187–90; and Merecedes González de la Rocha, "Familias y política social en México: El caso de Oportunidades," paper presented at the Conference Welfare Regime and Social Actors in Inter-Regional Perspective: The Americas, Asia and Africa (University of Texas at Austin, 2006). A more general analysis of focused social policy is found in Julia Sant'Anna, "Governos de esquerda e o gasto social na América Latina," *Observador on-line,* vol. 2. no. 2 (2007) (http://www.opsa.iuperj.br).
49. Víctor Nunes Leal, *Coronelismo, enxada e voto* (São Paulo: Alfa Omega [1948] 1976); Glaucio A. Dillon Soares, *A democracia interrompida* (Rio de Janeiro: FGV Editora, 2001).
50. For the strong hypothesis of a mere administration of poverty, see B. Lautier, *op. cit.,* p. 184. A milder view, which stresses the more universalist but yet fragmented nature of Brazilian social policy, is found in his "Les politiques sociales au Brasil durant le gouvernement de Lula: aumône d'État ou droits sociaux," *Problèmes d'Amérique latine,* no. 63 (2006–2007).
51. Avritzer, *Democracy and the Public Space in Latin America,* chap. 6, and "El ascenso del Partido de los Trabajadores en Brasil: la democracia y la distribución participativas como alternativas al neoliberalismo," in César A. Rodríguez Garavito, Patrik S. Barret, and Daniel Chavez (eds.), *La nueva izquierda en América Latina: Sus orígenes y trayectoria futura* (Bogotá: Norma, 2005).
52. Cf. N. G. Canclini, *Culturas híbridas: Estrategias para entrar y salir de la modernidad* (Mexico: Grijalbo, 1990); Avritzer, *op. cit.,* chap. 3.
53. Lautier, *op. cit.,* p. 184; Barrientos, *op. cit.;* Clarisa Hardy, "Una nueva generación de reformas sociales en América Latina," in Rolando Cordera, Leonardo Lomelí, and Rosa Elena Montes de Oca (eds.), *La cuestión social: superación de la pobreza y política social a 7 años de Copenhague* (Mexico: UNAM, IETD, and INDS, 2003), especially p. 205. I quote those data drawing upon her, who draws upon the Economic Commission for Latin America (ECLAC). See Cepal, *Panorama Social de América Latina* (2000–2001) and (2006).

Notes 139

54. Domingues, *Modernity Reconstructed,* chaps. 3–4, and "Sociologia brasileira, a América Latina e a terceira fase da modernidade" (2005), in Domingues and Maneiro, op. cit.
55. Asa Cristina Laurel (ed.), *Estado e políticas sociais no neoliberalismo* (São Paulo: Cortez [1992] 1995); Kaufman and Haggard, *op. cit.;* Sara Gordon, "Equidad social y justicia social," *Revista mexicana de sociología,* vol. 2 (1995); René Millán, "Cultura de la justicia y cultura política," *Revista mexicana de sociología,* vol. 2 (1995); Philip Oxhorn, "Desigualdad social, sociedad civil y los límites de la ciudadanía en América Latina," *Economía, sociedad y territorio,* vol. 3, no. 9 (2001); Martín Hopenhayn, "Old and new forms of citizenship," *Cepal Review,* no. 73 (2001); Carlos Sojo, "The idea of citizenship in the Latin American debate," *Cepal Review,* no. 76 (2002); Lautier, *op. cit.,* pp. 184, 182ff, 194–95; J. M. Domingues, "Amartya Sen, freedom and development" (2002), in Sérgio Costa, J. M. Domingues, Wolfgang Knöbl, and Josué Pereira da Silva (eds.), *The Plurality of Modernity: Decentring Social Theory* (Mehring: Hampp, 2006) and *Modernity Reconstructed.* Some want to lend a philosophical and even Rawlsian dressing to it: Henio Millán Valenzuela, "Política social y fundamentos del combate a la pobreza extrema en México," *Economía, sociedad y territorio,* vol. 3, no. 9 (2001). This is, however, more than arguable, and in any case has nothing to do with citizenship as such.
56. G. Esping-Andersen, *The Three Worlds of Welfare Capitalism* (Princeton, NJ: Princeton University Press, 1990).
57. Laurel, *op. cit.;* Christopher Abel and Colin M. Lewis, "Exclusion and engagement: A diagnosis of social policy in Latin America in the long run," in Abel and Lewis (eds.), *Exclusion & Engagement: Social Polity in Latin America* (London: Institute of Latin American Studies, 2002); Silvia Tamez González and Pedro Moreno Salazar, "Seguridad social en América Latina," in Enrique de la Garza Toledo (ed.), *Tratado latinoamericano de sociología del trabajo* (Mexico: El Colegio de México, FLACSO, UAM, and Fondo de Cultura Económica, 2000); Barrientos, *op. cit.*
58. J. M. Domingues, "Le premier governement Lula. Un bilan critique," *Problèmes d'Amérique latine,* no. 63 (2006–2007)—also in *Aproximações à América Latina.*
59. B. Lautier, "Citoyenneté et politiques d'ajustement," in Bérengère Marques-Pereira and Ilán Bizberg (eds.), *La citoyenneté sociale en Amérique latine* (Paris: L'Harttman, 1995), pp. 23–24.
60. Pablo Dávalos (ed.), *Pueblos indígenas, Estado y democracia* (Buenos Aires: CLACSO, 2005).
61. Josefina Saldaña-Portillo, "Who's the Indian in Aztlán? Re-writing mestizaje, indianism, and chicanismo from the Lancandón," in Ileana Rodríguez (ed.), *The Latin American Subaltern Studies Reader* (Durham and London: Duke University Press, 2001).
62. Alvarez, Dagnino, and Escobar, *op. cit.;* Garavito, Barret, and Chavez *op. cit.*
63. Domingues, "Nationalism in Central and South America."
64. Garavito, Barret, and Chavez, *op cit.,* p. 31. Plus D. Chavez and Benjamin Goldfrank (eds.), *La izquierda en la cuidad. Participación en gobiernos locales en América Latina* (Barcelona: Icaria, 2005). See also Alvarez, Dagnino, and Escobar, *op. cit.*
65. Domingues, *Modernity Reconstructed,* chap. 8.
66. See especially L. Avritzer and S. Costa, "Teoria crítica, democracia e esfera pública" (2004), in Domingues and Maneiro, *op. cit.*
67. For such usages, see Dagnino, *op. cit.;* L. Avritzer et al., "Special section on civil society in Latin America," *Constellations,* vol. 4 (1997).

140 Notes

68. J. M. Domingues and Andrea C. Pontual, "Environmental responsibility and the public sphere in Latin America," in Tuama Ó Seamus (ed.), *The Critical Theory of Piet Strydom* (New York: IB Taurus, 2007)—also in *Aproximações à América Latina*.

69. Rubem César Fernandes, *Privado porém público: O terceiro setor na América Latina* (Rio de Janeiro: Relume Dumará, 1994); Jasmine Gideon, "The politics of social service provision through NGOs: A study of Latin America," *Bulletin of Latin American Research*, vol. 17 (1998); Dagnino, Olvera, and Panfichi, *op. cit;* Marriane Braig, "Zwischen Menschenrechten und Rechtsstaatlichkeit: Zivile Frauenorganizationen und Demokratisierung des Staates in Lateinamerika," in S. Costa and Hauke Brunkhorst (eds.), *Jenseits von Zentrum und Peripherie: Zur Verfassung der fragmentierten Weltgesellschaft* (Mering: Hampp, 2005); Bernardo Sorj, "Civil societies North–South relations: NGOs and/beyond dependency," *The Edelstein Center for Social Research, Working Paper,* no. 1 (2005).

70. Gideon, *op. cit.,* p. 304.

71. See A. J. Olvera, "Sociedade civil e governabilidade no México," in E. Dagnino (ed.), *Sociedade civil e espaços públicos no Brasil* (São Paulo: Paz e Terra, 2002), and Dagnino, Olvera, and Panfichi, *op. cit.;* for more theoretical views, see Antonio Gramsci, *Quaderni del carcere*, vol. 3 (Turin: Einaudi, [1929–1935] 2001), vol. 2, pp. 763–64, 865–66, vol. 3, pp. 2287–89; plus Jeffrey Alexander, "Contradictions: The uncivilizing pressures of space, time, and function," *Soundings,* vol. 16 (2000).

72. See Boaventura de Sousa Santos, *O Fórum Social Mundial: manual de uso* (São Paulo: Cortez, 2005). For global civil society and cosmopolitan democracy, see David Held, *Democracy and the Global Order: From the Modern State to Cosmopolitan Governance* (Cambridge: Polity, 1995).

73. Pérez-Perdomo and Friedman, *op. cit.,* p. 17.

74. Cristina Carvalho Pacheco, "Directrices del Banco Mundial para la Reforma Judicial en América Latina," *El otro derecho,* vol. 25 (2000); Lawyers Committee for Human Rights, *Building in Quicksand: The Collapse of the World Bank's Judicial Reform Project in Peru* (New York and Washington, DC: Lawyers Committee for Human Rights, 2000); José Renato Nailini, "Judicial reform in Brazil," in *Judicial Reform in Latin America and the Caribeean: Proceedings of a World Bank Conference* (Washington, DC: The World Bank, 1995); World Bank, "Judicial reform in Latin American courts: The experience in Argentina and Ecuador," *World Bank Technical Paper,* no. 350 (1996); Linn Hammergen et al., *América Latina hoy*, vol. 30 (2005); C. Rodríguez Garavito, "Globalización, reforma judicial y Estado de derecho en Colombia y América Latina: el regreso de los programas de derecho y desarrollo" and Rodrigo Uprimny, C. Rodríguez Garavito, and Mauricio García Villegas, "¿Justicia para todos o seguridad para el mercado? El neoliberalismo y la reforma judicial en Colombia," both in R. Uprimny, C. Rodríguez Garavito, and M. García Villegas (eds.), *¿Justicia para todos? Sistema judicial, derechos sociales y democracia en Colombia* (Bogotá: Norma, 2006); Thamy Pogrebinschi, "Law and society in Latin America: Brazil, Argentina and Mexico in a comparative perspective," paper presented at the 24th Annual ILASSA Conference on Latin America, University of Texas, Austin (2004).

75. Ibrahim F. I. Shihata, "Legal framework for development: The World Bank's role in legal and judicial reform," in *Judicial Reform in Latin America and the Caribeean:Proceedings of a World Bank Conference* (Washington, DC: The World Bank, 1995), "Judicial reform in developing countries and the role of the World Bank," in *Judicial Reform in Latin America and the Caribeean: Proceedings of a World Bank Conference* (Washington, DC: The World Bank, 1995), plus "The World Bank," in E. Jarquín and F. Carrillo (eds.), *Justice Delayed: Judicial Reform*

Notes 141

in Latin America (Washington, DC: Inter-American Bank of Development, 1998), plus the World Bank *Technical Papers* no. 280 (1994) and no. 350 (1996).

76. Mauro Cappelletti and Bryan Garth, *The Judicial Process in Comparative Perspective* (Oxford: Clarendon, 1978).
77. See Merryman, *op. cit.*, p. 153; and Domingues, *Modernity Reconstructed*, chap. 5.
78. L. Werneck Vianna et al., *Corpo e alma da magistratura brasileira* (Rio de Janeiro: Revan, 1997) and *A judicialização da política e das relações sociais* (Rio de Janeiro: Revan, 1999). Plus L. Werneck Vianna, "Revolução processual do direito e democracia progressiva," in L. Werneck Vianna (ed.), *A democracia e os três poderes no Brasil* (Belo Horizonte: Editora UFMG, 2000). And Fiona Macaulay, "Democratización y poder judicial: agendas de reforma en competencia," *América Latina hoy*, vol. 39 (2005).
79. Sergio López-Ayllón and Héctor Fix-Fierro, "'Faraway, so close!' The rule of law and legal change in Mexico, 1970–2000," in Pérez-Perdomo and Friedman, *op. cit.*; Miguel Carbonel, "El poder judicial: ¿el tercero ausente?," *Metapolítica*, no. 230, vol. 7 (2003); Catharine Conighan, "Más allá del minimalismo: una agenda para unir democracia y desarrollo," in G. O'Donnell et al., *op. cit.*, p. 114.
80. Inés Bergoglio, "Argentina: The effects of democratic institutionalization," in Pérez-Perdomo and Friedman, (eds.), *op. cit.*; Felipe Fucito, *¿Podrá cambiar la justicia en la Argentina?* (Fondo de Cultura Económica: Buenos Aires, 2002); M. Maneiro, *Encuentros y desencuentros. Estado y movimientos de trabajadores desocupados del Gran Buenos Aires (1996–2005)*. PhD Thesis (Rio de Janeiro: IUPERJ, 2007).
81. R. Uprimny, C. Rodríguez Garavito, and M. García Villegas, "Introducción: Una nueva aproximación al debate sobre la justicia, los derechos sociales y la democracia en Colombia" and "Las cifras de la justicia," in Idem, *op. cit.* See, for the ombudsman, Mark Ungar, "The defensoría del pueblo," in Jo-Marie Burt and Philip Mauceri (eds.), *Politics in the Andes. Identity, Conflict, Reform* (Pittsburgh: Pittsburgh University Press, 2004), and Fredrik Uggla, "The Ombudsman in Latin America," *Journal of Latin American Studies*, vol. 36 (2004).
82. Gladys Acosta, Germán Burgos, and Margarita Flórez, "Los servicios legales y las campañas de fin de siglo: preguntas y respuestas," *El otro derecho*, vol. 5, no. 3 (1994); G. Burgos, "Los servicios legales populares y los extravíos de la pregunta por el político," *El otro derecho*, vol. 7, no. 3 (1996).
83. Burgos, op.cit.; Pogrebinschi, op. cit.
84. Deborah J. Yashar, "Indigenous politics and democracy: Contesting citizenship in Latin America," *Comparative Politics*, vol. 31 (1998); Donna Lee Van Cott, "A political analysis of legal pluralism in Bolivia and Colombia," *Journal of Latin American Studies*, vol. 32 (2000); Catherine Walsh, "Interculturalidad, reformas constitucionales y pluralismo jurídico," *Boletim ICCI-Rimai*, año 4, no. 36 (2002); Toomas Gross, "Community and dissent: Religious intolerance in rural Oaxaca," *Finish Anthropologist*, vol. 26 (2003).
85. "Arbitragem: confusão com a justiça," *O Globo*, May 10, 2003.
86. José Eduardo Faria, *O direito na sociedade globalizada* (São Paulo: Malheiros, 1999); Germán Palacio, "Pluralismo jurídico, neoamericanismo y postfordismo: notas para descifrar la naturaleza de los cambios jurídicos de fines de siglo," *Crítica jurídica*, vol. 17 (2000).
87. The problem here is also to which extent the model of the individual—typically applied to companies in the "principal-agent" scheme—is still valid, or whether the networked business firm has been in some degree replacing it. Cf. Gunther Teubner, "La coupole invisible: de l'attribution causale à la l'attribution collective de la responsabilité ecologique," in *Droit et reflexivité: L'Auto-reference dans l'organisation* (Paris: L.G.D.J and Bruyant, [1992] 1996).

142 Notes

88. Boaventura de Sousa Santos, *Toward a New Common Sense* (New York: Routledge, 1995).
89. Manuel A. Garretón, *Incomplete Democracy: Political Democratization in Chile and Latin America* (Chapel Hill and London: University of North Carolina Press, 2003), part II.
90. Merryman, *op. cit.*, 156; Werneck Vianna et al., *A judicialização da política e das relações sociais*; Bergogli, *op. cit.*; Lopéz-Ayllon and Fix-Fierro, *op. cit.*, and "Legitimidad contra legalidad. Los dilemas de la transición jurídica y el Estado de derecho en México," *Política y gobierno*, vol. 3 (1999); Pilar Domingo, "Judicial independence: The politics of Supreme Court in Mexico," *Journal of Latin American Studies*, vol. 32 (2000); Luis Pásara, "Justicia, régimen político y sociedad en América Latina," *Política y gobierno*, vol. 10 (2003); Macaulay, *op. cit.*; Al Giordano, "Mexico presidencial swindle," *New Left Review*, no. 41 (2006).
91. M. García Villegas, "El derecho como esperanza: constitucionalismo y cambio social en América Latina, con algunas ilustraciones a partir de Colombia," in Uprimny, Rodríguez Garavito, and García Villegas, *op. cit.*
92. Wanderley Guilherme dos Santos, *Paradoxos do liberalismo: teoria e história* (Rio de Janeiro: IUPERJ; São Paulo: Vértice, 1988), chap. 4.
93. O'Donnell, "Notas sobre la democracia en América Latina"; Conighan, *op. cit.*
94. See J. M. Domingues, "Instituições formais no Brasil do século XXI" (2006), in *Aproximações à América Latina*, for a discussion of the Brazilian case within the Latin American context.
95. José Eisenberg and T. Pogrebinschi, "Pragmatismo, direito e política," *Novos Estudos CEBRAP*, vol. 62 (2002).
96. Axel Honneth, *Kampf um Anerkennung* (Frankfurt am Main: Suhrkamp, 1992). But with much greater room for particularities than he perceives in his *Leiden an Unbestimmtheit: Eine Reaktualisierung der Hegelschen Rechtsphilosophie* (Stuttgart: Phillip Reclam, 2001). See Chapter 3.
97. Habermas, *Faktizität und Geltung*.
98. J. Habermas, "Die postnationale Konstellation und die Zukunft der Demokratie," in *Die postnationale Konstellation* (Frankfurt am Main: Suhrkamp, 1998).
99. As is well-known, this is where the "immanent critique" of modernity started: The understanding of a fundamental contradiction between the promises of modernity and the impossibility of making those practices come true within its limits. Socialism and communism translated those aspirations into a different language, aggregating new elements to their phrasing and changing them somehow. Cf. Seyla Benhabib, *Critique, Norm and Utopia* (New York: Columbia University Press, 1986).

NOTES TO CHAPTER 2

1. See Seymour Martin Lipset, "Values, Education, and Entrepreneurship," in S. M. Lipset and Aldo Solari (eds.), *Elites in Latin America* (New York: Oxford University Press, 1967).
2. Talcott Parsons, "Evolutionary universals in Society" (1964), in *Sociological Theory and Modern Society* (New York: Free Press, 1967). See also his *The System of Modern Society* (Englewood Cliffs, NJ: Prentice-Hall, 1971).
3. Jürgen Habermas, *Theorie des kommunikativen Handelns*, vols. 1–2 (Frankfurt am Main: Suhrkamp, 1981). For a critique, which draws upon the strong and recent economic sociology, see José Maurício Domingues, *Social Creativity, Collective Modernity and Contemporary Modernity* (London: Macmillan; and New York: St. Martin's Press, 2000), chap. 6.

Notes 143

4. Karl Polanyi, *The Great Transformation* (Boston, MA: Beacon, [1944] 1975); J. M. Domingues, *Modernity Reconstructed* (Cardiff: University of Wales Press, 2006), chaps. 2 and 8–10.

5. I cannot tackle such a debate here, whose main references are listed in J. M. Domingues, "Global modernity, civilization analysis, Latin American issues," in Gerard Delanty (ed.), *European Handbook of Social Theory* (London: Routledge, 2005). In any case, it may be worth stressing that relations of production, rather than trade as such, underlie my understanding of capitalism, bringing me closer to Marxism, hence at variance with a Wallersteinian standpoint.

6. See Florestan Fernandes, *A revolução burguesa no Brasil* (Rio de Janeiro: Zahar, 1975), chap. 2; Tulio Halperin Donghi, "Economy and society," in Leslie Bethel (ed.), *The Cambridge History of Latin America*, vol. III (Cambridge: Cambridge University Press: 1985); William Glade, "Latin America and the international economy, 1870–1914" and Arnold Bauer, "Rural Spanish America, 1870–1930," both in L. Bethel (ed.), *The Cambridge History of Latin America*, vol. IV (Cambridge: Cambridge University Press, 1986).

7. Celso Furtado, *Formação econômica da América Latina* (Rio de Janeiro: Lia, 1967, 2nd ed.), chaps. IV and VII. Especially in mining they created actual "enclaves."

8. Karl Marx, *Das Kapital,* book I, vol. 1 (Berlin: Dietz, [1867] 1965), chap. 1.

9. Furtado, *op. cit.,* chaps. IV and X–XI; Rosemary Thorp, "Latin America and the international economy from the First World War to the World Depression," in Bethel, *op. cit,* vol. IV. The First World War in particular, due to the difficulty of carrying out foreign trade, was a moment of rapid advancement of industry in Latin America, concentrated on light and simple consumption goods.

10. See Peter Wagner, *A Sociology of Modernity: Liberty and Discipline* (London: Routledge, 1994); and, for a summary and advanced argument, Robert Boyer, "Du fordisme canonique à une variété de modes de développement," in R. Boyer and Yves Saillard (eds.), *Théorie de la régulation: L'Etat des savoirs* (Paris: La Découverte, 2002).

11. For the following paragraphs, see Furtado, *op. cit.,* especially chaps. V, X–XII, and XV–XVIII; Fernando Henrique Cardoso and Enzo Faletto, *Dependência e desenvolvimento na América Latina* (Rio de Janeiro: Zahar, 1970); José Serra (ed.), *América Latina: Ensaios de interpretação econômica* (Rio de Janeiro: Paz e Terra, 1976); Carlos Ominami, "Chili: Échec du monetarisme périphérique" and Ricardo Haussmann and Gustavo Márquez, "Venezuela: Du bon coté du choc pétrolier," both in R. Boyer (ed.), *Capitalismes fin de siècle* (Paris: Presses Universitaires de France, 1986); R. Boyer and Julio C. Neffa (eds.), *La economía argentina y sus crises (1976–2001): Visiones institucionalistas y regulacionistas* (Buenos Aires: Miño y Dávila, 2004); Jaime Marques Pereira and Bruno Théret, "Regime politiques, médiation sociales et trajectoires économiques: A propos de la bifurcation des économies brésilienne et mexicaine depuis les années 1970" plus Brasílio Sallum Jr, "Crise économique et changement politique au Brésil et au Méxique: Une critique de l'analyse comparative des héritages institutionnels," in Bruno Lautier and Jaime Marques Pereira (eds.), *Brèsil, Méxique: Deux trajectories dans la mondialisation* (Paris: Karthala, 2003); Robert R. Kaufman, "How societies change developmental models or keep them: Reflections on the Latin American experience in the 1930s and the Postwar World" and René Villareal, "The Latin American strategy of import substitution: Failure or paradigm for the region?," both in Gary Gereffi and Donald L. Wyman (eds.), *Manufacturing Miracles: Paths of*

144   Notes

Industrialization in Latin America and East Asia (Princeton, NJ: Princeton University Press, 1990). See also Larbi Talha, "Théorie de la régulation et développement," plus Jaime Aboites, Luis Miotti, and Carlos Quenan, "Les approches régulationes et l'accumulation en Amérique Latine," in Boyer and Saillard, *op. cit.* For further discussion, see J. M. Domingues, "Modelos de desenvolvimento e desafios latino-americanos" (2006), in *Aproximações à América Latina* (Rio de Janeiro: Civilização Brasileira, 2007).

12. The Departments I and II, respectively of means of production and of means of consumption (basically to reproduce the labor force of the working class), were defined as such by Marx in his study of the theory of "equilibrium" and especially of the dynamic of capitalist social formations. Others have introduced varied definitions of a Department III (production of weapons or superfluous and luxurious means of consumption for the ruling classes). See K. Marx, *op. cit.*, book II, vol. 3 (Berlin: Dietz, [1885] 1965), chap. XX; and Ernest Mandel, *Late Capitalism* (London: New Left Books, [1972] 1975), chaps. 1 and 4.

13. Peter Evans, *Embedded Autonomy. States and Industrial Transformation* (Princeton, NJ: Princeton University Press, 1995), especially pp. 109, 149–60, and 167.

14. Cuba of course chose a very specific and divergent, "real socialist" path since the 1960s.

15. José Nun, "La teoría de la masa marginal (Superpoblación relativa, ejército industrial de reserva y masa marginal" (1969) and "La respuesta a la crítica (Marginalidad y otras cuestiones)" (1971); plus F. H. Cardoso, "La crítica de Cardoso (Comentarios sobre los conceptos de sobrepoblación relativa y marginalidad)" (1970), all now in J. Nun, *Marginalidad y exclusión social* (Buenos Aires and Mexico: Fondo de Cultura Económica, 2001).

16. Aníbal Pinto, "Heterogeneidade e padrão de desenvolvimento recente," in Serra, *op. cit.* Plus Maria da Conceição Tavares and J. Serra, "Além da estagnação. Uma discussão sobre o estilo de desenvolvimento recente do Brasil," in Serra, *op. cit.*, pp. 234–36. These two latter authors warn however against the introduction of any sort of dualistic interpretation in this regard, since there were dynamic connections between sectors. They noted too that heterogeneity was not an impediment for further expansion.

17. R. Boyer, *La Théorie de la régulation: Une analyse critique* (Paris: La Découverte, 1986), p. 102; Manuel Castells, *La Crise économique et la société américaine* (Paris: Presses Universitaires de France, 1976); Luciano Coutinho and Luiz Gonzaga de Mello Belluzzo, "O desenvolvimento do capitalismo avançado e a reorganização da economia mundial no pós-guerra," in L. G. M. Belluzzo and Renata Coutinho (eds.), *Desenvolvimento capitalista e crise no Brasil* (São Paulo: Brasiliense, 1982).

18. Barbara Stallings, "International influence on economic policy: Debt, stabilization, and structural reform," in Stephan Haggard and R. R. Kauffman (eds.), *The Politics of Economic Adjustment: International Constraints, Distributive Conflicts, and the State* (Princeton, NJ: Princeton University Press, 1992), p. 58. Answers to the debt crisis varied from country to country, but increasingly the creditors' cartel and the IMF managed to have uniform perspectives and policies.

19. Serra, *op. cit.*; Marques-Pereira and Théret, *ops. cits.*; Demian Panigo and Edgardo Torija-Zane, "Une approche regulationiste des crisis de l'économie argentine: 1930–2002," *Document de travail* no. 2004–07, CEPREMAP (http://www.cepremap.cnrs.fr); Aboites, Miotti, and Quenan, *op. cit.*; Cepal, "Transformação produtiva com eqüidade: A tarefa prioritária do desenvolvimento da América Latina e do Caribe nos anos 1990" (1990), in Ricardo

Bielschowsly (ed.), *Cinqüenta anos de pensamento na CEPAL,* vol. 2 (Rio de Janeiro: Record, Cepal, and Cofecon, 2000), p. 889. Plus Domingues, "Modelos de desenvolvimento e desafios latino-americanos."

20. Institutionalists may be said to have made a contribution to some extent against the grain, not exactly in terms of political economy, though.

21. Michel Aglietta, *Régulation et crises du capitalisme: L'experience des Etats-Unis* (Paris: Calmon-Levy, 1976).

22. Boyer, *La Théorie de la régulation,* pp. 36–56. The theory of value, he notes, is not actually a point of divide within the broad school. Fordism, on the other hand, has been at the centre of their debate. Idem, "Du fordisme canonique à une variété de modes de développement."

23. Idem, *La Théorie de la régulation,* pp. 60–64.

24. Michel Julliard, "Regimes d'accumulation," in Boyer and Saillard, *op. cit.* See also R. Boyer, "Introduction. Les crises ne sont plus ce qu'elle étaient," in Boyer (ed.), *Capitalismes fin de siècle,* pp. 20–22.

25. Bruno Amable, "La théorie de la régulation et le changement technique," in Boyer and Saillard, *op. cit.;* Boyer, *La Théorie de la régulation,* p. 104.

26. M. Castells, *The Rise of the Network Society: The Information Age: Economy, Society and Culture* (Oxford: Blackwell, 2000, 2nd ed.). I do not see, however, as useful his little argued distinction between "mode of accumulation" and "mode of development" (pp. 13–18).

27. Boyer, "Introduction. Les crises ne sont plus ce qu'elle étaient," p. 19.

28. See David Harvey, *The Postmodern Condition* (Oxford: Blackwell, 1989), Part II.

29. Mandel, *op. cit.,* chap. 6.

30. José Eduardo Cassiolato, Jorge Nogueira de Paiva Brito, and Marcio Antonio Vargas, "Arranjos cooperativos e inovação na indústria brasileira," in João Alberto De Negri and Sérgio Salerno (eds.), *Inovações, padrões tecnológicos e desempenho das firmas industriais* (Brasília: IPEA, 2005), p. 518. Castells, *The Rise of the Network Society,* pp. 174–75.

31. Castells, *The Rise of the Network Society,* passim, but especially pp. 500ff; Luke Boltanski and Eve Chiapello, *Le Nouvel Esprit du capitalisme* (Paris: Gallimard, 1999); Domingues, *Modernity Reconstructed,* chap. 8.

32. Talha, *op. cit.,* pp. 452–53; Aboites, Miotti and Quenan, *op. cit.,* p. 467. It must be noted that especially Cardoso and Faletto (*op. cit.*) stressed the role of internal class alliances for the paths taken by each Latin American country.

33. Talha, *op. cit.,* pp. 454–55. Besides, he notes (p. 456) that most studies about underdevelopment privilege either the salary relationship or the regime of accumulation (the former being stronger in Latin America). See also Alain Lipietz, "Le kaléidoscope des 'Sud,'" in Boyer (ed.), *Capitalismes fin de siècle;* see also Francisco de Oliveira, "Padrões de acumulação, olipólios e Estado no Brasil (1950–1976)," in *A economia da dependência imperfeita* (Rio de Janeiro: Graal, 1977), especially pp. 84–85.

34. Harvey, *op. cit.,* p. 159.

35. See R. Bielschowsly, *op. cit.,* vol. 1, which includes an enlightening introduction by the editor, as well as Prebischi's pieces from the 1940s–1950s, especially his "O desenvolvimento econômico da América Latina e alguns de seus principais problemas" (1962).

36. See, for instance, for mostly technical and labor-related aspects, Jorge Walter and Cecília Senén González (eds.), *La privatización de las telecomunicaciones en América Latina* (Buenos Aires: Eudeba, 1998).

37. Castells, *La Crise économique et la société américaine,* p. 258, and *The Rise of the Network Society,* pp. 95–96.; Susan Strange, *The Retreat of the State: The*

146 Notes

Diffusion of Power in the World Economy (Cambridge: Cambridge University Press, 1996), pp. 42–43 and 199, plus chap. 7.

38. Andrew Nickson and Peter Lambert, "State reform and the 'privatized state' in Paraguay," *Public Administration and Development,* vol. 22 (2002).

39. See Domingues, "Modelos de desenvolvimento e desafios latino-americanos"; C. Quenan, "Peut-on parler d'économies émergentes en Amérique latine?," *Amérique latine, tournant de siècle* (Paris: La Découverte, 1997); Aldo Ferrer, *La economía argentina* (Buenos Aires: Fondo de Cultura Económica, 2005); Ibarra, *op. cit.;* James M. Cypher, "Developing desarticulation within the Mexican economy," *Latin American Perspectives,* vol. 28 (2001); Milton Santos and Maria Laura Silveira, *O Brasil: território e sociedades no início do século XXI* (Rio de Janeiro: Civilização Brasileira, 2004); Roberto Laserna, "Bolivia: La crisis de octubre y el fracaso del ch'enko. Una visión desde la economía política," *Anuario social y político de América Latina y el Caribe,* vol. 7 (2005); M. L. da Silveira (ed.), *Continente em chamas: Globalização e território na América Latina* (Rio de Janeiro: Civilização Brasileira, 2005).

40. The evolution of the auto industry in Argentina, the exemplary branch of the period of state-organized modernity and Fordism as well as of its period of "intensive accumulation," expresses this trend dramatically, when compared to Brazil and Mexico. In 1970, Brazil produced 416,000 motor vehicles, Mexico, 193,000, while Argentine produced 220,000, being the only one to export such products, albeit modestly (1,000 in that same year). In 1989, Brazil produced 914,000 motor vehicles and in 1990 it exported 254,000, whereas Mexico in 1990 achieved the marks of 821,000 and 279,000, respectively (although export of parts was much higher). In 1989, Argentina produced only 100,000 motor vehicles and exported the reduced number of 2,000 in 1990. Cf. Naeyoung Lee and Jeffrey Cason, "Automobile commodity chains in the NICs: A comparison of South Korea, Mexico, and Brazil," in Gary Gereffi and Miguel Korzeniewicz (eds.), *Commodity Chains and Global Capitalism* (Westport, CT: Praeger, 1994), p. 224.

41. Haggard and Kaufman, "Introduction: institutions and economic adjustment," in Haggard and Kaufman, *op. cit.,* p. 3.

42. Idem; plus Moisés Naím, "Latin America: The second stage of reform," *Journal of Democracy,* vol. 5 (1994).

43. Idem; plus Manuel Pastor Jr. and Carol Wise, "The politics of second generation reform," *Journal of Democracy,* vol. 10 (1999).

44. B. Stallings, *op. cit.;* Miles Kahler, "External adjustment, conditionality, and the politics of adjustment," in Haggard and Kaufman, *op. cit.*

45. Between 1970 and 1981, net transfers of resources to Latin America, mainly through lending, achieved an amazing annual rate of 34 percent, interrupted by the Mexican 1982 moratorium; between 1982 and 1989, net transfer of resources in the opposite direction amounted to 1.9 percent. Debt restructuring and international liquidity, as well as a sharp increase in FDI (partly concentrated on privatizations), reversed the trend: In the 1990s, up to the 1998 Asian crisis, net transfers to Latin America picked to the annual average of 35.3 percent, with FDI answering for 44 percent of the net flux of capital. Since then it has remained relatively low, though payment of royalties has risen sharply; Brazil, Argentina, and Mexico concentrated circa 75 percent of this sort of investment between 1995 and 2000. See David Ibarra, "La inversión extranjera," in *Ensayos sobre economía mexicana* (Mexico: Fondo de Cultura Económica, 2005), pp. 196–207.

46. Alexander Gheventer, *Autonomia versus controle. Origens do novo marco regulatório antitruste na América Latina e seus efeitos sobre a democracia* (Belo Horizonte: UFMG, 2005), especially pp. 189–94; Jacint Jordana and David

Notes 147

Levi-Faur, "The diffusion of regulatory capitalism in Latin America: Sectoral and national channels in the making of a new order," *Annals of American Political and Social Sciences Academy*, no. 598 (2005); and "Towards a Latin American regulatory state? The diffusion of autonomous regulatory agencies across countries and sectors," *International Journal of Public Administration*, vol. 29 (2006); and (with Fabrizio Gilard), "Regulation in the age of globalization: The diffusion of regulatory agencies across Europe and Latin America," *IBEI Working Papers*, 2006/1 (2006).

47. Judith Mariscal, "Telecommunications reform in Mexico from a comparative perspective," *Latin American Politics and Society*, vol. 46 (2004).

48. Mônica Herz and Andréa Ribeiro Hoffman, *Organizações internacionais: História e práticas* (Rio de Janeiro: Campus, 2004), chap. 5; J. M. Domingues, "Regionalismos, poder de Estado e desenvolvimento" (2004), in *Aproximações à América Latina*. In any case, this is also an important counterpoint to the signature of free-trade agreements (FTAs) between many Latin American countries (Chile, Colombia, etc.) and the United States in the aftermath of the actual rejection of the Free Trade Area of the Americas (FTAA), as pushed forward by the latter.

49. Marta Novick, "La transformación de la organización del trabajo," in Enrique de la Garza Toledo (ed.), *Tratado Latinoamericano de sociología del trabajo* (Mexico: El Colegio de México, FLACSO, UAM, and Fondo de Cultura Económica, 2000).

50. E. de la Garza Toledo, "Las teorías de la restructuración productiva y América Latina," in Idem, *op. cit.*, p. 729.

51. Idem and also his "La flexibilidad del trabajo en América Latina," both in Idem, *op. cit.*

52. Oliver Williamson, *Markets and Hierarchies* (New York: Free Press, 1975).

53. Gereffi and Korzeniewicz, *op. cit.*; Martina Sproll, "Las redes transnacionales de producción. América Latina, Ásia y Europa del Este en la manufactura por contrato en la industria eletrónica," *Memória*, no. 176 (2003); Paul Hirst and Grahame Thompson, *Globalization in Question* (Cambridge: Polity, 1999, 2nd ed.), chap. 4.

54. Alejandro Portes, M. Castells, and Lauren A. Benton (eds.), *The Informal Economy. Studies in Advanced and Less Developed Countries* (Baltimore, MD and London: Johns Hopkins University Press, 1989).

55. Ferrer, *op. cit.*, pp. 338–39; Bernardo Kosacoff and Adrián Ramos, "Transformaciones estructurales de la producción industrial," in *Cambios contemporáneos en la estructura industrial argentina (1975–2000)* (Bernal: Universidad de Quilmes, 2002); Sano Makoto and Alberto Di Martino, "'Japanization' of the employment relationship: Three cases in Argentina," *Cepal Review*, no. 80 (2003); Martina Miravalles, M. Novick, and C. Senén González, "Vinculaciones interfirmas y competencias laborales en la Argentina. Los casos de la industria automotriz y de las telecomunicaciones," in M. Novick and María A. Gallart (eds.), *Competitividad, redes productivas y competencias laborales* (Montevideo: OIT/CINTRFOR-RE, 1997); J. Walter and C. Senén González, "Cambio tecnológico y redes formales e informales en la industria argentina," *Perfiles latinoamericanos*, año 4, no. 7 (1995).

56. Luciano Coutinho, "Especialização regressiva: um balanço do desempenho industrial pós-estabilização," in João Paulo dos Reis Velloso (ed.), *Brasil: Desafios de um país em transformação* (Rio de Janeiro: José Olympio, 1997); Marco Flávio C. Resende and Patrícia Anderson, "Mudanças estruturais na indústria brasileira de bens de capital," *Textos para discussão*, no. 658 (Brasília: IPEA, 1999); Ricardo Markwald, "O impacto da abertura comercial sobre a indústria brasileira," in J. P. dos Reis Velloso (ed.), *Como vão o desenvolvimento*

148 Notes

e a democracia no Brasil (Rio de Janeiro: José Olympio, 2001); João Carlos Ferraz, David Kupfer, and Mariana Iootty, "Industrial competitiveness in Brazil ten years after economic liberalization," *Cepal Review,* no. 82 (2004); Noela Invernizzi, "Disciplining the workforce. Controlling workers in the restructuring process," *Latin American Perspectives,* vol. 33 (2006); De Negri and Salerno, *op. cit.*

57. José Ricardo Ramalho, "Novas conjunturas industriais e participação em estratégias locais de desenvolvimento" (2005), in J. R. Ramalho and Marco Aurélio Santana (eds.), *Trabalho e desenvolvimento regional: Efeitos sociais da indústria automobilística no Brasil* (Rio de Janeiro: Mauad, 2006); Sproll, *op. cit.;* Ferraz, Kupfer, Iootty, *op. cit.,* p. 109. In this regard, the reflections by Lee and Cason (*op. cit.*) are useful to make clear that—especially in an industry such as motor vehicles, where a car is composed of more than 15,000 parts—outsourcing and networks have been a crucial issue for many years, certainly also in Latin America since the 1960s.

58. Francisco Zapata, *México: Tiempos neoliberales* (Mexico: El Colegio de México, 2005), chap. 2; Gerardo Fuli, Eduardo Candaudap, and Claudia Ganona, "Exportaciones, industria maquiladora y crecimiento económico en México a partir de la década de los noventa," *Investigación económica,* vol. LXIV, no. 254; Ibarra, *op. cit.,* pp. 68–69, 109, 243–86.

59. Sproll, *op. cit.;* Jorge Carrillo and Arturo Lara, "Nuevas capacidades de coordinación centralizadas. ¿Maquilas de cuarta generación en México?," *Estudios sociológicos,* vol. XXII, no. 66.

60. See Fabio S. Erber, "Perspectivas da América Latina em ciência e tecnologia," *Parcerias estratégicas*, no. 8 (2000)—also in J. M. Domingues and María Maneiro (eds.), *América Latina hoje: Conceitos e interpretações* (Rio de Janeiro: Civilização Brasileira, 2006); Fabio Grobart Sunshine, "Situación actual en América Latina respecto a la innovación y la competitividad," paper given at the V Encuentro Latinoamericano de estudios prospectivos, Guadelajara, México (2002); Alberto Melo, "The innovation systems of Latin America and the Caribbean," *Working Paper* #640, Interamerican Development Bank, Research Department (2001); Jorge Katz, "Reformas estruturais orientadas para o mercado, globalização e transformação dos sistemas de inovação latino-americanos," in Ana Célia Castro, Antonio Licha, and Helber Queiroz e João Sabóia (eds.), *Brasil em desenvolvimento*, vol. 1 (Rio de Janeiro: Civilização Brasileira, 2005).

61. M. Castells, *Globalización, desarrollo y democracia: Chile en el contexto mundial* (Mexico and Santiago: Fondo de Cultura Económica, 2005).

62. RICYT, *El estado de la ciencia 2004* (Buenos Aires: RICYT, 2005) (http://www.ricyt.edu.ar).

63. Isabel Bortagaray and Scott Tiffin, "Innovation clusters in Latin America," in M. Heitor, D. Gibson, and M. Ibarra (eds.), *Technology Policy and Innovation,* vol. 1 (New York: Quorum Books, 2002). For a critical view, see Renato Dagnino, "A relação universidade-empresa e o 'argumento da tripla hélice,'" *Convergência*, vol. 11, no. 35 (2000).

64. Kristian Thorn, "Ciencia, tecnología e innovación en Argentina. Un perfil sobre temas y prácticas," World Bank Document, Latin American and Caribean Region (2005) (sitesources.worldbank.org/INTARGENTINASPANISH/).

65. Ibarra, *op. cit.,* p. 280.

66. João Furtado, "O comportamento inovador das empresas industriais no Brasil," *Estudos e pesquisas*, no. 88, INAE (2004).

67. See De Negri and Salerno, *op. cit.,* especially, therein, Cassiolato, Brito, and Vargas, *op. cit.*

Notes   149

68. José Maria Lladós and Samuel Pinheiro Guimarães (eds.), *Perspectivas Brasil y Argentina* (Brasília: IPRI, 1999); Domingues, "Regionalismo, poder de estado e desenvolvimento,"in *Aproximaõpes à América Latina.*
69. Katz, *op. cit.,* p. 375.
70. See, for a recovery of the debate, Aníbal Quijano, *La economía popular y sus caminos en América Latina* (Lima: Mosca Azul, 1998), chap. 2; and, for a contemporary critical discussion, Fernando Cortés, "Las metamorfosis de los marginales: la polémica sobre el sector informal en América Latina," in Garza Toledo, *op. cit.*
71. The main authors with strong positions about this are Offe, Gorz, and Rifkin. For an (excessively) critical discussion, with a Latin American slant, see E. de la Garza Toledo, "Fin del trabajo o trabajo sin fin," in Idem, *op. cit.*
72. J. Nun, "El futuro del empleo y la tesis de la masa marginal" (1999), in Nun, *op. cit.;* also in Domingues and Maneiro, *op. cit.*
73. Cortés, *op. cit.;* A. Portes, M. Castells, and L. A. Benton, "Conclusion: the policy implications of informality," as well as M. Castells and A. Portes, "World underneath: The origins, dynamics, and effects of the informal economy," plus the other articles contained in Portes, Castells, and Benton, *op. cit.;* Maria Cristina Cacciamali, "Régime d'accumulation et processus d'informalité: Le Brésil et le Mexique à l'unisson de l'Amérique Latine," in Lautier and Marques Pereira, *op. cit.*
74. Jürgen Weller, "Tertiary sector employment in Latin America: Between modernity and survival," *Cepal Review,* no. 84 (2004).
75. David de Ferranti, Guillermo Perry, Francisco H. G. Ferreira, Michael Walton et al., *Inequality in Latin America: Breaking with History?* (Washington, DC: World Bank, 2004), pp. 2–10 and chap. 2. Most astonishing is the decay of Argentina into social polarization and the rampant poverty of large amounts of the population, dramatizing the rise of inequality that affected the whole region in the 1990s (with marginal gains in countries such as Brazil). They refrain from the obvious conclusion, though: that the "promarket" reforms of the time were, in this sense, let alone others, devastating, assuming a supposedly more neutral position (p. 10).
76. Fernando Fajnzynlber, "Industrialização na América Latina: Da 'caixa preta' ao conjunto vazio" (1990), in Bielschowsky, *op. cit.,* pp, 863–66. Gino Germani, *Política y sociedad en una época de transición* (Buenos Aires: Paidos, 1965), pp. 102–3.
77. See Silveira, *op. cit.;* for the views from ECLA (and especially Raúl Prebisch's), see Bielschowsly, *op. cit.,* and, especially for Marxism, Mandel, *op. cit.,* chap. 11. Both currents, despite their distinct conceptual apparatuses and understandings, focus on the concentration of technical progress and forms of less labor-intensive production at the center as the means whereby it drains rent from the periphery, refusing the liberal theory of comparative advantages.
78. Jorge Bengoa, "25 años de estudios rurales," *Sociologias,* no. 10 (2003); Cristóbal Kay, "Agrarian reform and the neoliberal counter-reform in Latin America," in Jacquelyn Chase (ed.), *The Spaces of Neoliberalism: Land, Place and Family in Latin America* (Bloomfield, CT: Kumarian, 2002).
79. Domingues, "Modelos de desenvolvimento e desafios latino-americanos"; Enrique Arceo, *Argentina en la periferia próspera: Renta internacional, dominación oligárquica y modo de acumulación* (Bernal: Universidad Nacional de Quilmes, 2003); Ferrer, *op. cit.,* pp. 341–42; Norman Long and Bryan Roberts, "The agrarian structure of Latin America," in L. Bethel (ed.), *The Cambridge History of Latin America,* vol. VI, part I (Cambridge: Cambridge University Press, 1994); Walter A. Pengue, *Agricultura industrial y transnacionalización*

150 Notes

en América Latina (Mexico: UACM and PNUMA, 2005); Zapata, *op. cit.,* pp. 26–28; Heather L. Williams, *Social Movements and Economic Transition: Markets and Distributive Conflict in Mexico* (Cambridge: Cambridge University Press, 2001); Yolanda Massieu Trigo et al., "Consecuencias de la biotecnologia en México: El caso de los cultivos transgenicos," *Sociológica,* año 15, no. 43 (2000); Walter L. Goldfrank, "Fresh demand: the consumption of Chilean produce in the United States," in Gereffi and Korzeniewicz, *op. cit.;* Oscar Landerretche, C. P. Ominami, and Mario Lanzarotti, "El desarrollo de Chile en la encrucijada: O cómo viejas controversias impiden abordar nuevos problemas," *Foro 21,* no. 34 (2004); José Garcia Gasques et al., "Desempenho e crescimento do agronegócio no Brasil," *Textos para discussão,* no. 1009 (Rio de Janeiro: IPEA, 2004).

80. Suzane Wilson and Marta Zabrano, "Cocaine, commodity chains, and drug politics: a transnational approach," in Gereffi and Korzeniewicz, *op. cit;* César Enrique Ortiz, "Cultivos ilícitos y nueva ruralidad en Colombia," *Cuadernos de desarrollo rural,* no. 50 (2003).

81. Fernando Coronil, *El Estado mágico. Naturaleza, dinero y modernidad en Venezuela* (Caracas: Nueva Sociedad, 2002); Bernard Mommer, "Petróleo subversivo," in Steve Ellner and Daniel Hellinger (eds.), *La política venezoelana en la época de Chávez* (Caracas: Nueva Sociedad, [2002] 2003).

82. Quenan, "Peut-on parler d'économies emergentes en Amérique Latine?," p. 51.

83. Overall, growth in 2006 was a bit higher than 5 percent. Mexico and Brazil, with less than 3 percent, did especially badly. At least internal markets have shown some more strength, even though exports remain crucial for the model. Cepal, *Balance preliminar de las economías latinoamericanas 2006,* pp. 9–23; Domingues, "Modelos de desenvolvimento e desafios latinoamericanos."

84. See R. Boyer, "Is finance-led growth a viable alternative to Fordism? A preliminary analysis," *Economy and Society,* vol. 29; Graciela Moguillansky, Rogerio Studart, and Sebastián Vergara, "Foreign banks in Latin America: A paradoxical result," *Cepal Review,* no. 82 (2004).

85. See Benjamin Coriat, "Régimen de convertibilidad, acumulación y crisis en la Argentina de los años noventa. Un enfoque en términos de formas institucionales," in Neffa and Boyer, *op. cit.*

86. Ferrer, *op. cit.,* p. 355.

87. Cardoso and Faletto, *op. cit.,* pp. 25ff.

88. F. H. Cardoso, "Teoria da dependência ou análise concreta de situações de dependência?" (1975), in *O modelo político brasileiro* (São Paulo: Difel, 1977). See also Vladimir I. Lenin, *Imperialism, the Higher Stage of Capitalism: A Popular Outline* (1917), in *Collected* Works, vol. 22 (Moscow: Progressive Publishers, 1934).

89. See Marcos Nobre et al., *Desenvolvimento Sustentável: a institucionalização de um conceito* (Brasília: IBAMA; São Paulo: CEBRAP, 2002); and J. M. Domingues and Andrea C. Pontual, "Environmental responsibility and the public sphere in Latin America," in Tuama Ó Seamus (ed.), *The Critical Theory of Piet Strydom* (New York: IB Taurus, 2007); also in *Aproximações à América Latina.* María Pilar García-Guadilla, "El movimiento ambientalista y la constitucionalización de nuevas racionalidades: dilemmas y desafíos," *Revista venezoelana de economía y ciencias sociales,* vol. 7 (2001).

90. Cf. Theodor W. Adorno and Max Horkheimer, *Dialektik der Aufklärung* (Frankfurt am Main: Fisher, [1944] 1984); Ulrich Beck, *Risk Society* (London: Sage, [1986] 1992).

Notes 151

91. See Nestor García Canclini, *Consumidores e cidadãos: Conflitos multiculturais da globalização* (Rio de Janeiro: Editora UFRJ, 1995).

NOTES TO CHAPTER 3

1. It can be argued that racial classification and stratification were ever-lasting inventions of Europeans precisely at the initial moments of colonization. See Aníbal Quijano, "Colonialidad del poder, eurocentrismo y América Latina," in Edgardo Lander (ed.), *La colonialidad del saber: Eurocentrismo y ciencias sociales: Perspectivas latinoamericanas* (Buenos Aires: CLACSO, 1993).
2. Richard Morse, *El espejo de Próspero* (Mexico: Siglo XI, 1982).
3. Martin S. Lipset and Aldo Solari (eds.), *Elites in Latin America* (New York: Oxford University Press, 1967); Fernando Henrique Cardoso and Enzo Faletto, *Dependência e desenvolvimento na América Latina* (Rio de Janeiro: Zahar, 1970).
4. Göran Therborn, *Between Sex and Power: Family in the World* (London and New York: Routledge, 2004), pp. 18–19, 34–37, 90–91, 157–60 (quotation taken from the latter).
5. José Medina Echevarría, *Consideraciones sociológicas sobre el desarrollo económico* (Buenos Aires: Solar y Hachette, 1964), pp. 33–34, 38ff.
6. Theborn, *op. cit.*, pp. 90, 169–70, 282–83; Irma Arriagada, "Changes and inequality in Latin American families," *Cepal Review*, no. 77 (2002) and "Transformaciones sociales y demográficas de las familias latinoamericanas," *Papeles de población*, no. 40 (2004)—also in José Maurício Domingues and María Maneiro (eds.), *América Latina hoje: Conceitos e interpretações* (Rio de Janeiro: Civilização Brasileira, 2006); Thomas W. Merrick, "The population of Latin America, 1930–1990," in Leslie Bethel (ed.), *The Cambridge History of Latin America*, vol. 6, part 2 (Cambridge: Cambridge University Press, 1994).
7. Angel Rama, *La ciudad letrada* (Montevideo: Ediciones del Norte, 1984); José Luís Romero, *Latinoamérica. La ciudad y las ideas* (Buenos Aires: Siglo XX, [1976] 2004).
8. See Benedict Anderson, *Imagined Communities. Reflections on the Original Spread of Nationalism* (London: Verso, 1991).
9. J. M. Domingues, "Nationalism in South and Central America," in Gerard Delanty and Krishan Kumar (eds.), *Handbook of Nationalism* (London: Routledge, 2006)—also in J. M. Domingues, *Aproximações à América Latina* (Rio de Janeiro: Civilização Brasileira, 2007); José Murilo de Carvalho, *A construção da ordem: A elite política imperial* (Rio de Janeiro: Campus, 1980); Rama, *op. cit.*; Miguel Angel Centeno, *Blood and Debt. War and the Nation State in Latin America* (University Park: Pennsylvania University Press, 2002); Lawrence Whitehead, "State organization in Latin America since 1930," in Bethel, *op. cit.*, part 2.
10. Domingues, *op. cit.*; Peter Wade, *Race and Ethnicity in Latin America* (London: Pluto, 1997), chap. 3; Renato Ortiz, "From incomplete modernity to world modernity," *Daedalus*, vol. 129 (2000).
11. The bibliography for this topic, especially with respect to the working classes, is truly large. See Hobart Spalding Jr., *Organized Labor in Latin America* (New York: Harper & Row, 1987); Ian Roxborough, "The urban working class and labour movement since 1930," and (specifically for peasant corporatism, basically in Bolivia) Guillermo de la Peña, "Rural mobilizations in Latin America since c. 1920," in Bethel, *op. cit.*, part 2. For businesspeople, see especially Renato R. Boschi, "Democratización y restructuración del sector

152   Notes

privado en América Latina," *Síntesis*, no. 22 (1994)—also in Domingues and Maneiro, *op. cit.*; and Ben Ross Schneider, *Business Politics and the State in Twentieth Century Latin America* (Cambridge: Cambridge University Press, 2004). On a different note, but related to this, a couple of decades ago some even argued that Latin America, plagued by its Iberian heritage, was anti-individualist, authoritarian and had therefore corporatism as its, say, "natural" expression. For an overview, see João Feres Jr., *A história do conceito de América Latina nos Estados Unidos* (Bauru: EDUSC/ANPOCS, 2005), chap. 6. But only Morse's (*op. cit.*) later texts and culture-oriented account seem to me, despite tendencies toward essentialism, truly interesting insofar as he stops short of that, instead stressing a truly important point in the Iberian matrix: There was no contradiction between lending the state a prominent role in the organization of society and extreme individualism in what regards subjectivity and responsibility as for one's interests.

12. For general overviews and case studies, see Scott Mainwaring and Thimoty R. Scully (eds.), *Building Democratic Institutions* (Stanford, CA: Stanford University Press, 1995); Marcelo Cavarozzi and Juan Abal Medina, hj (eds.), *El asedio a la política: Los partidos latinoamericanos en la era neoliberal* (Rosario: Homo Sapiens, 2002).

13. For a review of the literature on the military regimes, see José Luis Fiori, "Para uma crítica da teoria latino-americana do Estado," in *Em busca do dissenso perdido* (Rio de Janeiro: Insight, 1995). The main classic on such regimes is Guillermo O'Donnell, *Bureaucratic Authoritarianism. Argentina, 1966–1973 in Comparative Perspective* (Berkeley and Los Angeles: University of California Press, 1988).

14. Juan Carlos Portantiero, "La múltiple transformación del Estado latinoamericano," *Nueva sociedad*, no. 104 (1989); Florestan Fernandes, *Capitalismo dependente e classes sociais* (Rio de Janeiro: Zahar, 1975), pp. 60, 73–74. Although empirically misguided in his views as to Latin America and in spite of a false opposition between (neo)patrimonialism and the nation-state, some conceptual clues can be found in Shmuel N. Eisenstadt, *Traditional Patrimonialism and Modern Neopatrimonialism* (Sage Research Papers in the Social Sciences, vol. 1—Beverly Hills, CA, and London: Sage, 1973).

15. Michael Mann, "La crisis del Estado-nación en América Latina," *Desarrollo económico*, vol. 44, no. 174 (2004)—also in Domingues and Maneiro, *op. cit.*

16. Whitehead, *op. cit.*; G. O'Donnell, "Acerca del Estado en América Latina contemporanea: Diez tesis para discusión," in G. O'Donnell et al., *La democracia en América Latina: Hacia una democracia de ciudadanas y ciudadanos—Contribuciones para el debate* (PNUD, 2004), especially pp. 175–77; Peter Spinx, "Possibilities and political imperatives: Seventy years of administrative reform in Latin America," in Luiz Carlos Bresser Pereira and P. Spinx (eds.), *Reforming the State. Managerial Public Administration* (Boulder, CO: Lynne Rinner, 1999). And, for a discussion of "conventionalizations" in the second phase of modernity, see once again Peter Wagner, *A Sociology of Modernity: Liberty and Discipline* (London: Routledge, 1994).

17. Orlandina de Oliveira and Bryan Roberts, "Urban growth and the social structure in Latin America, 1930–1990," in Bethel, *op. cit.*, part 1; Cardoso and Faletto, *op. cit.*, pp. 71ff, 91ff. When planning remained abstract and detached from such interests, state action seems to have been blocked, cf. Carlos A. de Mattos, "Estado, procesos de decision y planificación en América Latina," *Revista de la Cepal*, no. 31 (1987). A more balanced view is found in Albert O. Hirschman, *Journeys toward Progress: Studies of Economic Policy-Making in Latin America* (New York: Anchor Books, 1965). In any case, the

Notes   153

extreme developmentalist voluntarism of the Brazilian state under General Geisell's presidency in the mid-1970s was by no means ineffective. See José Luís Fiori, "Para uma economia política do Estado brasileiro," in *op. cit.*

18. Fernandes, *op. cit.*, pp. 58, 60–63, 69–70, 73–74, 105–8; F. H. Cardoso, *Política e desenvolvimento em sociedades dependentes: Ideologias do empresariado industrial argentino e brasileiro* (Rio de Janeiro: Zahar, 1971), especially pp. 201–5; Cardoso and Faletto, *op. cit.*, pp. 114ff; Oliveira and Roberts, *op. cit.*; Alejandro Portes, "Latin American class structures: Their composition and change during the last decades," *Latin American Research Review*, vol. 20 (1985). As Fernandes noted some decades ago, social classes were—and remain—a badly studied phenomena in Latin America. Within business associations, tensions between national and transnational capital can in any case be spotted. See Schneider, *op. cit.*, pp. 46–49.

19. Alain Touraine, *La Parole et le sang* (Paris: Odile Jacob, 1988), pp. 447–51. This is at variance, I believe, with the ideas contained in his *Le Retour de l'acteur* (Paris: Fayard, 1984). The concept of "populism" features prominently in Gino Germani, *Sociedad y política en una época de transición* (Buenos Aires: Paidós, 1965). However, differently from those who used it later (including some Marxist authors), he was much clearer about the role those "national-popular" movements meant for the working classes in terms of the increase of concrete *freedom*. See J. M. Domingues and M. Maneiro, "Revisiting Germani: The interpretation of modernity and the theory of action," *Dados* w/no. (Scielo, 2005—http://www.scielo.com.br)—also in *Aproximações à América Latina*. I shall not employ such a concept of "populism" at all here since I do not see analytical strength in it. It has in fact operated as an attempt to frame Latin American modernity in a teleological model—populism would represent then merely a distorted move in the transition to modernity. Or else it provides for a disqualification of popular-oriented governments, beyond occasional demagoguery, certainly not a privilege of the subcontinent. A more circumspect view, which points to the mix of elements with different class origins in its discourse, is found in Ernesto Laclau, "Towards a theory of populism," in *Politics and Ideology in Marxist Theory. Capitalism, Fascism, Populism* (London: New Left Books, 1977). For a mix of both, emphasizing the multiclass nature of "populism" and the manipulative role of new political leadership, see Octávio Ianni, *A formação do Estado populista na América Latina* (Rio de Janeiro: Civilização Brasileira, 1975).

20. Oliveira and Roberts, *op. cit.*, especially p. 315; de la Peña, *op. cit.*; Touraine, *op. cit.*

21. Portes, *op. cit.*; Ruth Corrêa L. Cardoso, "Movimentos sociais na América Latina," *Revista Brasileira de Ciências Sociais*, no. 3, vol. 1 (1987).

22. The theory of collective subjectivity was elaborated especially in J. M. Domingues, *Sociological Theory and Collective Subjectivity* (London: Macmillan; and New York: St. Martin's Press, 1995). See also my "Social and System Integration," *Sociology*, vol. 34 (2000), and "Collective Subjectivity and Collective Causality," *Philosophica*, vol. (2003).

23. See, for the main texts, Karl Marx and Friedrich Engels, "Manifest der kommunistischen Partei" (1848), pp. 466–67, 470–74, and *Die deutsche Ideologie* (1845), pp. 60–62, both in *Werke*, vol. 4 (Berlin: Dietz, 1939); K. Marx, *Misère de la Philosophie* (1847), in *Oeuvres*, vol. 1 (Paris: Gallimard, 1963), p. 135, and *Der 18te Brumaire Luis Bonapartes* (1852), in *Werke*, vol. 8 (Berlin: Dietz, 1960), p. 199. This sort of perspective is clearly reproduced, for instance, in Erik Olin Wright, *Class Counts* (Cambridge: Cambridge University Press; and Paris: Maison des Sciences de l'Homme, 1997), pp. 3, 379–88. Marx's later discussion in *Das Kapital,* especially in vols. I and III (Berlin:

154 Notes

Dietz, respectively *Mega-II*, [1867] 1987; and Marx & Engels, *Werke,* vol. 25, [1894] 1964) might be read in a way closer to the discussion about practical reflexivity as developed below, especially insofar as it is a critique of the economicist reification of Political Economy. Thereby he wanted to show that its economic categories (especially labor, capital, and land rent) were reified expressions of social collectivities and the differential appropriation of surplus value. However, he did not work the issue out.

24. Max Weber, *Wirtschaft und Gesellschaft* (Tübing: J. C. B. Mohr—Paul Siebeck, [1921–1922] 1980), pp. 177–79, 531–39.

25. Nicos Poulantzas, *Pouvoir politique et classes sociales* (Paris: Maspero, [1968] 1975), vol. 1, pp. 66ff.

26. Anthony Giddens, *The Class Structure of Advanced Societies* (New York: Harper & Row, [1973] 1975), pp. 101–13.

27. Giddens, *op. cit.,* pp. 160ff, 173ff; Wright, *op. cit.,* especially pp. 19–26.

28. I put forward these concepts in J. M. Domingues, *Social Creativity, Collective Subjectivity and Contemporary Modernity* (London: Macmillan; and New York: St. Martin's Press, 2000), chaps. 1–2; and in "Reflexividade, individualismo e modernidade" (2002), in *Ensaios de sociologia* (Belo Horizonte: Editora UFMG, 2003).

29. Weber, *op. cit.,* p. 240.

30. See, for a full exploration of such issues, Guillermo Trejo, "Etinicidad y movilización social: Una revisión teórica con aplicaciones a la 'cuarta ola' de movilizaciones indígenas en América Latina," *Política y gobierno,* vol. 7 (2000)—also in Domingues and Maneiro (eds.), *América Latina hoje.*

31. Carlos Hasenbalg, *Discriminação e desigualdades raciais no Brasil* (Belo Horizonte: Editora UFMG, [1979] 2005), chap. 3; Stuart Hall, "The question of cultural identity," in S. Hall, David Held, and Tony Magrew (eds.), *Modernity and Its Futures* (Cambridge: Polity, 1992), pp. 120ff; P. Wade, *Race, Nature, and Culture* (London: Pluto Press, 2002), especially chaps. 1–2. To some extent it is exact too that ethnicity often entails racial overtones as Wade (*Race and Ethnicity in Latin America,* pp. 37–39) argues; but the opposite is not necessarily true.

32. See Sylvia Walby, *Theorizing Patriarchy* (Oxford: Blackwell, 1990), pp. 3, 103–6, 111–12.

33. See Karl Mannheim, "The problem of generations" (1928), in *Essays on the Sociology of Knowledge* (London: Routledge & Kegan Paul, 1952); and J. M. Domingues, "Para uma teoria das gerações" (2002), in *Ensaios de sociologia.*

34. The rationalization of a previously existing collective subjectivity—German "traditionalists" become "conservatives"—was analyzed theoretically by K. Mannheim, "Conservative thought" (1925), in *Essays on Sociology and Social Psychology* (London: Routledge & Kegan Paul, 1953).

35. Luis Tapia, *La condición multisocietal: Multiculturalidad, pluralismo, modernidad* (La Paz: Muela del Diablo, 2002), pp. 101–14.

36. For social movements, see Sidney Tarrow, *Power in Movement. Social Movements, Collective Action and Politics* (Cambridge: Cambridge University Press, 1994); Alberto Melucci, *Challenging Codes. Collective Action in the Information Age* (Cambridge: Cambridge University Press, 1996); J. M. Domingues, "Vida cotidiana, história e movimentos sociais" (2003), in *Ensaios de sociologia;* and "Os movimentos sociais latino-americanos: Características e possibilidades" (2007), in *Aproximações à América Latina.* The idea of "costs" (and benefits), for which Tarrow draws upon Olson, is however too a priori and hardly agrees with much of what can be empirically observed, the same happening with Melucci's actual refusal of formal politics and absolutization of culture as the goal of contemporary social movements.

Notes 155

37. J. M. Domingues, *Modernity Reconstructed* (Cardiff: University of Wales Press, 2006), chap. 6, plus "Nationalism in South and Central America"; Hall, *op. cit.*

38. N. Poulantzas, *L'Etat, le pouvoir, le socialisme* (Paris: Presses Universitaires de France, 1978), pp. 18, 143–44, 153–56, 161–62, 170ff.

39. M. Mann, *The Sources of Social Power*, vol. 2. The Rise of Classes and Nation-States, 1760–1974 (Cambridge: Cambridge University Press, 1993), pp. 53–59, 75–81.

40. Poulantzas, *Pouvoir politique et classes sociales*, vol. II, chap. 4 (which includes a criticism of what he saw as Gramsci's "historicism"); Antonio Gramsci, *Quaderni dei carcere* (Turin: Einaudi, [1929–1935] 2001), vol. 2, pp. 1051–52, 1211–35; vol. 3, pp. 1559–66, 1569, 2010–11.

41. Domingues, *Modernity Reconstructed*, chaps. 1–2.

42. Néstor García Canclini, *Culturas híbridas: Estrategias para entrar y salir de la modernidad* (Mexico: Grijalbo, 1990). He is clearer about the meaning of hybridism in his "Antropología y estudios culturales: Una agenda de fin de siglo," in José Manuel Valenzuela Arce (ed.), *Los estudios culturales en México* (Mexico: Conaculta and Fondo de Cultura Económica, 2003), pp. 42, 48–49. There he speaks of hybridism in more than one register: As to "temporal heterogeneity" of subsisting social forms and in terms of a mix of "the traditional and the modern, the learned, the popular, and the massive;" it would consist of a descriptive category, which may be workable for explications as well as a resource for hermeneutics. He is interested in hybridization processes rather than in hybridism per se.

43. Cf. Jan Nederveen Pieterse, *Globalization & Culture* (Laham, MD: Rowman & Littlefield, 2004).

44. I cannot elaborate the issue here. Suffice it to say that by modern tradition I mean the imaginary and institutional elements of modernity as such. Cf. Domingues, *Social Creativity, Collective Subjectivity and Contemporary Modernity*, chap. 5.

45. Tapia, *op. cit.*, especially pp. 9–19, 57–72.

46. Sérgio Zermeño, *La sociedad derrotada. El desorden mexicano del fin de siglo* (Mexico: Siglo XXI, [1996] 2001).

47. Maristella Svampa (ed.), *Desde abajo: La transformación de las identidades sociales* (Buenos Aires: Biblos, 2000); Romeo Grompone, *Las nuevas reglas de juego: Transformaciones sociales, culturales y políticas en Lima* (Lima: IEP, 1999), especially pp. 13–14, 65–68, 299–302, 311; Norbert Lechner, "Os desafios das mudanças culturais sob a democracia," *Novos estudos CEBRAP*, no. 68 (2004); Manuel Castells, *Globalización, desarrollo y democracia: Chile en el contexto mundial* (Mexico and Santiago: Fondo de Cultura Económica, 2005), chap. 4.

48. Domingues, "Collective Subjectivity and Collective Causality."; *Sociological Theory and Collective Subjectivity*, chap 1.

49. Marcio Pochmann et al., *Atlas da exclusão social no Brasil*, vol. 3. Os ricos no Brasil (São Paulo: Cortez, 2004), especially chap. 2; A. Portes and Kelly Hoffman, "Latin American class structures: Their composition and change during the neoliberal era," *Latin American Research Review*, vol. 38 (2003), p. 42.

50. For a former overview, see Domingues, "Os movimentos sociais latino-americanos: características e possibilidades."

51. Cf. Chiara Saraceno, *Anatomia della famiglia* (Bari: De Donato, 1976).

52. Arriagada, *op. cit.*; Marina Ariza and O. de Oliveira, "Familias en transición y marcos conceptuales en redefinición," *Papeles de Población*, no. 28 (2001); Brígida García and Olga Lorena Rojas, "Cambios en la formación

156   Notes

y disolución de las uniones en América Latina," *Papeles de población,* no. 32 (2002); Julieta Quilodran, "La familia, referentes en transición," *Papeles de población,* no. 37 (2003); Jorge A. Rodriguez Vignoli, "¿Cohabitación en América Latina: Modernidad, exclusion o diversidad?," *Papeles de población,* no. 40 (2004).

53. Celad, *La transición demográfica en América Latina* (2000) (http://www. wclac.cl./Celade/SitDem/DE). In any case, family size does not seem to vary significantly if ethnic or racial variables are taken into account. Cf. David de Ferranti, Guillermo E. Perry, Francisco H. G. Ferreira, Michael Walton et al., *Inequality in Latin America. Breaking with History* (Washington, DC: The World Bank, 2004), p. 90.

54. Jeni Vaitsman, "Pluralidade de mundos entre mulheres urbanas de baixa renda," *Estudos feministas,* vol. 5; Arriagada, *op. cit.;* Ariza and Oliveira, *op. cit.;* Elsa S. Guevarra Ruiseñor, "Intimidad y modernidad. Precisiones conceptuales y su pertinencia para el caso de México," *Estudios sociológicos,* vol. 33 (2005).

55. Cepal, *Panorama social de América Latina* (2004), p. 35

56. Ferranti, Perry, Ferreira, Walton et al., *op. cit.,* pp. 85, 87–89, 104–5 (authors' tabulations using a mix of national samples). Gender statistics are directly derived from sex criteria (p. 90), an unproblematic move, I believe, insofar as the issue goes.

57. Nancy Saporta Sternbach, Narysa Navarro-Aranguren, Patricia Chuchryk, and Sonia E. Alvarez, "Feminisms in Latin America: From Bogotá to San Bernardo," in Arturo Escobar and S. E. Alvarez (eds.), *The Making of Social Movements in Latin America: Identity, Strategy, and Democracy* (Boulder, CO: Westview, 1992); S. E. Alvarez, "Latin America feminisms 'go global': Trends of the 19990s and challenges for the New Millennium," in S. E. Alvarez, Evelina Dagnino, and A. Escobar (eds.), *Culture of Politics, Politics of Culture: Revisioning Latin American Social Movements* (Boulder, CO: Westview, 1998).

58. Cepal, *op. cit.,* pp. 14, 27.

59. Michel Maffesoli, *Le temp des tribus: Le Déclin du individualisme dans les sociétés de masse* (Paris: Grasset, 1992).

60. *Nómadas,* no. 23 (2005); Mario Margulis and Marcelo Urresti, "Buenos Aires y los jóvenes: Las tribus urbanas," *Estudios sociológicos,* vol. 46 (1995); Cepal, *op. cit.,* pp. 26–34. For further conceptual insights, see Jesús Martín-Barbero, *Al sur de la modernidad: Comunicación, globalización y multiculturalidad* (Pittsburgh, PA: Instituto Internacional de Literatura—Pittsburgh University, 2001), pp. 197–201, 232ff.

61. Maritza Urteaga Castro-Pozo and Carlos Feixo Pámpolis, "De jóvenes, músicas y las dificultades de integrarse," in N. García Canclini (ed.), *op. cit.,* p. 285.

62. J. Martín-Barbero, "Proyectos de modernidad en América Latina," *Metapolítica,* no. 42 (2004)—also in Domingues and Maneiro (eds.), *América Latina hoje.* While I rather speak of modernizing moves related to availability and re-embeddings, it is worthwhile noting that "post-modernism" was in great measure originally defined in this connection—idleness and consumption versus the asceticism of the Protestant ethic. Cf. Daniel Bell, *The Coming of Post-Industrial Society* (New York: Basic Books, 1976).

63. Domingues, "Nationalism in South and Central America."

64. Manuel A. Vasquez and Philip J. Williams, "Introduction: The power of religious identities in the Americas," *Latin American Perspectives,* vol. 32 (2005).

65. There is a large debate here, of course. See mainly Jeffrey Hadden, "Toward desacralizing secularization theory," *Social Forces,* vol. 65 (1987); Steve Bruce.

Religion in the Modern World: From Cathedrals to Cult (Oxford: Oxford University Press, 1996); Flávio Pierruci, "Secularização em Max Weber: Da contemporânea serventia de voltarmos a acessar aquele velho conceito," *Revista Brasileira de Ciências Sociais*, no. 37 (1998).

66. I cannot do justice to the full range of literature on this topic. But see, for overviews: Cristián Parker Gumucio, "¿América Latina ya no es católica? Pluralismo cultural y religioso creciente," *América Latina Hoy*, vol. 41 (2000); Yvon le Bot, "Churches, sects and communities: Social cohesion recovered?" and Cristian Gros, "Evangelical Protestantism and indigenous populations," both in *Bulletin of Latin American Studies*, vol. 18 (1999); Toomas Gross, "Protestantism and modernity: The implications of religious change in contemporary rural Oaxaca," *Sociology of Religion: A Quartely Review*, vol. 64 (2003); Jean-Pierre Bastian, "Le Monopole de l'Église Catholique menacé," in Georges Couffignal (ed.), *Amérique Latine tournant de siècles* (Paris: La Découverte, 1997). See also, Martín-Barbero, *Al sur de la modernidad*, pp. 178–80.

67. Max Weber, *Gesammelte Aufsätze zur Religionssoziologie* (Tübingen: J. C. B. Mohr—Paul Siebeck, [1920] 1988).

68. Andrew Canessa, "Contesting hybridity: Evangelistas and Kataristas in Highland Bolivia," *Journal of Latin American Studies*, vol. 32 (2000).

69. Ferranti, Perry, Ferreira, Walton et al., *op. cit.*, pp. 78–84 (authors' tabulations using a mix of national samples).

70. Idem, pp. 92–96, 104–5 (authors' tabulations using a mix of national samples). To my best knowledge, there are no comprehensive statistics for the racial and ethnic composition of classes in Latin America. Nonetheless, income analyses, such as those reproduced above, as well as historical interpretations (Idem, chap. 4), strongly evince the overwhelming predominance of whites in the upper classes of the subcontinent.

71. Axel Honneth, *Kampf um Annerkenung* (Frankfurt am Main: Suhrkamp, 1992).

72. Trejo, *op. cit.;* Wade, *Race and Ethnicity in Latin America*, chaps. 6–7; Armando Bartra, "Los apocalípitcos y los integrados: Indios y campesinos en la encrucijada," *Memoria*, no. 190 (2004).

73. Xavier Albó, "Ethnic identity and politics in the Andes: The cases of Bolivia, Peru and Ecuador," in Jo-Marie Burt and Philip Mauceri (eds.), *Politics in the Andes. Identity, Conflict, Reform* (Pittsburgh, PA: University of Pittsburgh Press, 2004). See Grompone (*op. cit.*) for a colorful picture of Lima.

74. Othón Baños Ramírez, *Modernidad, imaginario e identidades rurales—el caso de Yucatán* (Mexico: El Colegio de México, 2003), especially pp. 266–67.

75. Wade, *Race and Ethnicity in Latin America*, chaps. 6–7; Livio Sansone, *Blackness without Ethnicity: Constructing Race in Brazil* (London and New York: Palgrave Macmillan, 2003); Pierre Bourdieu and Loïc Wacquant, "Sur les ruses de la raison imperialiste," *Actes de la recherche en sciences socials*, nos. 121–22 (1988); Sérgio Costa, *As cores de Ercília* (Belo Horizonte: Editora UFMG, 2002), chap. 7.

76. Marcela A. Hernández Romo, "Perspectiva sociológica de los actores empresariales," in Enrique de la Garza Toledo (ed.), *Tratado latinoamericano de sociología* (Rubí, Barcelona: Anthropos; and Mexico: UAM, 2006), p. 216.

77. Portes and Hoffman, op. cit. especially pp. 45–65. These numbers derive from the means of eight Latin American countries—Brazil, Chile, Colombia, Costa Rica, El Salvador, Mexico, Panama, Venezuela—which amount to three-fourths of the region's EAP; they draw upon ECLAC's data (Table 1). The obvious problem here is that their class "structure," due especially albeit not only to very distinct levels of industrialization, should be more differentiated.

158 Notes

However, strangely this does not show when Portes and Kelly present data from each country (Table 2). The data for other countries, such as Argentina (Great Buenos Aires), Bolivia, Uruguay, Paraguay (Asunción), Honduras, and Ecuador, present basically the same profile (Table 3). To be sure, their substantialist definition of an informal proletariat—as well as of a formal one—has to be criticized as inadequate: I have put forward in Chapter 2 a proposal to treat these two dimensions in analytical terms instead.

78. Pochmann et al., *op. cit.* For Brazil and Mexico, some further class analysis is available. In the former, two authors have dealt with the problem. Olin Wright's model has served for one detailed assessment of the countries' class "structure" (stopping right there, however). Santos has found in Brazil a very small percentage of capitalists (0.5 to 0.7), whereas the working class comprises exactly half of the population, with a huge number of intermediate layers (small-business owners, the petty bourgeoisie, middle classes, self-employed people) in between. Although data are not really comparable, his findings are not too far from Portes and Kelly's in a general way. In Mexico, the position of the very rich was studied in an approximate manner by More as well as by de la Torre García, with very partial data. The latter states that the number of millionaires in Mexico exceeds what is found in other countries; the former concentrates on physical and financial assets, which are even more concentrated than income. See José Alcides F. Santos, *Estrutura de posições de classe no Brasil: Mapeamento, mudanças e efeito na renda* (Belo Horizonte: Editora UFMG, 2002), chap. 2; Héctor Moreno, "Riqueza y niveles de vida de los hogares en México" and Rodolfo de la Torre García, "Los ricos en México," both in *Comercio Exterior—Revista de análisis económico y social,* vol. 56 (2006).
79. M. Svampa, *La sociedad excluyente. La Argentina bajo el signo del neoliberalismo* (Buenos Aires: Taurus, 2005), chaps. 4–6 (quotation from p. 119).
80. Enrique Arceo and Eduardo M. Basualdo, "Los cambios en los sectores dominantes en América Latina bajo el neoliberalismo: La problemática propuesta," in E. M. Basualdo and E. Arceo (eds.), *Neoliberalismo y sectores dominantes: Tendencias globales y experiencias nacionales* (Buenos Aires: CLACSO, 2006), pp. 18, 20–22; Daniel Aspiazu and E. Basualdo, "Las privatizaciones en la Argentina: Genesis, desarrollo y los impactos estructurales"; Atilio Borón and Mabel Thwaites Rey, "La expropriación neoliberal: El experimento privatista en Argentina"; and John Saxe-Fernández and M. T. Rey, "La desnacionalización integral de México," all in James Petras and Henry Veltmeyer (eds.), *Las privatizaciones y la desnacionalización de América Latina* (Buenos Aires: Prometeo, 2004).
81. Orlando Caputo Leiva, "La economía mundial a inicios del siglo XXI," *Globalizaciones,* January 2006 (http://www.rcci.net/globalizacion).
82. Graciela Moguillansky, Rogério Studart, and Sebastián Vergara, "Foreign banks in Latin America: a paradoxal result," *Cepal Review,* no. 82 (2004), especially p. 23, where they show also a very high level of concentration of the banking system.
83. Caputo Leiva, *op. cit.*
84. Geisa Maria Rocha, "Neo-Dependency in Brazil," *New Left Review,* no. 16 (2002), quotation at p. 22.
85. Portes and Kelly, *op. cit.,* pp. 66ff.
86. See the studies amassed in *Perfiles latinoamericanos,* año 10, no. 19 (2001).
87. Boschi, *op. cit.;* Ary Minella, "Globalização financeira e as associações de bancos na América Latina," *Cadernos de pesquisa PPGSP/UFSC,* no. 30 (2002).
88. Drawing upon "prospective theory" (indeed a variation of rational choice theory, which predicts that gains are moderately sought, while losses are

Notes 159

fiercely resisted), that is the argument put forward for governments and the whole of the population in Kurt Weyland, "Risk-taking in Latin American economic restructuring," *International Studies Quarterly,* vol. 40 (1996).

89. Cardoso and Faletto, *op. cit.,* chap. 6. The former curiously bet on the deepening of that. To be sure, "globalization" became a gloss in his and others' speech for the process that was really being pressed on Latin America.

90. Arceo and Basualdo, *op. cit.,* pp. 19, 23–24; Armando Boito Jr., "A burguesia no governo Lula" and Felipe Burlano de Lara, "Estratégias para sobrevivir a la crisis del Estado: Empresarios, política y partidos en Ecuador," both also in Basualdo and Arceo, *op. cit.;* J. M. Domingues, "Le premier governement Lula. Un bilan critique," *Problèmes d'Amérique latine,* no. 63 (2006–2007)—also in *Aproximações à América Latina.*

91. Cristóbal Kay, "Agrarian reform and the neoliberal counter-reform in Latin America," in Jacquelyn Chase (ed.), *The Spaces of Neoliberalism. Land, Place and Family in Latin America* (Bloomfield, CT: Kumarian, 2002), especially pp. 40–43.

92. The literature is large here. I shall rest content with a selection of titles: Marina Farinetti, "¿Qué queda del 'movimiento obrero'? Las formas del reclamo laboral en la nueva democracia argentina," *Trabajo y sociedad,* no. 1 (1999); Javier Auyero, "Los cambios en el repertorio de la protesta social en Argentina," *Desarrollo económico,* vol. 42 (2002); M. Svampa and Sebastián Pereyra, *Entre la ruta y el barrio* (Buenos Aires: Biblos, 2003); Svampa, *La sociedad excluyente,* chaps. 6–9; Guillermo Almeyra, *La protesta social en la Argentina (1990–2004)* (Buenos Aires: Continente, 2004); M. Maneiro, "Movimentos sociais e Estado: Uma perspectiva relacional," in Maneiro and Domingues (eds.), *América Latina hoje,* and *De encuentros y desencuentros. Estado y movimientos de trabajadores desocupados del Gran Buenos Aires (1996–2005).* PhD thesis (Rio de Janeiro: IUPERJ, 2007); Adalberto M. Cardoso, *A década neoliberal e a crise dos sindicatos no Brasil* (São Paulo: Boitempo, 2003); José Othón Quiroz Trejo, "Sindicalismo, núcleos de agregación obrera y corporativismo en México: Inercias, cambios y reacomodos," *Cotidiano,* vol. 128 (2004); Francisco Zapata, *México: Tiempos neoliberales* (Mexico: Colegio de México, 2005), chap. 4, and "¿Crisis en el sindicalismo en América Latina?," University of Notre Dame, Kellog Institute, *Working Paper* no. 302 (2003).

93. Kay, *op. cit.;* J. M. Domingues, "A diálética da modernização conservadora e a nova história do Brasil" (2002), in *Ensaios de sociologia;* Pablo Stefanoni, "Acción colectiva y desplazamientos identitarios en Bolivia: El caso del MAS," clase 14 del curso "Crisis y conflicto en el capitalismo latinoamericano" (Buenos Aires: CLACSO, 2004); Heather L. Williams, *Social Movements and Economic Transition: Markets and Distributive Conflict in Mexico* (Cambridge: Cambridge University Press, 2001).

94. Eduardo Viola, "The environment movement in Brazil: Institutionalization, sustainable development, and crisis of governance since 1987," in Gordon J. MacDonald, Daniel L. Nielson, and Marc A. Stern (eds.), *Latin American Environmental Policy in International Perspective* (Boulder, CO: Westview, 1997); Manuel Garretón, *Incomplete Democracy. Political Democratization in Chile and Latin America* (Chapel Hill and London: University of Carolina Press, 2003), chap. 7; J. M. Domingues and Andrea C. Pontual, "Environmental responsibility and the public sphere in Latin America," in Tuama Ó Seamus (ed.), *The Critical Theory of Piet Strydom* (New York: IB Taurus, 2007)—also in *Aproximações à América Latina;* Sternbach, Navarro-Aranguren, Chuchryk, and Alvarez, *op. cit.;* Alvarez, *op. cit.*

95. Svampa, *La sociedad excluyente,* chap. 5; Minor Mora Salas and Juan Pablo Pérez Sáinz, "De la vulnerabilidad social al riesgo de empobrecimiento de los

160 Notes

sectores medios: Un giro conceptual y metodológico," *Estudios sociológicos,* vol. 24, no. 70 (2006).

96. Boaventura de Sousa Santos, *Pela mão de Alice: O social e o político na pós-modernidade* (São Paulo: Cortez, 1995), pp. 256–69.
97. Douglas A. Chalmers, Scot B. Martin, and Kerianne Piester, "Associative networks: New structures of representation for the popular sectors?," in D. A. Chalmers et al. (eds.), *The New Politics of Inequality in Latin America: Rethinking Participation and Representation* (Oxford: University of Oxford Press, 19997), pp. 157–58. See also S. E. Alvarez, E. Dagnino, and A. Escobar, "Introduction: The cultural and the political in Latin American social movements," in Idem (eds.), *op. cit.,* pp. 9, 14–16.
98. Cf. Domingues, *Modernity Reconstructed,* chap. 8.
99. Josée Johnston and Gordon Laxers, "Solidarity in the age of globalization: Lessons from the Zapatista struggle," *Theory and Society,* vol. 32 (2003).
100. Robert Michels, *Political Parties* (New York: Dover, [1915] 1959); Wanderley Guilherme dos Santos, *Paradoxos do liberalismo: Teoria e história* (Rio de Janeiro: IUPERJ; and São Paulo: Vértice, 1988), chap. 4; Cavarozzi and Abal Medina, *op. cit.;* Garretón, *op. cit.,* chap. 6; "Balance de las democracias Latinoamericanas: Incertidumbres y procesos de consolidación," special issue of *Política,* no. 42 (2004); César A. Rodríguez Garavito, Patrik S. Barret, and Daniel Chavez (eds.), *La nueva izquierda en América Latina: Sus orígenes y trayectoria futura* (Bogotá: Norma, 2005).
101. See, respectively, Scott Mainwaring and Timothy Scully (eds.), *Building democratic institutions* (Stanford, CA: Stanford University Press, 1995); Fátima Anastasia, Carlos Ranulfo Melo, and Fabiano Santos, *Governabilidade e representação política na América do Sul* (Rio de Janeiro: Konrad Adenauer; and São Paulo: Editora da UNESP, 2004).
102. Garativo, Barret, and Chavez, *op. cit.;* Christian Adeal Mirza, *Movimientos sociales y sistemas políticos en América Latina* (Buenos Aires: CLACSO, 2006); Domingues, "Le Premier gouvernement Lula: Un bilan critique." For cesarism, as stemming from a stalemate in the relation of social forces, with "catastrophic" perspectives, see Gramsci, *op. cit.,* vol. 3, pp. 1619–20. Maybe it is not exactly a stalemate what happens in Venezuela, but the lack of organized social basis against powerful opponents brings the situation closer to that analyzed by Gramsci. A further concern has been the participation of women in politics, which has been circumscribed especially as to party politics. Cf. Celia Jardim Pinto, "Ciudadanía y democracia: Los aportes de una perspectiva de género," in G. O'Donnell et al., *op. cit.;* and Line Bareiro, Oscar López, Clyde Soto, and Lílian Soto, "Sistemas electorales y representación femenina en América Latina," *Cepal—Serie Mujer y Desarrollo,* no. 54 (2004).
103. Chalmers, Martin, and Piester, *op. cit.,* pp. 543–62. See also Chapter 1.
104. Álvaro García Linera, "El evismo: Lo nacional-popular en acción," *Revista del OSAL,* no. 19 (2006). This includes the reconstruction of the state in a multinational direction, whereby non-Western institutions are then constitutionalized, providing for change and autonomy. Cf. Tapia, *op. cit.,* pp. 15–19.
105. See Claudio Rama, *Economia de las industrias culturales en la globalización digital* (Buenos Aires: Eudeba, 2003), chap. 5; Germán Rey, "A situação do jornalismo na América Latina," *Observatório da imprensa,* May 16, 2006 (http://observatorio.ultimosegundo.ig.com.br); John Sinclair, *Latin American Television: A Global View* (Oxford: Oxford University Press, 1999); Elizabeth Fox and Silvio Waisbord (eds.), *Latin Politics, Global Media* (Austin: University of

Notes 161

Texas Press, 2002); Valério Cruz Brittos and César Ricardo Bolaño (eds.), *Rede Globo: 40 anos de poder e hegemonia* (São Paulo: Paulus, 2005).

106. Mann, *op. cit.;* see also Darío I. Restrepo, "Luchas por el control territorial en Colombia," *Economía, sociedad y territorio,* vol. 3 (2002).

107. Marcus André Melo, "Estado, governo e políticas públicas," in Sérgio Miceli (ed.), *O que ler na ciência social brasileira (1970–1995): Ciência política,* vol. III (São Paulo: Sumaré and Anpocs, 1999).

108. Corruption seemingly remains high, in any case. See the contributions to B. Schneider and Blanca Heredia (eds.), *Reinventing the Leviathan: The Politics of Administrative Reform in Developing Countries* (Miami, FL: North-South Center Press at the University of Miami, 2003); as well as to Bresser Pereira and Spink (eds.), *op. cit.* See also Oscar Ozlak, "El mito del Estado mínimo: Una década de reforma estatal en la Argentina," *Desarrollo económico,* no. 168, vol. 42 (2003) and the issues of *Revista del CLAD.*

109. Bob Jessop, *The Future of the State* (Cambridge: Polity, 2002). Some features of this renewed state form would be: a subordination of social to economic policy (but with very different regimes being possible) and its postnational character, plus the shift from the primacy of state intervention against market failure to emphasis on public-private partnerships and self-organized governance in a networked economy.

110. Castells, *op. cit., passim,* but especially pp. 39–40, 105. His discussion of identities (communitarian and defensive versus project-oriented) is found in M. Castells, *The Power of Identity: The Information Age,* vol. 2 (Oxford: Blackwell, 1997). I have critically discussed his ideas in "Modelos de desenvolvimento e desafios latino-americanos" (2006), in *Aproximações à América Latina.*

111. Basualdo and Arceo, *op. cit.,* p. 20.

112. Gramsci, *op. cit.,* vol. 3, pp. 962–64, 2011.

113. For the Brazilian case, see Luiz Werneck Vianna, "Caminhos e descaminhos da revolução passiva à brasileira," in *A revolução passiva: Iberismo e americanismo no Brasil* (Rio de Janeiro: Revan, 1997). For history and social movements, drawing upon phenomenology, see Domingues, "Vida cotidiana, história e movimentos sociais."

114. Domingues, "Le premier gouvernement Lula. Un bilan critique."

115. See J. M. Domingues, "Instituições formais no Brasil do século XXI" (2006) in *Aproximações à América Latina*; and *Modernity Reconstructed,* parts III–IV.

116. Touraine, *La Parole et le sang,* p. 474.

NOTES TO THE CONCLUSION

1. Enrique Dussel, *The Underside of Modernity: Apel, Ricouer, Rorty, Taylor, and the Philosophy of Liberation* (Atlantic Highlands, NJ: Humanities Press [1993] 1996), chap. 7. For the discussion of "neo-episodic" visions of history (Gellner, Mann, Giddens), as opposed to evolutionary theories, see José Maurício Domingues, *Social Creativity, Collective Subjectivity and Contemporary Modernity* (London: Macmillan; and New York: St. Martin's Press, 2000), chap. 4.

2. Benjamin Nelson, *Der Ursprung der Moderne. Vergleichende Studien zum Zivilisationsprozess* (Frankfurt am Main: Suhrkamp, 1977); J. M. Domingues, "Social theory, Latin America and modernity," in Gerard Delanty (ed.), *Handbook of European Social Theory* (London: Routledge, 2005).

3. Renato Ortiz, *A moderna tradição brasileira* (São Paulo: Brasiliense, 1988), pp. 208–10.

162 Notes

4. This is the core of his general critique of political economy, although the "commodity fetishism" and the "Trinitarian formula" concentrate this intensively. Karl Marx, *Das Kapital,* books I and III, in, respectively, *Mega* II-5 (Berlin: Dietz, [1867] 1965) and *Werke,* vol. 37 (Berlin: Dietz, [1894] 1967). Collective subjectivities and class struggle were his conceptual alternatives.
5. Domingues, "Social Theory, Latin America and modernity."
6. These are the contributions, as well as limits, to be found in Walter D. Mignolo, *Local Histories/Global Designs: Coloniality, Subaltern Knowledges and Border Thinking* (Princeton, NJ: Princeton University Press, 2000) and *The Idea of Latin America* (Oxford: Blackwell, 2005). He entirely misses the multifarious character of modernity, and its heterogeneous tissue at present. To some extent we can say that, rather than a precise interpretation of contemporary modernity, his work is an *expression* of it at the cultural-academic level.
7. Catherine Walsh, "Políticas y significados conflictivos," *Nueva sociedad,* no. 165 (2000).
8. Pablo González Casanova, "Internal colonialism and national development," *Studies in Comparative International Development,* vol. 1 (1965); Rodolfo Stavenhagen, "Classes, colonialism and acculturation," *Studies in Comparative International Development,* vol. 1 (1965); Javier Sanjinés C., "Outside in and inside out: Visualizing society in Bolivia," in Ileana Rodríguez (ed.), *The Latin American Subaltern Studies Reader* (Durham, NC, and London: Duke University Press); Mignolo, *op. cit.,* pp. 104, 281–12, 313.
9. The main texts here may be the following: Shmuel Eisenstadt, "Multiple modernities," *Daedalus,* vol. 129 (2000) and "The civilizational dynamic of modernity: Modernity as a distinct civilization," *International Sociology,* vol. 16 (2001); Johann Arnason, *Social Theory and the Japanese Experience: The Dual Civilization* (London and New York: Kegan Paul International, 1997) and "Civilizational Patterns and Civilizing Processes," *International Sociology,* vol. 16 (2001). For a very detailed and critical overview, see Wolfgang Knöbl, *Spielräume der Modernisierung: Das Ende der Eindeutigkeit* (Weilerwist: Velbrück, 2001), chaps. 5, 7, and 9.
10. A similar view of social totality can be found in Aníbal Quijano, "Colonialidad del poder y clasificación social," in *Journal of World-Systems Research* (Special Issue. Festschrift for Immanuel Wallerstein, Part I), vol. XI (2000).
11. Leon Trotsky, *History of the Russian Revolution,* vol. 1 (London: Sphere Books, [1932–1933] 1967), chap. 1. This concept was already appropriated in a more general sociological manner for the analysis of development in Latin America in the 1950s and the 1960s. Cf., amog others, Luis Costa Pinto, *Desenvolvimento econômico e transição social* (Rio de Janeiro: Civilização Brasileira, 1970, 2nd ed.), pp. 21–23, 31ff.
12. For the post-Kantian and post-Newtonian space-time conception supposed here, see J. M. Domingues, *Sociological Theory and Collective Subjectivity* (London: Macmillan; and New York: St. Martin's Press, 1995), chap. 8. For evolution and creativity, see my *Social Creativity, Contemporary Modernity and Collective Subjectivity,* especially chaps. 2 and 4.
13. Gino Germani, *Política y sociedad en una época de transición* (Buenos Aires: Paidós, 1965), pp. 16–17, 98–109.
14. While this is more or less generalized in the literature—in Spanish, Portuguese, English, or French—with different views being sustained, a sample may be offered by most pieces collected in Guillermo O'Donnell et al., *La democracia en América Latina. Hacia una democracia de ciudadanas y ciudadanos—Contribuciones para el debate* (PNUD, 2004).

Notes 163

15. A summary is found in Manuela Boatca, "Semiperipheries in the world-system: Reflecting Eastern European and Latin America Experiences," *Journal of World Systems Research,* vol. 12 (2006).
16. Social movements are in bad shape in the West, likewise social democracy; Islamic radical movements of course beg the question, which cannot, it goes without saying, be discussed here.
17. I do not want to go into such a discussion here in any detail, but it seems pretty clear to me that, if we should not take a naïve view especially of political parties—which are prone to oligarchic structuration—neither should we embark on radical "autonomist" ideas, which often strangely mix an absolutely totalist view of power with a radical refusal of institutionalization, along with an exaggerated apology of the spontaneity of action and a politically dangerous and empty revolutionary outlook.

Bibliography

Abel, Christopher, and Colin M. Lewis (eds.), *Exclusion & Engagement: Social Policy in Latin America* (London: Institute of Latin American Studies, 2002).

Acosta, Gladys, Gérman Burgos, and Margarita Flórez, "Los servicios legales y las campañas de fin de siglo: Preguntas y respuestas," *El otro derecho,* vol. 5, no. 3 (1994).

Adeal Mirza, Christian, *Movimientos sociales y sistemas políticos en América Latina* (Buenos Aires: CLACSO, 2006).

Adorno, Theodor W., *Minima Moralia* (Frankfurt am Main: Suhrkamp, [1945–1947] 1997).

Adorno, Theodor W., and Max Horkheimer, *Dialektik der Aufklärung* (Frankfurt am Main: Fisher, [1944] 1984).

Aglietta, Michel, *Régulation et crises du capitalisme: L'experience des Etats-Unis* (Paris: Calmon-Levy, 1976).

Alexander, Jeffrey, "Contradictions: The uncivilizing pressures of space, time, and function," *Soundings,* vol. 16 (2000).

Almeyra, Guillermo, *La protesta social en la Argentina (1990–2004)* (Buenos Aires: Continente, 2004).

Alvarez, Sonia E., Evelina Dagnino, and Arturo Escobar (eds.), *Cultures of Politics, Politics of Culture: Re-envisioning Latin American Social Movements* (Boulder, CO: Westview, 1998).

Anastasia, Fátima, Carlos Ranulfo Melo, and Fabiano Santos, *Governabilidade e representação política na América do Sul* (Rio de Janeiro: Konrad Adenauer; and São Paulo: Editora da UNESP, 2004).

Anderson, Benedict, *Imagined Communities: Reflections on the Original Spread of Nationalism* (London: Verso, 1991).

"Arbitragem: Confusão com a justiça," *O Globo,* May 10, 2003.

Arceo, Enrique, *Argentina en la periferia próspera: Renta internacional, dominación oligárquica y modo de acumulación* (Bernal: Universidad Nacional de Quilmes, 2003).

Arceo, Enrique, and Eduardo M. Basualdo (eds.), *Neoliberalismo y sectores dominantes: Tendencias globales y experiencias nacionales* (Buenos Aires: CLACSO, 2006).

Ariza, Marina, and Orlandina de Oliveira, "Familias en transición y marcos conceptuales en redefinición," *Papeles de Población,* no. 28 (2001).

Arnason, Johann, *Social Theory and the Japanese Experience: The Dual Civilization* (London and New York: Kegan Paul International, 1997).

Arnason, Johann, "Civilizational Patterns and Civilizing Processes," *International Sociology,* vol. 16 (2001).

Arriagada, Irma, "Changes and inequality in Latin American families," *Cepal Review,* no. 77 (2002).

166   Bibliography

Auyero, Javier, *La política de los pobres: Las prácticas clientelistas del peronismo* (Buenos Aires: Manantial, 2001).

Auyero, Javier, "Los cambios en el repertorio de la protesta social en Argentina," *Desarrollo económico*, vol. 42 (2002).

Avritzer, Leonardo, *A moralidade da democracia* (São Paulo: Perspectiva; and Belo Horizonte: Editora UFMG, 1996).

Avritzer, Leonardo, *Democracy and the Public Space in Latin America* (Princeton, NJ: Princeton University Press, 2002).

Avritzer, Leonardo et al., "Special section on civil society in Latin America," *Constellations*, vol. 4 (1997).

Baños Ramírez, Othón, *Modernidad, imaginario e identidades rurales—el caso de Yucatán* (Mexico: El Colegio de México, 2003).

Bareiro, Line, Oscar López, Clyde Soto, and Lílian Soto, "Sistemas electorales y representación femenina en América Latina," *Cepal—Serie Mujer y Desarrollo*, no. 54 (2004).

Bartra, Armando, "Los apocalípitcos y los integrados: Indios y campesinos en la encrucijada," *Memoria*, no. 190 (2004).

Beck, Ulrich, *Risk Society* (London: Sage, [1986] 1992).

Bell, Daniel, *The Coming of Post-Industrial Society* (New York: Basic Books, 1976).

Belluzzo, Luiz Gonzaga de Mello, and Renata Coutinho (eds.), *Desenvolvimento capitalista e crise no Brasil* (São Paulo: Brasiliense, 1982).

Bendix, Reinhard, *Kings or People: Power and the Mandate to Rule* (Berkeley: University of California Press, 1978).

Benhabib, Seyla, *Critique, Norm and Utopia* (New York: Columbia University Press, 1986).

Bethel, Leslie (ed.), *The Cambridge History of Latin America*, vols. I–VI (Cambridge: Cambridge University Press, 1984–1994).

Bielschowsly, Ricardo (ed.), *Cinqüenta anos de pensamento na CEPAL*, vols. 1–2 (Rio de Janeiro: Record, Cepal and Cofecon, 2000).

Boatca, Manuela "Semiperipheries in the world-system: Reflecting Eastern European and Latin America Experiences," *Journal of World Systems Research*, vol. 12 (2006).

Boltanski, Luke, and Eve Chiapello, *Le Nouvel Esprit du capitalisme* (Paris: Gallimard, 1999).

Borón, Atílio, *Estado, capitalismo y democracia en América Latina* (Buenos Aires: CLACSO, 2003).

Bortagaray, Isabel, and Scott Tiffin, "Innovation clusters in Latin America," in M. Heitor, D. Gibson, and M. Ibarra (eds.), *Technology Policy and Innovation*, vol. 1 (New York: Quorum Books, 2002).

Bourdieu, Pierre, and Loïc Wacquant, "Sur les ruses de la raison imperialiste," *Actes de la recherche en sciences socials*, nos. 121–22 (1988).

Boyer, Robert, *La Théorie de la régulation: Une analyse critique* (Paris: La Découverte, 1986).

Boyer, Robert, "Is finance-led growth a viable alternative to Fordism? A preliminary analysis," *Economy and Society*, vol. 29 (2000).

Boyer, Robert (ed.), *Capitalismes fin de siècle* (Paris: Presses Universitaires de France, 1986).

Boyer, Robert, and Yves Saillard (eds.), *Théorie de la régulation. L'Etat des savoirs* (Paris: La Découverte, 2002).

Boyer, Robert, and Julio C. Neffa (eds.), *La economía argentina y sus crises (1976–2001): Visiones institucionalistas y regulacionistas* (Buenos Aires: Miño y Dávila, 2004).

Braig, Marriane, "Zwischen Menschenrechten und Rechtsstaatlichkeit: Zivile Frauenorganizationen und Demokratisierung des Staates in Lateinamerika," in Sérgio

Bibliography 167

Costa and Hauke Brunkhorst (eds.), *Jenseits von Zentrum und Peripherie: Zur Verfassung der fragmentierten Weltgesellschaft* (Mering: Hampp, 2005).

Brittos, Valério Cruz, and César Ricardo Bolaño (eds.), *Rede Globo: 40 anos de poder e hegemonia* (São Paulo: Paulus, 2005).

Bruce, Steve, *Religion in the Modern World: From Cathedrals to Cult* (Oxford: Oxford University Press, 1996).

Burgos, Germán, "Los servicios legales populares y los extravíos de la pregunta por el político," *El otro derecho*, vol. 7, no. 3 (1996).

Burt, Jo-Marie, and Philip Mauceri (eds.), *Politics in the Andes. Identity, Conflict, Reform* (Pittsburgh, PA: Pittsburgh University Press, 2004).

Canessa, Andrew, "Contesting hybridity: Evangelistas and Kataristas in Highland Bolivia," *Journal of Latin American Studies*, vol. 32 (2000).

Cappelletti, Mauro, and Bryan Garth, *The Judicial Process in Comparative Perspective* (Oxford: Clarendon, 1978).

Caputo Leiva, Orlando, "La economía mundial a inicios del siglo XXI," *Globalizaciones*, January 2006 (http://www.rcci.net/globalizacion).

Carbonel, Miguel, "El poder judicial: ¿el tercero ausente?," *Metapolítica*, no. 230, vol. 7 (2003).

Cardoso, Adalberto M., *A década neoliberal e a crise dos sindicatos no Brasil* (São Paulo: Boitempo, 2003).

Cardoso, Fernando Henrique, *Política e desenvolvimento em sociedades dependentes: Ideologias do empresariado industrial argentino e brasileiro* (Rio de Janeiro: Zahar, 1971).

Cardoso, Fernando Henrique, "Teoria da dependência ou análise concreta de situações de dependência?" (1975), in *O modelo político brasileiro* (São Paulo: Difel, 1977).

Cardoso, Fernando Henrique, and Enzo Faletto, *Dependência e desenvolvimento na América Latina* (Rio de Janeiro: Zahar, [1970] 1979).

Cardoso, Ruth Corrêa L., "Movimentos sociais na América Latina," *Revista Brasileira de Ciências Sociais*, no. 3, vol. 1 (1987).

Carrillo, Jorge, and Arturo Lara, "Nuevas capacidades de coordinación centralizadas. ¿Maquilas de cuarta generación en México?," *Estudios sociológicos*, vol. XXII, no. 66 (2004).

Carvalho, José Murilo de, *A construção da ordem: A elite política imperial* (Rio de Janeiro: Campus, 1980).

Carvalho, José Murilo de, *Desenvolvimiento de la ciudadania en Brasil* (Mexico: Fondo de Cultura Económica, 1995).

Carvalho Pacheco, Cristina, "Directrices del Banco Mundial para la Reforma Judicial en América Latina," *El otro derecho*, vol. 25 (2000).

Castañeda, Jorge, *Unarmed Utopia: The Latin American Left after the Cold War* (New York: Vintage, 1993).

Castells, Manuel, *La Crise économique et la société américaine* (Paris: Presses Universitaires de France, 1976).

Castells, Manuel, *The Information Era: Economy, Society and Culture*, vols. 1–3 (Oxford: Blackwell, 1996–2000).

Castells, Manuel, *Globalización, desarrollo y democracia: Chile en el contexto mundial* (Mexico and Santiago: Fondo de Cultura Económica, 2005).

Castro, Ana Célia, Antonio Licha, and Helber Queiroz e João Sabóia (eds.), *Brasil em desenvolvimento*, vol. 1 (Rio de Janeiro: Civilização Brasileira, 2005).

Cavarozzi, Marcelo, and Juan Abal Medina, hj (eds.), *El asedio a la política: Los partidos latinoamericanos en la era neoliberal* (Rosario: Homo Sapiens, 2002).

Cecilia Bobes, Velia, *Los laberintos de la imaginación: Repertorio simbólico, identidades y actores del cambio social en Cuba* (Mexico: El Colegio de México, 2000).

168   Bibliography

Celad, *La transición demográfica en América Latina* (2000) (http://www.wclac.cl./ Celade/SitDem/DE).

Centeno, Miguel Angel, *Blood and Debt: War and the Nation State in Latin America* (University Park: Pennsylvania University Press 2002).

Cepal, *Balance preliminar de las economías latinoamericanas 2006* (2006).

Cepal, *Panorama social de América Latina* (2000–2001).

Cepal, *Panorama social de América Latina* (2004).

Cepal, *Panorama social de América Latina* (2006).

Chalmers, Douglas A. et al. (eds.), *The New Politics of Inequality in Latin America: Rethinking Participation and Representation* (Oxford: Oxford University Press, 1997).

Chase, Jacquelyn (ed.), *The Spaces of Neoliberalism: Land, Place and Family in Latin America* (Bloomfield, CT: Kumarian, 2002).

Chavez, Daniel, and Benjamin Goldfrank (eds.), *La izquierda en la cuidad: Participación en gobiernos locales en América Latina* (Barcelona: Icaria, 2005).

Coronil, Fernando, *El Estado mágico: Naturaleza, dinero y modernidad en Venezuela* (Caracas: Nueva Sociedad, 2002).

Costa, Sérgio, *As cores de Ercília* (Belo Horizonte: Editora UFMG, 2002).

Costa, Sérgio, "Desprovincializando a teoria sociológica: A contribuição pós-colonial," *Revista brasileira de ciências sociais,* vol. 21, no. 60 (2006).

Costa Pinto, Luis, *Desenvolvimento econômico e transição social* (Rio de Janeiro: Civilização Brasileira, 1970, 2nd ed.).

Couffignal, Georges (ed.), *Amérique Latine tournant de siècles* (Paris: La Découverte, 1997).

Cypher, James M., "Developing desarticulation within the Mexican economy," *Latin American Perspectives,* vol. 28 (2001).

Dagnino, Evelina (ed.), *Sociedade civil e espaços públicos no Brasil* (São Paulo: Paz e Terra, 2002).

Dagnino, Evelina, Alberto J. Olvera, and Aldo Panfichi (eds.), *A disputa pela construção democrática na América Latina* (São Paulo: Paz e Terra, 2005).

Dagnino, Renato, "A relação universidade-empresa e o 'argumento da tripla hélice'," *Convergência,* vol. 11, no. 35 (2000).

Dahl, Robert, *Poliarchy: Participation and Opposition* (New Haven, CT: Yale University Press, 1971).

Dávalos, Pablo (ed.), *Pueblos indígenas, Estado y democracia* (Buenos Aires: CLACSO, 2005).

De Negri, João Alberto, and Sérgio Salerno (eds.), *Inovações, padrões tecnológicos e desempenho das firmas industriais* (Brasília: IPEA, 2005).

Diniz, Eli, *Voto e máquina política: Patronagem e clientelismo no Rio de Janeiro* (Rio de Janeiro: Paz e Terra, 1982).

Domingo, Pilar, "Judicial independence: The politics of Supreme Court in Mexico," *Journal of Latin American Studies,* vol. 32 (2000).

Domingues, José Maurício, *Sociological Theory and Collective Subjectivity* (London: Macmillan; and New York: St. Martin's Press, 1995).

Domingues, José Maurício, *Social Creativity, Collective Subjectivity and Contemporary Modernity* (London: Macmillan; and New York: St. Martin's Press, 2000).

Domingues, José Maurício, "Social and System Integration," *Sociology,* vol. 34 (2000).

Domingues, José Maurício, "Amartya Sen, freedom and development" (2002), in Sérgio Costa, J. M. Domingues, Wolfgang Knöbl, and Josué Pereira da Silva (eds.), *The Plurality of Modernity: Decentring Social Theory* (Mehring: Hampp, 2006).

Domingues, José Maurício, "Collective Subjectivity and Collective Causality," *Philosophica,* vol. 71 (2003).

Bibliography 169

Domingues, José Maurício, *Estudos de sociologia* (Belo Horizonte: Editora UFMG, 2004).

Domingues, José Maurício, "Social theory, Latin America and modernity," in Gerard Delanty (ed.), *Handbook of European Social Theory* (London: Routledge, 2005).

Domingues, José Maurício, *Modernity Reconstructed* (Cardiff: University of Wales Press, 2006).

Domingues, José Maurício, *Aproximações à América Latina* (Rio de Janeiro: Civilização Brasileira, 2007).

Domingues, José Maurício and María Maneiro (eds.), *América Latina hoje: Conceitos e interpretações* (Rio de Janeiro: Civilização Brasileira, 2006).

Dussel, Enrique, *1492: El encubrimiento del Otro. Hacia el origen del "mito de la modernidad"* (La Paz: Plural Editores, Universidad Mayor de San Andrés, 1994).

Dussel, Enrique, *The Underside of Modernity: Apel, Ricouer, Rorty, Taylor, and the Philosophy of Liberation* (Atlantic Highlands, NJ: Humanities Press [1993] 1996).

Eisenberg, José, and Thamy Pogrebinschi, "Pragmatismo, direito e política," *Novos Estudos CEBRAP,* vol. 62 (2002).

Eisenstadt, Shmuel, "Multiple modernities," *Daedalus,* vol. 129 (2000).

Eisenstadt, Shmuel, "The civilizational dynamic of modernity: Modernity as a distinct civilization," *International Sociology,* vol. 16 (2001).

Eisenstadt, Shmuel, *Traditional Patrimonialism and Modern Neopatrimonialism* (Sage Research Papers in the Social Sciences, vol. 1; Beverly Hills, CA; and London: Sage, 1973).

Ellner, Steve, and Daniel Hellinger (eds.), *La política venezoelana en la época de Chávez* (Caracas: Nueva Sociedad, [2002] 2003).

Enrique Ortiz, César, "Cultivos ilícitos y nueva ruralidad en Colombia," *Cuadernos de desarrollo rural,* no. 50 (2003).

Escobar, Arturo, "The Latin American Modernity/Coloniality Research Program," in Guillermo O'Donnell et al., *Cruzando fronteras en América Latina* (Amsterdan: CEDLA, 2003).

Escobar, Arturo, and Sonia E. Alvarez (eds.), *The Making of Social Movements in Latin America: Identity, Strategy, and Democracy* (Boulder, CO: Westview, 1992).

Esping-Andersen, Goran, *Politics against Markets: The Social-Democratic Road to Power* (Princeton. NJ: Princeton University Press, 1985).

Esping-Andersen, Goran, *The Three Worlds of Welfare Capitalism* (Princeton, NJ: Princeton University Press, 1990).

Evans, Peter, *Embedded Autonomy: States and Industrial Transformation* (Princeton, NJ: Princeton University Press, 1995).

Faria, José Eduardo, *O direito na sociedade globalizada* (São Paulo: Malheiros, 1999).

Feres Jr., João, *A história do conceito de América Latina nos Estados Unidos* (Bauru: EDUSC/ANPOCS, 2005).

Fernandes, Florestan, *A revolução burguesa no Brasil* (Rio de Janeiro: Zahar, 1975).

Fernandes, Florestan, *Capitalismo dependente e classes sociais* (Rio de Janeiro: Zahar, 1975).

Fernandes, Rubem César, *Privado porém público: O terceiro setor na América Latina* (Rio de Janeiro: Relume Dumará, 1994).

Fiori, José Luis, *Em busca do dissenso perdido* (Rio de Janeiro: Insight, 1995).

Garretón, Manuel A., *Incomplete democracy: Political Democratization in Chile and Latin America* (Chapel Hill and London: University of North Carolina Press, 2003).

Garza Toledo, Enrique de la (ed.), *Tratado latinoamericano de sociología del trabajo* (Mexico: El Colegio de México, FLACSO, UAM and Fondo de Cultura Económica, 2000).

170 Bibliography

Germani, Gino, *Política y sociedad en una época de transición* (Buenos Aires: Paidós 1965).

Gideon, Jasmine, "The politics of social service provision through NGOs: A study of Latin America," *Bulletin of Latin American Research*, vol. 17 (1998).

Harvey, David, *The Postmodern Condition* (Oxford: Blackwell, 1989).

Farinetti, Marina, "¿Qué queda del 'movimiento obrero'? Las formas del reclamo laboral en la nueva democracia argentina," *Trabajo y sociedad,* no. 1 (1999).

Ferranti, David de, Guillermo Perry, Francisco H. G. Ferreira, Michael Walton et al., *Inequality in Latin America. Breaking with History?* (Washington, DC: World Bank, 2004).

Ferraz, João Carlos, David Kupfer, and Mariana Iootty, "Industrial competitiveness in Brazil ten years after economic liberalization," *Cepal Review*, no. 82 (2004);

Ferrer, Aldo, *La economía argentina* (Buenos Aires: Fondo de Cultura Económica, 2005).

Forment, Carlos A., *Democracy in Latin America, 1760–1900*, vol. 1 (Chicago: University of Chicago Press, 2003).

Fox, Elizabeth, and Silvio Waisbord (eds.), *Latin Politics, Global Media* (Austin: University of Texas Press, 2002).

Fucito, Felipe, *¿Podrá cambiar la justicia en la Argentina?* (Buenos Aires: Fondo de Cultura Económica, 2002).

Fuli, Gerardo, Eduardo Candaudap, and Claudia Ganona, "Exportaciones, industria maquiladora y crecimiento económico en México a partir de la década de los noventa," *Investigación económica,* vol. LXIV, no. 254

Furtado, Celso, *Formação econômica da América Latina* (Rio de Janeiro: Lia, 1967, 2nd ed.).

Furtado, João, "O comportamento inovador das empresas industriais no Brasil," *Estudos e pesquisas,* no. 88, INAE (2004).

García, Brígida, and Olga Lorena Rojas, "Cambios en la formación y disolución de las uniones en América Latina," *Papeles de población,* no. 32 (2002)

Garcia Canclini, Néstor, *Culturas híbridas: Estrategias para entrar y salir de la modernidad* (Mexico: Grijalbo, 1990).

Garcia Canclini, Néstor, *Consumidores e cidadãos: Conflitos multiculturais da globalização* (Rio de Janeiro: Editora UFRJ, 1995).

García-Guadilla, María Pilar, "El movimiento ambientalista y la constitucionalización de nuevas racionalidades: Dilemmas y desafíos," *Revista venezoelana de economía y ciencias sociales,* vol. 7 (2001).

García Linera, Álvaro, "El evismo: lo nacional-popular en acción," *Revista del OSAL,* no. 19 (2006).

Gasques, José Garcia et al., "Desempenho e crescimento do agronegócio no Brasil," *Textos para discussão,* no 1009 (Rio de Janeiro: IPEA, 2004).

Gereffi, Gary, and Donald L. Wyman (eds.), *Manufacturing Miracles: Paths of Industrialization in Latin America and East Asia* (Princeton, NJ: Princeton University Press, 1990).

Gereffi, Gary, and Miguel Korzeniewicz (eds.), *Commodity Chains and Global Capitalism* (Westport, CT: Praeger, 1994).

Gheventer, Alexander, *Autonomia versus controle: Origens do novo marco regulatório antitruste na América Latina e seus efeitos sobre a democracia* (Belo Horizonte: UFMG, 2005).

Giddens, Anthony, *The Class Structure of Advanced Societies* (New York: Harper & Row, [1973] 1975).

Giddens, Anthony, *The Nation State and Violence* (Cambridge: Polity Press, 1985).

Giddens, Anthony, *The Consequences of Modernity* (Cambridge: Polity, 1990).

Bibliography 171

Giordano, Al, "Mexico presidencial swindle," *New Left Review,* no. 41 (2006).
González Casanova, Pablo, "Internal colonialism and national development," *Studies in Comparative International Development,* vol. 1 (1965).
González de la Rocha, Mercedes, "Familias y política social en México: El caso de Oportunidades," paper presented at the Conference Welfare Regime and Social Actors in Inter-Regional Perspective: The Americas, Asia and Africa (University of Texas at Austin, 2006).
Gordon, Sara, "Equidad social y justicia social," *Revista mexicana de sociología,* vol. 2 (1995).
Gough, Ian, and Geof Wood (eds.), *Insecurity and Welfare Regimes in Asia, Africa and Latin America* (Cambridge: Cambridge University Press, 2004).
Gramsci, Antonio, *Quaderni del carcere,* vols. 1–3 (Turin: Einaudi, [1929–1935] 2001).
Grompone, Romeo, *Las nuevas reglas de juego: Transformaciones sociales, culturales y políticas en Lima* (Lima: IEP, 1999).
Gros, Cristian, "Evangelical Protestantism and indigenous populations," *Bulletin of Latin American Studies,* vol. 18 (1999).
Gross, Toomas, "Community and dissent: Religious intolerance in rural Oaxaca," *Finish Anthropologist,* vol. 26 (2003).
Gross, Toomas, "Protestantism and modernity: The implications of religious change in contemporary rural Oaxaca," *Sociology of Religion: A Quartely Review,* vol. 64 (2003).
Guevarra Ruiseñor, Elsa S., "Intimidad y modernidad: Precisiones conceptuales y su pertinencia para el caso de México," *Estudios sociológicos,* vol. 33 (2005).
Gumucio, Cristián Parker, "¿América Latina ya no es católica? Pluralismo cultural y religioso creciente," *América Latina Hoy,* vol. 41 (2000)
Habermas, Jürgen, *Theorie des kommunikativen Handelns,* vols. 1–2 (Frankfurt am Main: Suhrkamp, 1981).
Habermas, Jürgen, "Die Moderne—ein unvollendetes Projekt," in *Kleine politische Schriften I–IV* (Frankfurt am Main: Suhrkamp, 1981).
Habermas, Jürgen, *Fakzität und Geltung* (Frankfurt am Main: Suhrkamp, 1992).
Habermas, Jürgen, "Die postnationale Konstellation und die Zukunft der Demokratie," in *Die postnationale Konstellation* (Frankfurt am Main: Suhrkamp, 1998).
Hadden, Jeffrey, "Toward desacralizing secularization theory," *Social Forces,* vol. 65 (1987).
Hagopian, Frances, and Scott P. Mainwaring (eds.), *The Third Wave of Democratization in Latin America: Advancements and Setbacks* (Cambridge: Cambridge University Press, 2005).
Hall, Stuart, "The question of cultural identity," in S. Hall, David Held, and Tony Magrew (eds.), *Modernity and Its Futures* (Cambridge: Polity, 1992).
Halperin Donghi, Tulio, *Historia contemporánea de América Latina* (Madrid: Alianza [1969] 1993).
Hammergen, Linn et al., *América Latina hoy,* vol. 30 (2005).
Hardy, Clarisa, "Una nueva generación de reformas sociales en América Latina," in Rolando Cordera, Leonardo Lomelí, and Rosa Elena Montes de Oca (eds.), *La cuestión social: superación de la pobreza y política social a 7 años de Copenhague* (Mexico: UNAM, IETD and INDS, 2003).
Hasenbalg, Carlos, *Discriminação e desigualdades raciais no Brasil* (Belo Horizonte: Editora UFMG, [1979] 2005).
Held, David, *Democracy and the Global Order: From the Modern State to Cosmopolitan Governance* (Cambridge: Polity, 1995).
Herz, Mônica, and Andréa Ribeiro Hoffman, *Organizações internacionais: História e práticas* (Rio de Janeiro: Campus, 2004).

172   Bibliography

Hirschman, Albert O., *Journeys toward Progress. Studies of Economic Policy-Making in Latin America* (New York: Anchor Books, 1965).

Hirst, Paul, and Grahame Thompson, *Globalization in Question* (Cambridge: Polity, 1999, 2nd edition).

Hopenhayn, Martín, "Old and new forms of citizenship," *Cepal Review,* no. 73 (2001).

Honneth, Axel, *Kampf um Anerkennung* (Frankfurt am Main: Suhrkamp, 1992).

Honneth, Axel, *Leiden an Unbestimmtheit: Eine Reaktualisierung der Hegelschen Rechtsphilosophie* (Stuttgart: Phillip Reclam, 2001).

Ianni, Octávio, *A formação do Estado populista na América Latina* (Rio de Janeiro: Civilização Brasileira, 1975).

Ibarra, David, *Ensayos sobre economía mexicana* (Mexico: Fondo de Cultura Económica, 2005).

Invernizzi, Noela, "Disciplining the workforce: Controlling workers in the restructuring process," *Latin American Perspectives,* vol. 33 (2006).

Jessop, Bob, *The Future of the State* (Cambridge: Polity, 2002).

Johnston, Josée, and Gordon Laxers, "Solidarity in the age of globalization: Lessons from the Zapatista struggle," *Theory and Society,* vol. 32 (2003).

Lenin, Vladimir I., *Imperialism, the Higher Stage of Capitalism: A Popular Outline* (1917), in *Collected Works,* vol. 22 (Moscow: Progressive Publishers, 1934).

Jordana, Jacint, and David Levi-Faur, "The diffusion of regulatory capitalism in Latin America: Sectoral and national channels in the making of a new order," *Annals of American Political and Social Sciences Academy,* no. 598 (2005).

Jordana, Jacint, and David Levi-Faur, "Towards a Latin American regulatory state? The diffusion of autonomous regulatory agencies across countries and sectors," *International Journal of Public Administration,* vol. 29 (2006).

Jordana, Jacint, David Levi-Faur, and Fabrizio Gilard, "Regulation in the age of globalization: The diffusion of regulatory agencies across Europe and Latin America," *IBEI Working Papers,* 2006/1 (2006).

Kaufman, Robert R., and Stephan Haggard (eds.), *The Politics of Economic Adjustment: International Constraints, Distributive Conflicts, and the State* (Princeton, NJ: Princeton University Press, 1992).

Knöbl, Wolfgang, *Spielräume der Modernisierung: Das Ende der Eindeutigkeit* (Weilerwist: Velbrück, 2001).

Kosacoff, Bernardo, and Adrián Ramos, "Transformaciones estructurales de la producción industrial," in *Cambios contemporáneos en la estructura industrial argentina (1975–2000)* (Bernal: Universidad de Quilmes, 2002).

Kurtz, Marcus J., "Understanding the Third World Welfare State after Neoliberalism," *Comparative Politics,* vol. 24 (2002).

Laclau, Ernesto, "Towards a theory of populism," in *Politics and Ideology in Marxist Theory: Capitalism, Fascism, Populism* (London: New Left Books, 1977).

Lambert, Jacques, *Amérique Latine. Structures sociales et institutions politiques* (Paris: Presses Universitaires de France, 1963).

Landerretche, Oscar, Cesar P. Ominami, and Mario Lanzarotti, "El desarrollo de Chile en la encrucijada: O cómo viejas controversias impiden abordar nuevos problemas," *Foro 21,* no. 34 (2004).

Laserna, Roberto, "Bolivia: la crisis de octubre y el fracaso del ch'enko: Una visión desde la economía política," *Anuario social y político de América Latina y el Caribe,* vol. 7 (2005).

Lawyers Committee for Human Rights, *Building in Quicksand: The Collapse of the World Bank's Judicial Reform Project in Peru* (New York and Washington, DC: Lawyers Committee for Human Rights, 2000).

Leal, Víctor Nunes, *Coronelismo, enxada e voto* (São Paulo: Alfa Omega [1948] 1976).

Bibliography 173

Laurel, Asa Cristina (ed.), *Estado e políticas sociais no neoliberalismo* (São Paulo: Cortez [1992] 1995).

Lautier, Bruno, "Les politiques sociales au Brasil durant le gouvernement de Lula: Aumône d'Etat ou droits sociaux," *Problèmes d'Amérique latine*, no. 63 (2006–07).

Lautier, Bruno, and Jaime Marques Pereira (eds), *Brèsil, Mexique: Deux trajectories dans la mondialisation* (Paris: Karthala, 2004).

le Bot, Yvon, "Churches, sects and communities: Social cohesion recovered?," *Bulletin of Latin American Studies*, vol. 18 (1999).

Lechner, Norbert, "Os desafios das mudanças culturais sob a democracia," *Novos estudos CEBRAP*, no. 68 (2004).

Lipset, Martin S., and Aldo Solari (eds.), *Elites in Latin America* (New York: Oxford University Press, 1967).

Lladós, José Maria, and Samuel Pinheiro Guimarães (eds.), *Perspectivas Brasil y Argentina* (Brasília: IPRI, 1999).

López-Ayllón, Sergio, and Héctor Fix-Fierro, "Legitimidad contra legalidad: Los dilemas de la transición jurídica y el Estado de derecho en México," *Política y gobierno*, vol. 3 (1999).

Lo Vuolo, Ruben, and Alberto Barbeito, *La nueva oscuridad: Del estado populista al neoconservador* (Buenos Aires: Miño y Dávila, 1998).

Lukács, Gyorg, *Geschichte und Klassenbewusstsein* (Berlin: Herman Luchterhand, [1923] 1977).

Macaulay, Fiona, "Democratización y poder judicial: Agendas de reforma en competencia," *América Latina Hoy,* vol. 39 (2005).

MacDonald, Gordon, J. Daniel L. Nielson, and Marc A. Stern (eds.), *Latin American Environmental Policy in International Perspective* (Boulder, CO: Westview, 1997).

Makoto, Sano, and Alberto Di Martino, "'Japanization' of the employment relationship: three cases in Argentina," *Cepal Review,* no. 80 (2003).

Mainwaring, Scott, and Thimoty R. Scully (eds.), *Building Democratic Institutions* (Stanford, CA: Stanford University Press, 1995).

Maffesoli, Michel, *Le temp des tribus: Le Déclin du individualisme dans les sociétés de masse* (Paris: Grasset, 1992).

Mandel, Ernest, *Late Capitalism* (London: New Left Books, [1972] 1975).

Maneiro, María, *Encuentros y desencuentros .Estado y movimientos de trabajadores desocupados del Gran Buenos Aires (1996–2005).* PhD thesis (Rio de Janeiro: IUPERJ, 2007). "Maneiro, María," Os movimentos sociais na América Latina: Uma perspectiva a partir das relações do Estado com a sociedade civil," in José Maurício Domingues and María Maneiro (eds.) *América Latina hoje. Conceitos e interpretações* (Rio de Janeiro: Civilização Brasileira, 2006).

Mann, Michael, *The Sources of Social Power,* vol. 2. The Rise of Classes and Nation-States, 1760–1974 (Cambridge: Cambridge University Press, 1993).

Mannheim, Karl, "Conservative Thought" (1925), in *Essays on Sociology and Social Psychology* (London: Routledge & Kegan Paul, 1953).

Mannheim, Karl, "The problem of generations" (1928), in *Essays on the Sociology of Knowledge* (London: Routledge & Kegan Paul, 1952).

Marshall, T. H., "Citizenship and social class" (1950), in *Class, Citizenship and Social Development* (Garden City, NY: Doubleday & Co, 1964).

Marx, Karl, *Zur Judenfrage* (1847) in Marx & Engels, *Werke,* vol. 1 (Berlin: Dietz, 1956).

Marx, Karl, *Misère de la Philosophie* (1847), in *Oeuvres,* vol. 1 (Paris: Gallimard, 1963).

Marx, Karl, *Der 18te Brumaire Luis Bonapartes* (1852), in *Werke,* vol. 8 (Berlin: Dietz, 1960).

174 Bibliography

Marx, Karl, *Das Kapital*, books I, II (Berlin: Dietz, [1867 and 1885] 1965) in *Mega* II-5; and III, in *Werke*, vol. 37 (Berlin: Dietz, [1894] 1967).

Marx, Karl, and Friedrich Engels, *Die deutsche Ideologie* (1845), in *Werke*, vol. 4 (Berlin: Dietz, 1939).

Marx, Karl, and Friedrich Engels, "Manifest der kommunistischen Partei" (1848), in *Werke*, vol. 4 (Berlin: Dietz, 1939).

Marques-Pereira, Bérengère, and Ilán Bizberg (eds.), *La citoyenneté sociale en Amérique latine* (Paris: L'Harttman, 1995).

Margulis, Mario, and Marcelo Urresti, "Buenos Aires y los jóvenes: las tribus urbanas," *Estudios sociológicos,* vol. 46 (1995).

Mariscal, Judith, "Telecommunications reform in Mexico from a comparative perspective," *Latin American Politics and Society,* vol. 46 (2004).

Martín-Barbero, Jesús, *Al sur de la modernidad: Comunicación, globalización y multiculturalidad* (Pittsburgh, PA: Instituto Internacional de Literatura—Pittsburgh University, 2001).

Massieu Trigo, Yolanda, "Consecuencias de la biotecnologia en México: el caso de los cultivos transgenicos," *Sociológica,* año 15, no. 43 (2000).

Mattos, Carlos A. de, "Estado, procesos de decisión y planificación en América Latina," *Revista de la Cepal,* no. 31 (1987).

Medina Echevarría, José, *Consideraciones sociológicas sobre el desarrollo económico de América Latina* (Buenos Aires: Solar and Hachette, 1964).

Melo, Alberto, "The innovation systems of Latin America and the Caribbean," *Working Paper* no. 640, Interamerican Development Bank, Research Department (2001).

Melo, Marcus André, "Estado, governo e políticas públicas," in Sérgio Miceli (ed.), *O que ler na ciência social brasileira (1970–1995). Ciência política,* vol. III (São Paulo: Sumaré and Anpocs, 1999).

Melucci, Alberto, *Challenging Codes: Collective Action in the Information Age* (Cambridge: Cambridge University Press, 1996).

Méndez, Juan, Guillermo O'Donnell, and Paulo Sérgio Pinheiro (eds.), *La (in)efectividad da ley y la exclusión en América Latina* (Buenos Aires: Paidós, [1997] 2003).

Merryman, John Henry, *The Civil Law Tradition: An Introduction to the Legal Systems of Western Europe and Latin America* (Stanford, CA: Stanford University Press, 1985, 2nd ed.).

Michels, Robert, *Political Parties* (New York: Dover, [1915] 1959).

Millán, René, "Cultura de la justicia y cultura política," *Revista mexicana de sociología,* vol. 2 (1995).

Millán Valenzuela, Henio, "Política social y fundamentos del combate a la pobreza extrema en México," *Economía, sociedad y territorio,* vol. 3, no. 9 (2001).

Mignolo, Walter D., *Local Histories/Global Designs: Coloniality, Subaltern Knowledges and Border Thinking* (Princeton, NJ: Princeton University Press, 2000).

Mignolo, Walter D., *The Idea of Latin America* (Oxford: Blackwell, 2005).

Minella, Ary, "Globalização financeira e as associações de bancos na América Latina," *Cadernos de pesquisa PPGSP/UFSC,* no 30 (2002).

Moguillansky, Graciela, Rogerio Studart, and Sebastián Vergara, "Foreign banks in Latin America: A paradoxical result," *Cepal Review,* no. 82 (2004).

Moreno, Héctor, "Riqueza y niveles de vida de los hogares en México," *Comercio Exterior—Revista de análisis económico y social,* vol. 56 (2006).

Morse, Richard, *El espejo de Próspero* (Mexico: Siglo XXI, 1982).

Nailini, José Renato, "Judicial reform in Brazil," in *Judicial Reform in Latin America and the Caribeean: Proceedings of a World Bank Conference* (Washington, DC: The World Bank, 1995).

Bibliography 175

Naím, Moisés, "Latin America: The second stage of reform," *Journal of Democracy,* vol. 5 (1994).

Nelson, Benjamin, *Der Ursprung der Moderne: Vergleichende Studien zum Zivilisationsprozess* (Frankfurt am Main: Suhrkamp, 1977).

Nickson, Andrew, and Peter Lambert, "State reform and the 'privatized state' in Paraguay," *Public Administration and Development,* vol. 22 (2002).

Nobre, Marcos et al., *Desenvolvimento Sustentável: a institucionalização de um conceito* (Brasília: IBAMA; São Paulo: CEBRAP, 2002).

Nómadas, no. 23 (2005).

Novick, Marta, and María A. Gallart (eds.), *Competitividad, redes productivas y competencias laborales* (Montevideo: OIT/CINTRFOR-RE, 1997).

Nun, José, *Marginalidad y exclusión social* (Buenos Aires and Mexico: Fondo de Cultura Económica, 2001).

O'Donnell, Guillermo, *Bureaucratic Authoritarianism: Argentina, 1966–1973 in Comparative Perspective* (Berkeley and Los Angeles: University of California Press, 1988).

O'Donnell, Guillermo, "Delegative democracy," *Journal of Democracy,* vol. 5 (1994).

O'Donnell, Guillermo, "Illusions about consolidation," *Journal of Democracy,* vol. 7 (1996).

O'Donnell, Guillermo, Philippe C. Schmitter, and Laurence Whitehead (eds.), *Transitions from Authoritarian Rule* (Baltimore, MD: Johns Hopkins University Press, 1986).

O'Donnell, Guillermo et al., *La democracia en América Latina. Hacia una democracia de ciudadanas y ciudadanos—contribuciones para el debate* (PNUD, 2004).

Offe, Claus, "The attribution of public status to interest groups," in *Disorganised Capitalism: Contemporary Transformations of Work and Politics* (Cambridge: Polity, 1985).

Oliveira, Francisco de, *A economia da dependência imperfeita* (Rio de Janeiro: Graal, 1977).

Ornelas Delgado, Jaime, "La política de combate a la pobreza en México, 1982–2005," *Papeles de población,* no. 47 (2006).

Ortiz, Renato, *A moderna tradição brasileira* (São Paulo: Brasiliense, 1988).

Ortiz, Renato, "From incomplete modernity to world modernity," *Daedalus,* vol. 129 (2000).

Ozlak, Oscar, "El mito del Estado mínimo: una década de reforma estatal en la Argentina," *Desarrollo económico,* no. 168, vol. 42 (2003).

Oxhorn, Philip, "Desigualdad social, sociedad civil y los límites de la ciudadanía en América Latina," *Economía, sociedad y territorio,* vol. 3, no. 9 (2001).

Palacio, Germán, "Pluralismo jurídico, neoamericanismo y postfordismo: Notas para descifrar la naturaleza de los cambios jurídicos de fines de siglo," *Crítica jurídica,* vol. 17 (2000).

Panigo, Demian, and Edgardo Torija-Zane, "Une approche regulationiste des crisis de l'économie argentine: 1930–2002," *Document de travail,* no. 2004–07, CEPREMAP (http://www.cepremap.cnrs.fr).

Parsons, Talcott, "Evolutionary universals in society" (1964), in *Sociological Theory and Modern Society* (New York: Free Press, 1967).

Parsons, Talcott, *The System of Modern Society* (Englewood Cliffs, NJ: Prentice-Hall, 1971).

Pásara, Luis, "Justicia, régimen político y sociedad en América Latina," *Política y gobierno,* vol. 10 (2003).

Pastor, Manuel, Jr., and Carol Wise, "The politics of second generation reform," *Journal of Democracy,* vol. 10 (1999).

176 Bibliography

Pengue, Walter A., *Agricultura industrial y transnacionalización en América Latina* (Mexico: UACM and PNUMA, 2005).

Pereira, Luiz Carlos Bresser, and Peter Spinx (eds.), *Reforming the State: Managerial Public Administration* (Boulder, CO: Lynne Rinner, 1999).

Pérez-Perdomo, Rogelio, and Lawrence Friedman (eds.), *Legal Culture in the Age of Globalization: Latin America and Latin Europe* (Stanford, CA: Stanford University Press, 2003).

Peruzzotti, Enrique, "Modernization and juridification in Latin America: A reassessment of the Latin American developmental path," *Thesis Eleven,* vol. 58 (1999).

Petras, James, and Henry Veltmeyer (eds.), *Las privatizaciones y la desnacionalización de América Latina* (Buenos Aires: Prometeo, 2004).

Pierruci, Flávio, "Secularização em Max Weber: Da contemporânea serventia de voltarmos a acessar aquele velho conceito," *Revista Brasileira de Ciências Sociais,* no. 37 (1998).

Pieterse, Jan Nederveen, *Globalization & Culture* (Laham, MD: Rowman & Littlefield, 2004).

Pochmann, Marcio et al., *Atlas da exclusão social no Brasil,* vol. 3, Os ricos no Brasil (São Paulo: Cortez, 2004).

Pogrebinschi, Thamy, "Law and society in Latin America: Brazil, Argentina and Mexico in a comparative perspective," paper presented at the 24th Annual ILASSA Conference on Latin America, University of Texas, Austin (2004).

Polanyi, Karl, *The Great Transformation* (Boston, MA: Beacon, [1944] 1975).

Política, no. 42 (2004).

Portantiero, Juan Carlos, "La múltiple transformación del Estado latinoamericano," *Nueva sociedad,* no 104 (1989).

Portes, Alejandro, "Latin American class structures: Their composition and change during the last decades," *Latin American Research Review,* vol. 20 (1985).

Portes, Alejandro, and Kelly Hoffman, "Latin American class structures: Their composition and change during the neoliberal era," *Latin American Research Review,* vol. 38 (2003).

Portes, Alejandro, M. Castells, and Lauren A. Benton (eds.), *The Informal Economy. Studies in Advanced and Less Developed Countries* (Baltimore, and London: Johns Hopkins University Press, 1989).

Poulantzas, Nicos, *L'Etat, le pouvoir, le socialisme* (Paris: Presses Universitaires de France, 1978).

Poulantzas, Nicos, *Pouvoir politique et classes sociales* (Paris: Maspero, [1968] 1975), vol. 1.

Quenan, Carlos, "Peut-on parler d'économies émergentes en Amérique latine?," *Amérique latine, tournant de siècle* (Paris: La Découverte, 1997).

Quijano, Aníbal, "Coloniality and modernity/rationality," *Cultural Studies,* vol. 21 ([1989] 2007).

Quijano, Aníbal, "Colonialidad del poder, eurocentrismo y América Latina," in Edgardo Lander (ed.), *La colonialidad del saber: Eurocentrismo y ciencias sociales: Perspectivas latinoamericanas* (Buenos Aires: CLACSO, 1993).

Quijano, Aníbal, *La economía popular y sus caminos en América Latina* (Lima: Mosca Azul, 1998).

Quijano, Aníbal, "Colonialidad del poder y clasificación social," in *Journal of World-Systems Research* (Special Issue: Festschrift for Immanuel Wallerstein, Part I), vol. XI (2000).

Quilodran, Julieta, "La familia, referentes en transición," *Papeles de población,* no. 37 (2003).

Quiroz Trejo, José Othón, "Sindicalismo, núcleos de agregación obrera y corporativismo en México: inercias, cambios y reacomodos," *Cotidiano,* vol. 128 (2004).

Bibliography   177

Rama, Angel, *La ciudad letrada* (Montevideo: Ediciones del Norte, 1984).

Rama, Claudio, *Economia de las industrias culturales en la globalización digital* (Buenos Aires: Eudeba, 2003).

Ramalho, José Ricardo, and Marco Aurélio Santana (eds.), *Trabalho e desenvolvimento regional: Efeitos sociais da indústria automobilística no Brasil* (Rio de Janeiro: Mauad, 2006).

Restrepo, Darío I., "Luchas por el control territorial en Colombia," *Economía, sociedad y territorio,* vol. 3 (2002).

RICYT, *El estado de la ciencia 2004* (Buenos Aires: RICYT, 2005) (http://www. .ricyt. edu.ar).

Reigadas, Cristina, "Modernización e identidad en el pensamiento argentino contemporáneo: Revisando el argumento de la inferioridad," *Revista latinoamericana de filosofía y ciencias sociales,* segunda época, año XXV, no. 22 (2000).

Resende, Marco Flávio C., and Patrícia Anderson, "Mudanças estruturais na indústria brasileira de bens de capital," *Textos para discussão,* no. 658 (Brasília: IPEA, 1999).

Revista del CLAD, several issues.

Rey, Germán, "A situação do jornalismo na América Latina," *Observatório da imprensa,* 16/05/2006 (http://observatorio.ultimosegundo.ig.com.br).

Robertson, Roland, *Globalization. Social Theory and Global Culture* (London: Sage, 1992).

Robertson, Roland, Scott Lash, and Mike Featherstone (eds.), *Global Modernities* (London: Sage, 1995).

Rocha, Geisa Maria, "Neo-Dependency in Brazil," *New Left Review,* no. 16 (2002).

Rodríguez, Ileana (ed.), *The Latin American Subaltern Studies Reader* (Durham, NC, and London: Duke University Press).

Rodríguez Garavito, César A., Patrik S. Barret, and Daniel Chavez (eds.), *La nueva izquierda en América Latina: Sus orígenes y trayectoria futura* (Bogotá: Norma, 2005).

Romero, José Luís, *Latinoamérica: La ciudad y las ideas* (Buenos Aires: Siglo XX, [1976] 2004).

Rodriguez Vignoli, Jorge A., "¿Cohabitación an América Latina: Modernidad, exclusion o diversidad?," *Papeles de población,* no. 40 (2004).

Salas, Minor Mora, and Juan Pablo Pérez Sáinz, "De la vulnerabilidad social al riesgo de empobrecimiento de los sectores medios: un giro conceptual y metodológico," *Estudios sociológicos,* vol. 24, no. 70 (2006).

Salmerón Castro, Fernando I., "Modernidad y prácticas políticas: Democracia, eslabonamientos y mediaciones en la sociedad civil," *Revista mexicana de sociología,* vol. 1 (2002).

Sansone, Livio, *Blackness without Ethnicity: Constructing Race in Brazil* (London and New York: Palgrave Macmillan, 2003).

Sant'Anna, Julia, "Governos de esquerda e o gasto social na América Latina," *Observador on-line,* vol. 2. no. 2 (2007) (http://www.opsa.iuperj.br).

Santos, José Alcides F., *Estrutura de posições de classe no Brasil: Mapeamento, mudanças e efeito na renda* (Belo Horizonte: Editora UFMG, 2002).

Santos, Milton, and Maria Laura Silveira, *O Brasil: Território e sociedades no início do século XXI* (Rio de Janeiro: Civilização Brasileira, 2004).

Santos, Wanderley Guilherme dos, *Paradoxos do liberalismo: Teoria e história* (Rio de Janeiro: IUPERJ; and São Paulo: Vértice, 1988).

Saraceno, Chiara, *Anatomia della famiglia* (Bari: De Donato, 1976).

Schmitter, Philippe C., "Still the century of corporatism?," *Review of Political Studies,* vol. 36 (1974).

Schneider, Ben Ross, *Business Politics and the State in Twentieth-Century Latin America* (Cambridge: Cambridge University Press, 2004).

178   Bibliography

Schneider, Ben Ross, and Blanca Heredia (eds.), *Reinventing the Leviathan: The Politics of Administrative Reform in Developing Countries* (Miami, FL: North-South Center Press at the University of Miami, 2003).

Serra, José (ed.), *América Latina: Ensaios de interpretação econômica* (Rio de Janeiro: Paz e Terra, 1976).

Shihata, Ibrahim F. I., "Legal framework for development: The World Bank's role in legal and judicial reform," in *Judicial Reform in Latin America and the Caribbean: Proceedings of a World Bank Conference* (Washington, DC: The World Bank, 1995).

Shihata, Ibrahim F. I., "Judicial reform in developing countries and the role of the World Bank," in *Judicial Reform in Latin America and the Caribbean: Proceedings of a World Bank Conference* (Washington: The World Bank, 1995).

Shihata, Ibrahim F. I., "The World Bank," in E. Jarquín and F. Carrillo (eds.), *Justice Delayed: Judicial Reform in Latin America* (Washington, DC: Inter-American Bank of Development, 1998).

Silveira, Maria Laura da (ed.), *Continente em chamas: Globalização e território na América Latina* (Rio de Janeiro: Civilização Brasileira, 2005).

Sinclair, John, *Latin American Television: A Global View* (Oxford: Oxford University Press, 1999).

Soares, Glaucio A. Dillon, *A democracia interrompida* (Rio de Janeiro: FGV Editora, 2001).

Sociologias, no. 10 (2004).

Sojo, Carlos, "The idea of citizenship in the Latin American debate," *Cepal Review,* no. 76 (2002).

Sorj, Bernardo, "Civil societies North-South relations: NGOs and/beyond dependency," *The Edelstein Center for Social Research, Working Paper* no. 1 (2005).

Sousa Santos, Boaventura de, *Toward a New Common Sense* (New York: Routledge, 1995).

Sousa Santos, Boaventura de, *Pela mão de Alice: O social e o político na pós-modernidade* (São Paulo: Cortez, 1995).

Sousa Santos, Boaventura de, *O Fórum Social Mundial: Manual de uso* (São Paulo: Cortez, 2005).

Spalding Jr. Hobart, *Organized Labor in Latin America* (New York: Harper & Row, 1987).

Sproll, Martina, "Las redes transnacionales de producción: América Latina, Ásia y Europa del Este en la manufactura por contracto en la industria eletrónica," *Memória,* no. 176 (2003).

Stavenhagen, Rodolfo, "Classes, colonialism and acculturation," *Studies in Comparative International Development,* vol. 1 (1965).

Stefanoni, Pablo, "Acción colectiva y desplazamientos identitarios en Bolivia: El caso del MAS," clase 14 del curso "Crisis y conflicto en el capitalismo latinoamericano" (Buenos Aires: CLACSO, 2004).

Strange, Susan, *The Retreat of the State: The Diffusion of Power in the World Economy* (Cambridge: Cambridge University Press, 1996).

Strydom, Piet, *Discourse and Knowledge: The Making of Enlightenment Sociology* (Liverpool: Liverpool University Press, 2000).

Sunshine, Fabio Grobart, "Situación actual en América Latina respecto a la innovación y la competitividad," paper presented at the V Encuentro Latinoamericano de estudios prospectivos, Guadelajara, México (2002).

Svampa, Maristella, *La sociedad excluyente: La Argentina bajo el signo del neoliberalismo* (Buenos Aires: Taurus, 2005).

Svampa, Maristella (ed.), *Desde abajo: La transformación de las identidades sociales* (Buenos Aires: Biblos, 2000).

Svampa, Maristella, and Sebastián Pereyra, *Entre la ruta y el barrio* (Buenos Aires: Biblos, 2003)

Bibliography 179

Tarrow, Sidney, *Power in Movement: Social Movements, Collective Action and Politics* (Cambridge: Cambridge University Press, 1994).

Teubner, Gunther, "La coupole invisible: De l'attribution causale à la l'attribution collective de la responsabilité ecologique," in *Droit et reflexivité: L'Auto-reference dans l'organisation* (Paris: L.G.D.J and Bruyant, [1992] 1996).

Therborn, Göran, *Between Sex and Power: Family in the World* (London and New York: Routledge, 2004).

Thorn, Kristian, "Ciencia, tecnología e innovación en Argentina: Un perfil sobre temas y prácticas," World Bank Document, Latin American and Caribean Region (2005) (http://www.worldbank.org/INTARGENTINASPANISH/).

Torre García, Rodolfo de la, "Los ricos en México," *Comercio Exterior—Revista de análisis económico y social,* vol. 56 (2006).

Torres, Pablo, *Votos, chapas y fideos: Clientelismo y ayuda social* (La Plata: de la campana, 2002).

Touraine, Alain, *La Parole et le sang* (Paris: Odile Jacob, 1988).

Trotsky, Leon, *History of the Russian Revolution,* vol. 1 (London: Sphere Books, [1932–1933] 1967).

Uggla, Fredrik, "The Ombudsman in Latin America," *Journal of Latin American Studies,* vol. 36 (2004).

Uprimny, Rodrigo, Cesar Rodríguez Garavito, and Mauricio García Villegas (eds.), *¿Justicia para todos? Sistema judicial, derechos sociales y democracia en Colombia* (Bogotá: Norma, 2006).

Vaitsman, Jeni, "Pluralidade de mundos entre mulheres urbanas de baixa renda," *Estudos feministas,* vol. 5 (1997).

Valenzuela Arce, José Manuel (ed.), *Los estudios culturales en México* (Mexico: Conaculta and Fondo de Cultura Económica, 2003).

Van Cott, Donna Lee, "A political analysis of legal pluralism in Bolivia and Colombia," *Journal of Latin American Studies,* vol. 32 (2000).

Vasquez, Manuel A., and Philip J. Williams, "Introduction. The power of religious identities in the Americas," *Latin American Perspectives,* vol. 32 (2005).

Velloso, João Paulo dos Reis (ed.), *Brasil: desafios de um país em transformação* (Rio de Janeiro: José Olympio, 1997).

Velloso, João Paulo dos Reis (ed.), *Como vão o desenvolvimento e a democracia no Brasil* (Rio de Janeiro: José Olympio, 2001).

Vianna, Luiz Werneck, *A revolução passiva: Iberismo e americanismo no Brasil* (Rio de Janeiro: Revan, 1997).

Vianna, Luiz Werneck et al., *Corpo e alma da magistratura brasileira* (Rio de Janeiro: Revan, 1997).

Vianna, Luiz Werneck et al., *A judicialização da política e das relações sociais* (Rio de Janeiro: Revan, 1999).

Vianna, Luiz Werneck (ed.), *A democracia e os três poderes no Brasil* (Belo Horizonte: UFMG, 2002).

Wacquant, Loic, *As prisões da miséria* (Rio de Janeiro: Zahar, 2001).

Wade, Peter, *Race and Ethnicity in Latin America* (London: Pluto, 1997).

Wagner, Peter, *A Sociology of Modernity: Liberty and Discipline* (London: Routledge, 1994).

Walby, Sylvia, *Theorizing Patriarchy* (Oxford: Blackwell, 1990).

Wallerstein, Immanuel, *The Politics of World-Economy. The States, the Movements and the Civilizations* (Cambridge: Cambridge University Press; and Paris: Editions de la Maison des Sciences de l'Homme, 1984).

Walsh, Catherine, "Políticas y significados conflictivos," *Nueva sociedad,* no. 165 (2000).

Walsh, Catherine, "Interculturalidad, reformas constitucionales y pluralismo jurídico," *Boletim ICCI-Rimai,* año 4, no. 36 (2002).

180   Bibliography

Walter, Jorge, and C. Senén González, "Cambio tecnológico y redes formales e informales en la industria argentina," *Perfiles latinoamericanos*, año 4, no. 7 (1995).

Walter, Jorge, and Cecília Senén González (eds.), *La privatización de las telecomunicaciones en América Latina* (Buenos Aires: Eudeba, 1998).

Weber, Max, *Wirtschaft und Gesellschaft* (Tübing: J. C. B. Mohr—Paul Siebeck, [1921–1922] 1980).

Weber, Max, *Gesammelte Aufsätze zur Religionssoziologie* (Tübingen: J.C.B. Mohr—Paul Siebeck, [1920] 1988).

Weller, Jürgen, "Tertiary sector employment in Latin America: Between modernity and survival," *Cepal Review*, no. 84 (2004).

Weyland, Kurt, "Risk-taking in Latin American economic restructuring," *International Studies Quarterly*, vol. 40 (1996).

Williamson, Oliver, *Markets and Hierarchies* (New York: Free Press, 1975).

Williams, Heather L., *Social Movements and Economic Transition: Markets and Distributive Conflict in Mexico* (Cambridge: Cambridge University Press, 2001).

World Bank Technical Paper, nos. 280 (1994) and 350 (1996).

Wright, Erik Olin, *Class Counts* (Cambridge: Cambridge University Press; and Paris: Maison des Sciences de l'Homme, 1997).

Yashar, Deborah J., "Indigenous politics and democracy: Contesting citizenship in Latin America," *Comparative Politics*, vol. 31 (1998).

Zapata, Francisco, "¿Crisis en el sindicalismo en América Latina?," University of Notre Dame, Kellog Institute, *Working Paper* no. 302 (2003).

Zapata, Francisco, *México: Tiempos neoliberales* (Mexico: El Colegio de México, 2005).

Zermeño, Sérgio, *La sociedad derrotada: El desorden mexicano del fin de siglo* (Mexico: Siglo XXI, [1996] 2001).

Index

A

1492, x, 125
Adorno, 11, 12
Africa, 125
Afro-descendents, 102–105 (see also Blacks)
Agency, xi, 126
Agencies, regulatory, 56–57, 118
Aglietta, 47
Agrarian property, 4, 5, 15, 77
Agrarian reform, 16, 70, 104, 111
Agribusiness (see Agriculture)
Agriculture, 45, 53, 62, 68, 69–71, 110, 112, 120
Albó, 104
Alliances, 145(n32)
Amable, 48
Amazon, 70
America, 125
Anarchism, 42
Andean Community (CAN), 57
Andean region, 80
Arbitrage, 31
Arceo, 120
Argentina vii, 4, 6, 8, 9, 17, 21, 23, 25, 30, 31, 42, 45, 46, 53, 54, 55, 56, 56, 57, 59, 61, 62, 63, 64, 70, 72, 73, 74, 80, 81, 82, 96, 101, 102, 106, 107, 108, 111, 112, 113, 115, 116, 117, 120, 130, 135(n16), 146(n40), 146(n45), 158(n77), 149(n75)
Arms, 117
Arnason, xvi, 128
Asia, 62, 71, 146
Asunción, 158(n77)
Atlantic, 1, 126
Auto industry, 146(n40)
Autonomism, 163(n17)
Avritzer, 9

Ayllu, 104
Aymaras, 102, 104

B

Banks, 72, 107, 108
Basualdo, 107, 120
Biotechnology, 64 (see also Transgenics)
Blacks, 6, 24, 76, 77, 78, 80, 102–105, 123
Black Panthers, 104
Bogotá, 30
Bolcheviques, 128
Bolivia vii, xvii, 6, 17, 21, 23, 30, 31, 45, 52, 74, 80, 93–94, 96, 100, 101–102, 103, 104, 112, 115–116, 121, 131, 158(n77)
 1952 Revolution, 6
Bolivian Workers Confederation (COB), 115
Bolivarianism, 116
Boltanski, 49
Border thinking, 127
Bourdieu, 105
Boyer, 47
Brazil vii, xvi, 3, 6, 8, 9, 16, 17, 21, 22, 23, 25, 27, 28, 29, 31, 42, 45, 52, 52, 55, 56, 57, 60–61, 62, 64, 68, 70, 72, 73, 77, 79, 80, 81, 82, 96, 101, 102–103, 104–105, 106, 108, 111, 112, 115, 116, 117, 121, 135(n13), 137(n17), 146(n40), 146(n45), 149(n75), 150(n83), 153(n17), 158(n78)
 1930 Revolution, 6
 1988 Constitution, 29
 Old Republic, 4
 racial democracy/biracial pattern, 105
 Real Plan, 120
Brazilian Black Front, 105
Bresser Pereira, 117–118
Britain, vii

182 Index

Buenos Aires, 53, 63, 107, 109
Bureaucracy
  NGOs, 27
  parties, 114
  regulatory agencies, 56–57
  state, 1, 29, 45, 79, 81, 91, 116, 117
Business associations, 106, 109, 152(n18)

C

CAN (see Andean Community)
Canada, 61
Capital, 4, 45, 46, 47, 48, 54
  finance, 52, 53, 54, 55, 70, 71, 73–74, 120, 124
  mode of development, 47, 71–75, 124
  modes of regulation, 39ff, 47, 51ff, 52, 55, 71–75
  primitive accumulation, xiv
  regimes of accumulation, 39ff, 42, 43, 44, 45, 47, 48, 51, 52, 65–66, 69, 71–75
  venture, 63
Capitalism x, xiii, 5, 6, 12, 37, 39, 41, 42, 48, 51, 57, 74, 75, 81, 87, 91, 99, 106, 124, 128, 143(n5)
Caputo, 107–108
Caracas, 109
Carcerary option, 17
Cardoso, 73–74, 108, 110
Caribbean, 96
Carvalho, 135(n13)
Castells, 48, 49, 62, 63, 118
Causality, 106
Center-Periphery-Semiperiphery, vii-viii, xv, 43, 44, 45, 46, 49, 50, 73, 110, 131, 133(n1), 135(n5), 149(n75)
Central America, 28, 45, 53, 57, 71, 82
Cesarism, 116, 121, 160(n102)
Chalmers, 113
Chávez, 10, 116
Chiapas, 101, 104
Chiapello, 49
Children, 90, 96, 97
Chile, 8, 9, 10, 21, 23, 32, 42, 45, 53, 54, 56, 62, 69–70, 74, 76, 80, 81, 82, 102–103, 106, 108, 115, 117, 118, 147(n48)
China, 71
Christianity, 76 (see also Church, Religion)
Churchs/Sects, 84 (see also Religion)
  Catholic, 42, 76, 77, 104
  Electronic, 101
  Evangelism, 101
  of God's Kingdom, 100

Pentecostal, 100
Protestant, 100–101, 104
Cisneros, 116
Cities, 53 (see also Urbanization)
Citizenship, xii, 1, 14, 17, 20, 22, 36, 76, 92, 122, 123–124, 135(n13), 135(n26)
  active, 25–26, 38
  definition, 11
  and identity, 12
  instituting and instituted, 10, 13, 119, 123
  and real abstractions, 11–13
Ciudad Juárez, 61
Civil rights movement, 104
Civil service, 81, 117
Civil society, 26, 98
Civilization, vii, ix, 93–94
  encounters, 126
  modern, x, xv, 1, 5, 37–38, 74, 75, 123–132
  theory, 128
Civilization and barbarism, 78
Class, xi-xii, xiv, xvii, 11–12, 24–25, 40, 41, 76, 89, 91, 94, 99, 104, 105–116, 119, 120, 124, 153(n18), 158(n77), 158(n78)
  bourgeois, 7, 46, 80, 81, 82–83, 92, 106, 109–110, 119, 120, 131, 151(n11)
  concept, 85–87
  middle/petty bourgeoisie, 6–7, 28, 45, 68, 72, 78, 92, 104, 106, 111–112, 120, 130
  peasants, 6, 16, 17, 23, 69–70, 80, 103–104, 112, 151(n11)
  popular, 45, 68, 77, 80, 84, 93, 96, 110, 111–114, 119, 120, 122, 123, 130, 132
  rulling/upper, 7, 42, 43, 45, 68, 72, 73, 78, 82–83, 92, 107–111, 120, 124, 130
  subaltern, 124, 130
  small proprietors, 69–70
  working, 6ff, 15, 17, 23, 42, 43, 45, 58, 60, 61, 71–72, 78, 80–81, 83, 92, 106, 151(n11), 153(n18)
Clientelism, 17–20, 25, 34, 101, 116, 119
  bureaucratic, 19
COB (see Bolivian Workers Confederation)
Coca/Cocaine, 70, 112
Cocaleros, 112
Cochabamba, 112

Index 183

Cold War, 10
Collective subjectivity, ix-xiii, xvii, 10, 12, 51, 76–77, 78, 84ff, 102, 105–116, 119, 122, 124–132
   definition, 84–85
   and solidarity, 91–92
Colombia, 6, 8, 21, 23, 28, 31, 45, 70, 74, 81, 82, 96, 102–103, 104–105, 106, 108, 115, 117, 147(n48)
   1991 Constitution, 30
Colonialism, internal, 127
Coloniality of power, xv
Colonization, 6, 76
Commodities, 41, 53, 60, 64, 69–71, 74
Commodity fetishism, 42, 75, 99
Common Market of the South (Mercosur), 57, 64
Communism, xii, 142(n99)
Competition, 47, 72
Complexification of society, 6, 26, 36, 49, 92–93, 114, 121, 124
CONAIE (see National Indian Confederation of Ecuador),
Conventionalizations, 82
Conighan, 34
Constitutions, 9, 29, 30, 32–33
Constitutionalization, 31–32
Consumption, 68–69, 71, 72, 75, 99–100
Contingency, 3, 12, 48
Corporatism, 7–8, 15, 16–17, 45, 80–81, 99, 109, 112, 115, 121, 136(n16), 136(n17), 151(n11)
   and Iberian heritage, 152(n11)
   post, 122
Corruption, 55, 81, 161(n108)
Costa Rica, 21, 102
Creativity, xii, 90, 100, 129, 131–132
Crisis (see also Argentina)
   Asian, 146(n45)
   economic/financial, 39, 43, 46, 47–48, 51
   of modernity, 5, 9, 43
Cuba, 39, 80, 96, 102–103, 133, 143(n14)
Culture (see also Social movements)
   dependency, 68–69
   political, 9

I

Debt, 54, 55, 143(n18), 146(n45)
Democracy/Democratization, 1ff, 9–11, 72–73, 80, 83, 84, 98, 105, 113, 115, 117, 119, 120, 121, 123–125, 131

delegative, 18
Demographic transitions, 78, 95–97
Denationalization, 55, 107, 108, 116
Departments I and II (of the economy), 44, 45, 46, 47, 48, 50, 53, 60
   definition, 144(n12)
Dependency theory, viii, xiii, 47, 76
Dependency, 73–74, 80, 110 (see also Culture)
Development, 39ff, 46, 52, 54, 73, 94, 110, 122
   dependent and associated, 73, 110
   mode of, 47, 122, 124 (see also Capital)
   uneven and combined, xv, 128–132
   and contradictory, 97, 129–132
Dialectic, 130
Dictatorships (see Military)
Discipline, 3
Discursive turn, xvi
Disembeddings, 12, 15, 77, 92–93, 94, 95, 97, 99, 121, 124 (see also Reembeddings)
Dollar, 72
   parity with Peso, 120
Domination, xiii, 2, 6, 12, 76, 105, 111, 120, 127, 130, 135(n13)
   of nature, 75
Dominican Republic, 21, 96, 102–103
Drugs, 117 (see also Coca)

E

Economic Commission for Latin America/ and for the Caribbean (ECLA/ ECLAC), xvii, 47, 50, 58, 73, 95
Ecuador, 23, 30, 31, 45, 72, 74, 93, 96, 102–103, 104, 111, 115, 130, 158(n77)
Education, 79, 104
Eisenstadt, xvi, 128
Ejido, 16, 70, 104
El Alto, 101
El Barzón, 70, 112
El Salvador, 21, 30, 96, 102–103
Elites, xi, 9, 76
Emancipation, xv, 6, 37, 80, 125, 127, 131, 132
Embrapa, 70
Empires (colonial), xiv, 76, 79, 125
Environment, 27, 74, 98, 113
Environmentalism, 75, 92, 113
Epistemic communities, ix
Equality, xiii, 1–2, 7, 14, 130
Equity, 22

184 *Index*

Ethnicity, xi, xvii, 6, 76, 78, 88, 91, 92, 94, 98, 99, 105, 111, 112, 119, 124, 154(n31)
Europe, vii, x, xiv, 3, 7, 9, 13, 22, 25, 34, 43, 51, 56, 61, 62, 79, 82, 110, 114, 126, 136(n19), 151(n1), 100
Evangelization, 76
Evolution, viii, 40, 92–93, 124, 125, 129, 135(n5), 161(n1)

F

Faletto, 73, 110
Family, xvii, 77, 78, 119
  colonial, 77
  decentered, 97
  female leadership, 78, 96, 97
  nuclear/extended, 78, 96
  patriarch, 77
  male absenteeism, 77, 96
  modern, 77–78, 90–91, 95–98
Feminism, 98, 113
Fernandes, xi, 3, 83
Fertility/Mortality rates, 78, 95
Fetishism of modernity, 126
Firms, 43, 49, 51, 56, 57–61, 72, 110, 124, 141(n87)
Flexible accumulation, 48–49, 50
Ford Foundation, 105
Fordism/Post-Fordism, 9, 32, 43, 46, 49, 50, 57, 69, 99, 112 145(n22), 146(n40)
Foreign Direct Investment (FDI), 51, 55, 56, 108, 146(n45)
Fragmentation, social, 93–94, 130
France, vii, 63
Frankfurt School, 11
Free Trade Agreements (FTAs), 147(n48)
Free Trade Area of the Americas (FTAA), 147(n48)
Freedom, xiii, 1–3, 5, 7, 32, 33–34, 41, 121, 130, 135(n13), 153(n19)
  equal, 2, 6–7, 12, 15, 37, 127, 131–132
  equal versus targeted social policy, 20
Freud, 87
Friedman, 27
FTA (see Free Trade Agreements)
FTAA (see Free Trade Area of the Americas)
Functionalism, xii, 65, 129

G

García Canclini, 93
Garza Toledo, 58

GATT (General Agreement on Trade and Tariffs)
Geisell, 153(n17)
Gender, xi, xvii, 12, 41, 77–78, 88–89, 92, 94, 95–98, 102, 119, 124
General Agreement on Trade and Tariffs (GATT), 51, 55, 73
Generations, xvii, 89, 91, 95, 102, 119
Germani, xi, 8, 129
Giddens, 86–88
Gini coefficients, 68
Global commodity chains, 59, 61, 70
Globalization, x-xi, 15, 24, 27, 73, 91, 100
  economic, 39, 42, 45, 46, 50, 51–52, 72, 112, 118, 119, 120, 124, 159(n89)
Globo Network, 116
Gorz, 149(n71)
Gramsci, 26–27, 120, 160(n102)
Guatemala, 93, 96, 101, 102–103, 104
Guerrilla, 104, 117

H

Habermas, 11, 25–27, 36, 40, 135(n5)
Haiti, 96
Hartlyn, 1
Hegel, 36, 129
Hegemony, 83, 92, 113, 114, 119, 120, 122
Heterogeneity, 27, 36–37, 46, 48, 52, 60, 62, 75, 76, 77, 84, 90, 93, 99, 127, 128, 143(n16), 155(n42)
Hierarchy, xvii, 24, 41, 42, 49, 97, 114
  command, xvii, 41, 114
Historical block (see Hegemony)
Historical Structuralism, xvii, 47, 73
History, 2, 12, 128–129
  episodic, 125, 161(n1)
  long duration, 121
  as a teleological process, 2
Homogenization, 10, 12–13, 40, 42, 43, 45, 46, 49, 76, 77, 79, 80, 93, 99, 106, 121
Honduras, 21, 96, 102, 158(n77)
Honneth, 103
Horkheimer, 11
Hybridism, 20, 93, 155(n42)

I

Identities, 12, 24, 76, 77, 79, 79, 83, 89, 90, 92, 97, 98–99, 100, 104, 105, 114, 161(n110)
  politics, 113
  quasi ascriptive/further optional, 90, 102, 105

Index 185

ILO (see International Labor Organization)
Imaginary, xii-xiii, xiv, 1–2, 5, 10, 13, 23, 36, 37, 84, 119, 123
IMF (see International Monetary Fund)
Immanent critique, 142(n99)
Immigrants, 71, 78
Imperialism, 73–74, 83
Import substitution industrialization, 43, 44, 46, 50, 53
Inclusion, 6, 8, 127
Income distribution, 44, 105
Independences, viii, 3–4, 11, 41, 76, 77, 78, 127
India, 60, 71
Indians/Indigenous peoples, 6, 23, 24, 42, 76, 77, 78, 80, 101, 102–105, 112, 123, 127
Forth wave of mobilization, 103–104
Indigenism, 80
Individualism, 7, 94, 152(n11)
Inequality, 2, 5, 6–7, 10, 68, 75, 97, 103, 105, 149(n75)
Inflation, 51, 52, 55, 110
Informality, 65–67, 72, 77–78, 81, 84, 96, 97, 106, 111 (see also Labor, Family, Patrimonialism)
Informatics, 45, 49, 61, 62, 90
Innovation (see Technology)
clusters, 63
Institutions, xii, 1–2, 5, 9–10, 13, 36, 37, 47, 48, 51, 84, 119, 123–132
Integration, regional, 57
Intellectuals, vii
Interculturality, 31, 127
Interest, xii, 113
International Labor Organization (ILO), 65
International Monetary Fund (IMF), 28, 51, 54, 55, 73, 120, 143(n18)
Internet, 62
Islam, 125, 163(n16)
Italy, 120

J

Japan, vii, 52, 61, 62
Judicialization, 29–30
Judiciary/Judicial system, 1, 10, 25, 27–32, 34, 121
Julliard, 48
Juridification, 11, 29
Justice, 1, 4–5, 10–11, 119, 123, 130
discourse, 5

K

Kant, 36

Katarism, 101–102
Kelly, 106
Kelsen, 36
Keynesianism, 7, 9, 43, 47, 48, 51, 64
Kirchner, 25
Korea, 50, 61

L

Labor (see also Reestructuration)
legislation, 8, 21, 55, 58, 66, 109, 111
markets, 44, 46, 64–68, 72, 96, 98
regimes, 47
Landless Workers Movement (MST), 16, 25, 112
La Paz, 101
Latin American studies, 134(n10)
Law, 1, 10–11, 27–32, 119, 123, 130
civil and common, 11, 29
legal pluralism, 30–32, 37
Lawyers, 28
Lenin, 73
Leninism, 24
Liberalism, 1, 4–5, 6, 7
Liberty (see Freedom)
Lifestyle, 86, 98–99, 101, 105–116
Lima, 23, 53, 66, 104
Lost decade, 36, 52, 109
Lukács, 11, 13
Lula da Silva, 22, 121

M

Macroeconomic measures/policies, 39, 52, 54, 56, 71–72, 161(n109)
Maffesoli, 98
Maiwaring, 115
Mann, 91
Mapuches, 118
Marginality (theories of), 64–66
Market, xvii, 3, 40, 42, 48, 49, 51, 55, 75, 99
voluntary exchange, xviii, 40, 41
Maquiladoras, 53, 61, 63–64, 70
Marriage, 41, 77–78, 90
Marshall, 11, 135 (n 12)
Martin, 113
Marx, xii, 11, 40, 42, 46, 47, 48, 67, 126, 85–87, 144(n12)
Marxism, 47, 65, 83, 86–87, 91, 104, 121, 126, 143(n5)
MAS (see Movement Toward Socialism)
Mechanisms of coordination, xvii, 51
Media, 97, 116, 119
Melucci, 101, 154(n36)
Memory, xii, 89–90, 98, 99, 100, 104

186 *Index*

Mercosur (see Common Market of the South)
Mestizaje/Miscigenation/Mixed people, 23, 76, 77, 78, 80, 93, 102–103
Mexico, vii, 6, 8, 16, 17, 18, 21, 23, 29, 30, 31, 32–33, 42, 45, 46, 53, 56, 57, 61, 62, 63, 64, 69–70, 73, 74, 80, 93, 94, 96, 102–103, 104, 108, 112, 115, 116, 117, 146(n40), 146(n45), 150(n83), 158(n78)
Mexico City, 53, 109
Mexican Revolution, 4, 6, 78
Michels, 114
Microelectronics, 45, 49, 58, 61, 64
Military, 9
  coups, 10
  regimes, 8ff, 47, 53, 59, 73, 81, 84, 98, 105, 136(n21)
Mode of production, 48
Modernity, vii-ix, xi, xiii-xiv, 2, 12, 20, 26, 37, 40, 76, 93, 100, 102, 122, 123–132, 135 (n5), 153(n19), 155(n44), 134–135(n5)
  and critique, 142(n99)
  global, viii, xvi, 128
  liberal and state organized phases, 3, 14, 41–42, 43, 45, 48, 76, 80, 82, 90, 92, 121, 127, 146(n40)
  third phase, viii, xvi, 3, 14ff, 35, 36, 49, 51, 53, 73, 75, 90, 95, 99, 114, 118, 111, 119, 121, 123–132, 133(n3), Modernization theory, viii, xiii, xiv, 40, 83, 96–97, 126, 129, 134(n10)
Molecular change, 26, 120, 121, 123–132
Money, 47
Morales, 116
Morse, 152(n11)
Mosca, xi, 9
Movement Toward Socialism (MAS), 104, 115
Moves, modernizing, 3, 5, 6, 9, 10, 14, 15, 18, 22–23, 26, 28, 29, 35, 40, 41, 43, 44, 61, 62, 65, 69, 76, 94, 98, 99, 100, 109, 110, 111, 116, 119, 122, 124, 126, 129, 156(n62)
  decentered, ix, 52, 54, 97, 118, 121
  definition, viii-ix, xiii
  episodic, 126
  offensive, ix, 41, 44, 51, 52, 54, 56, 57, 58, 74, 81, 118, 121
Music, 99

MST (see Landless Worker's Movement)

N

NAFTA (see North American Free Trade Area)
Nation/National identity/Nationalism, xiii, 24, 78–80, 85, 90, 91, 99, 102
National developmentalism, 39
National Indian Confederation of Ecuador (CONAIE), 104
Nationalist methodology, 125, 128
Neoclassical economics, 40, 47
Neocorporatism, 7–9, 25, 43
Neoliberalism, 13, 14, 27, 28–32, 33, 53, 54, 75, 94, 95, 100, 103, 109–110, 111, 112, 113, 116, 118, 119, 121, 123–132
Neo-Schumpterianism, 48, 49
Neo-Thomism, 7, 76
Network, xvii, 3, 24–25, 31, 35, 41, 49–50, 51, 52, 59, 101, 113–114, 118, 161(n109)
  voluntary collaboration, xvii, 41, 114
NGOs (see Non-governmental organizations)
Nicaragua, 21, 96, 102
Non-governmental organizations (NGOs), 26–27, 35, 74, 98, 105, 121
North American Free Trade Area (NAFTA), 57, 61, 69–70
Nun, 65–68

O

Occidentalism, xiv
O'Donnell, 18, 34
OECD (see Organization for Economic Development)
Offe, 149(n71)
Olin Wright, 158(n78)
Olson, 154(n36)
Organization for Economic Development (OECD), 51, 55, 71
Otro Derecho, 30
Oxaca, 23

P

Panama, 21, 82, 96
Paraguay, 21, 45, 52, 82, 96, 102, 158(n77)
Paramilitary, 117
Pareto, xi, 9
Parsons, xvi, 40
Participatory Budget, 20
Particularities, 12–13, 103, 123, 128
Parties, xvii, 7, 11, 24, 34, 114–116, 119, 120, 123, 160(n102), 163(n17)

Index 187

Brazilian Democratic Movement (PMDB), 115
Broad Front (FA), 20, 115, 121
Christian Democracy, 115
Democracy Party (PD)
Justicialista Party (PJ), 18, 115
National Action Party (PAN), 115
National Revolutionary Movement (MNR), 115
Party of Brazilian Social Democracy (PSDB), 115
Party of the Democratic Revolution (PRD), 115
Party of the Liberal Front (PFL), 115
Radical Civic Union (UCR), 4, 18
Revolutionary Institutional Party (PRI), 17, 19, 32–33, 115
Socialist Party (PS), 115
Workers' Party (PT), 20, 23, 115, 121
Passive adaptation (to globalization), 111, 118, 120, 131, 132
Passive revolution, 120, 124
Patriarchy, xiii, 77–78, 90, 98
Patrimonialism/Neopatrimonialism, 81, 152(n12)
PDVSA, 52
Pension Funds, 108
Pérez-Perdomo, 27
Periphery (see Center)
Peronism, 6, 18, 81, 107, 112, 115
Personal domination, 4, 5, 14, 41, 65, 80, 82
Peru, 9, 21, 28, 30, 45, 66, 74, 81, 96, 102–103, 104, 108, 115
Petrobras, 52
Philanthropy, 3, 15, 116, 119
Philosophy, xvi
Piester, 113
Pinochet, 32
Piqueteros, 17, 25, 112
Planning, 152(n17)
Plausibility, 90–91, 102
Pluralism/Pluralization, 13, 23, 28, 33–34, 35, 46, 48, 49, 76, 78, 91, 93, 94, 95, 96, 98, 99, 121, 123
Pochmann, 107
Polanyi, 40
Poliarchy, 9, 34
Political economy, 47, 154(n23)
Political system, 1
Populism, 83, 135(n16), 153(n19)
Portes, 106
Porto Alegre, 27
Postmodernity/Postmodernism, xiii, 37, 93, 127, 156(n62)

Poulantzas, 86–87, 91
Poverty, 21–22, 41, 75, 98, 149(n75), 188(n50)
Power, xii
Power blocks, 110, 120
Prebich, vii
Presidentialism, 115
Primordialism, 104
Privatization, 51, 52, 54–55, 107, 108, 118
Privilege, 2
Projetcs, 15, 38, 119, 134–135(n5)
Property, 105 (see also Rights)
Public officials, 8
Public sphere, 9, 25–27, 34, 35

Q

Quéchuas, 104
Quijano, xv

R

Race/Racism, xi, xiii, xvii, 12, 76, 78, 80, 88, 89, 91, 92, 94, 99, 102–105, 119, 124, 128, 151, 154(n31) (see also Blacks, Indigenous people, Mestizaje, Whites)
Rationality, 87–89, 125
Reagan, 56
Real abstractions, xvii, 34, 36–37, 119, 123
and citizenship, 11–13, 14
and passivity, 13
Recognition, 6, 36, 103, 127
Re-embeddings, 12, 37, 77, 92–93, 99, 124, 156(n62) (see also Disembeddings)
Reestructuration, economic, 23, 52, 54, 56, 57–61, 111, 119, 124
Reflexivity, 87–89, 93, 109, 154(n23)
Reification, 126
Religion, 99–102 (see also Churchs, Social Movements)
African-based, 100
Catholicism, 31, 100–101
Liberation Theology, 100
Magic, 100
New Age, 100
Protestantism, 31, 100–103, 156 (n 62)
Theology of Prosperity, 100
World, 128
Renaissance, x
Representation, proportional, 115
Reprimarization, 47, 52, 53, 110, 124
Research & Development, 61–64
Responsibility, xiii, 7, 14, 17, 21, 25, 32, 40, 42, 43, 121, 132, 152(n11)

188   *Index*

Rifkin, 149(n71)
Rights, 1ff, 119, 123, 130, 135(n26)
  civil, 1ff
  collective, 23
  discourse, 5, 10, 22–23
  political, 1ff
  and private property, 5, 135(n13)
  social, 1ff, 21ff, 124
Risk Assessment Agencies, 52, 124
Risks, 75
Risorgimento, 120
Russia, 128

S

São Paulo, 42, 53, 60, 107
Schumpeter, xi, 9
Science (see Technology)
Sects (see Churchs)
Secularization, 100–102
Semiperiphery (see Center)
Services, 66, 68, 96
Sexuality, 95–97
Silicon Valley, 63
Slavery, 4–5, 76, 77
Small groups, xi
Social Democracy, 8, 135(n16), 135(n19),
    163 (n16)
Social dimensions, 129
Social movements, xi, xvii, 9, 10, 24, 25,
    33, 89, 90, 93, 95, 112, 113,
    123, 154(n36), 163(n16) (see
    also Environmentalism, Landless
    Workers Movement, Feminism,
    Piqueteros, Unions)
  communitarian, 84, 111
  cultural, 93, 98
  modernity, 90
  new, 113
  religious, 93, 101, 102, 112
Social policy, 3, 21–22, 117, 161 (n109)
  targeted, 17–18, 21, 33, 119
    Argentina, 18
    Bolivia, 20
    Brazil, 19–20, 68, 188(n50)
    Chile, 19
    Mexico, 18–19
  universal versus means tested, 12
Social theory, xv
Socialism xii, 10, 42, 103, 142(n99),
    143(n14)
Society, xi
Sociology, 47, 48, 84, 126, 128
  Solidarity, xiii, 1–2, 6ff, 14, 17, 18, 24,
    31, 37, 48, 76, 77, 78, 101,

118, 119, 121, 130complex, 95,
    121–122, 124, 132
South American Community, 57
South Cone, 82
Soviet Union, 133(n3)
Space-time, 129
State, x-xi, xiii, xvii, 3, 6, 7, 8, 25, 35, 39,
    40, 43, 47, 51, 52, 54, 55, 72,
    73, 76, 77, 80, 85, 90–91, 114,
    116–119, 121, 125, 131, 132,
    161(n109) (see also Bureaucracy,
    Philanthropy, Secularization,
    Social Policy)
  Absolutist, 79
  developmental, 3, 9, 44, 104, 118, 152–
    153(n17)
  infra-structural versus despotic power,
    8, 10, 18, 57, 72, 80, 82, 91,
    116–117
  national, x, 4, 93, 125, 152(n12)
  as power container, x
  reform of, 82, 117–119
  and regulatory agencies, 56–57
  Schumpeterian Workfare Competition
    State, 118
Statistics, 82
Stratification, 105
Strydom, 5
Surplus-value, 59, 154(n23)
Sustainable development, 74–75, 113
Svampa, 107, 109
Sweat shops, 49, 59, 66

T

Tapia, 93
Tarrow, 101, 154(n36)
Taylorism, 49, 57–58
Technology, 43, 45, 46, 48, 49, 50, 51, 52,
    58, 61–64, 70, 74
Telecommunications, 51
Telefe, 116
Televisa, 116
Television, 116
Tertiarization of the economy, 23, 46,
    67–68, 84
Theborn, 77
Theory of regulation, xii, 47–51, 52
Third age, 98
Tocqueville, 135(n9)
Touraine, 8, 83–84, 122
Toyotism, 49, 58
Trade, terms of, 46, 69, 149(n77)
Tradition, viii, xiii, 18, 20, 76, 77, 93, 127,
    155(n42)

Index   189

modern, 155(n44)
Transgenics, 70
Transformism, 120–121, 131
Transnational corporations, 44, 50, 52, 54, 74, 107, 108, 109, 110, 120
Tribes, 98–99
Trotsky, 128–131

U

Underdevelopment, 50, 73–74, 110, 120, 124, 131
Unemployment, 24, 65–67
  structural, 65
Unions, 7, 9, 17, 23, 58, 66, 104, 111, 112
Unit of analysis, viii
United States, vii, xiv, 3, 7, 10, 11, 17, 28, 34, 43, 46, 51, 52, 55, 56, 61, 62, 63, 68, 69, 70, 73, 74, 82, 105, 110, 125, 133(n3), 135(n9), 147(n48)
Universalism/Universalization, 36–37, 123
University, 49, 63, 64, 79
  of Coimbra, 79
Urbanization, 78, 84, 96 (see also Cities)
Uruguay, 8, 21, 23, 45, 74, 77, 81, 82, 96, 102, 115, 121, 158(n77)

V

Value, Theory of, 145(n22)
Values, 1–2, 5
Vargas, 136(n17)
Venezuela, 6, 10, 21, 23, 45, 52, 74, 81, 96, 108, 115, 116, 121, 160(n102)
  oil, 53, 70–71
Violence, 6, 16, 82, 109

Volkswagen, 60

W

Wacquant, 105
Wagner, 3
Wallerstein, 133(n1), 143(n5)
War, 79
  World, 43, 143(n9)
Washington Consensus, 28, 54
  first generation reforms, 54
  second generation reforms, 28ff, 55
Wave (of democratization), 9–10, 36
Weber, xi, xii, 9, 86–88, 91, 100, 101, 106
Weberianism, 83
Welfare State, 9, 12, 13, 29
West, viii, xiv, xv, 2, 6, 9, 37, 41, 43, 52, 65, 95, 118, 125, 128, 163(n16)
Westcentrism, 125
Whites, 77, 78, 92, 102, 103, 135(n9), 157(n70)
Wittgenstein, xvi
Women, 6, 96, 103, 160(n102)
World Bank, 19, 28–31, 36, 51, 55, 56, 68, 73, 120
World Social Forum, 27, 132
World Trade Organization (WTO), 52, 73

Y

Youth, 98–100
Yrigoyen, 4

Z

Zapatismo, 23, 104, 114
Zavaleta, 93
Zermeño, 94